The Secret Śaṅkara

On Multivocality and Truth in Śaṅkara's Teaching

By

Yohanan Grinshpon

TUTA SUB AEGIDE PALLAS · 1683 ·

BRILL

LEIDEN • BOSTON
2011

This book is printed on acid-free paper.

Library of Congress Cataloging-in-Publication Data

Grinshpon, Yohanan, 1948–
The secret Śaṅkara : on multivocality and truth in Śaṅkara's teaching / by Yohanan Grinshpon.
p. cm. — (Jerusalem studies in religion and culture ; volume 12)
Includes bibliographical references and index.
ISBN 978-90-04-18926-3 (hardback : alk. paper) 1. Sankaracarya. 2. Hindu philosophy. I. Title.

B133.S5G75 2011
181'.482—dc22

2010042537

ISSN 1570-078X
ISBN 978 90 04 18926 3

PRINTED BY A-D DRUK BV - ZEIST, THE NETHERLANDS

In Memory of Wilhelm Halbfass (1940–2000),
A Philosopher and Teacher

CONTENTS

Preface and Acknowledgment ix

Chapter One On the Challenge of Listening to Śaṅkara's Voices: Dialogue and Monologue in Śaṅkara's Writing 1

Chapter Two On Doubt and Wonder in Advaita-Vedānta: Towards Perceiving a Śaṅkara and a Śaṅkarācārya 9

Chapter Three Ātman Disturbed: Self and Mind as its Other in the *Upadeśa-sāhasrī* 23

Chapter Four Individual Losses and Advaitic Consciousness: A Note on Īśvara's, Śaṅkara's and Śaṅkarācārya's Sorrow 33

Chapter Five On Doubt and Self-Understanding: The Omniscience of an Author and his Arch-Exponent 51

Chapter Six Śaṅkara's Śaṅkarācārya: The Invisible Author of BSBh and his Beloved *Siddhāntin* 63

Chapter Seven On Rice and Mokṣa: A Note on Śaṅkara's Voices and Aesthetics 91

Chapter Eight On Mud, Negation and the Hungry Space 101

Chapter Nine Advaita Messages and Foreign Voices: Some Philosophical Meanings of Śaṅkara's Art of Writing 115

Chapter Ten Commentator's Advaita, Exponent's Advaita 139

Epilogue The Useless Knowledge of Self as the Highest Good: A Note on Śaṅkara's Secret Teaching of Viveka-Vedānta 157

Bibliography 173

Index 175

PREFACE AND ACKNOWLEDGMENT

Primordial error with respect to a self that is intimately sensed yet little understood—this is the ground of life as we know it. We exist through a manifestion of self that is essentially false, blind to the relationship between our self and non-self even as we walk and speak, read or think. It is no wonder, then, that the sage who would articulate this stark truth remains in the shadows, concealed, as it were, behind alleged truths that are more acceptable and sanctioned by tradition.

In the introduction to his commentary on the *Brahma-sūtra*, Śaṅkara, author of the *Brahma-sūtra-bhāṣya* (BSBh), suggests that it is primordial error—the common lot of human beings and animals—that sustains our life (or embodied existence). The error, he states, comes about through the superimposition (*adhyāsa*) of that which sees—"having an object" (*viṣayin*)—on that which is seen (an object) (*viṣaya*), and vice versa. Every voluntary movement of the body requires a measure of false self-identification, or to quote his own words: "The body can only be set in motion through an inherently erroneous projection of the self on a non-self [which is the body]" (*na cânadhyastâtma-bhavena dehena kaścid vyāpriyate*).

This, as I read it, implies that a sage who has become wholly free of *adhyāsa* would cease to move his tongue (to speak) and his hands (to write), attaining thereby a high degree of dense silence. But for a philosopher committed to coherent speech, the condition of not moving his tongue and hands presents a paradox. Mindful of the theory of *adhyāsa* Śaṅkara realizes that the speech-act "I do not exist" (*nāham asmīti*; BSBh 1.1.1) presents a contradiction in terms. Nor can he ignore the existential meaning of the paradoxical statement that to live is to exist in error. In the thirteenth section of the metrical part of the *Upadeśa-sāhasrī*, the one and only self (*ātman*) speaks in Śaṅkara's voice: Having no eyes I do not see (*acakṣuṣṭvān na dṛṣṭir me*); with no ears, how is hearing possible (*tathâśrotrasya kā śrutiḥ*)?; having no organ of speaking, there is no speech in me (*avāktvān na tu vaktiḥ syāt*); without a mind, how can I think (*amanastvān matiḥ kutaḥ*)?[1]

---

[1] Upad 13.1.

By articulating a vision of life that is inherently (*naisargika*) a series of *adhyāsa*-moments, Śaṅkara expresses his innermost voice (or the position of his real self). The power to distinguish that which sees from that which is seen results in disembodiment and immobility (often referred to as *mokṣa*, freedom; *aśarīratvam mokṣaḥ*),[2] positing for all human beings, and especially philosophers, a terrible dilemma: a choice between true knowledge (*viveka*) or life. Thus, true knowledge implies the end of life as a series of activities that are embodied and dependent on the agency of the self. The implication here is that consciousness, the last stage of Darwinian evolution, turns on itself, risking its very survival. How then is audible speech possible? The philosopher's obvious predicament is that speech and writing ("noisy" existence) seem incompatible with true knowledge. Yet here the author of the BSBh finds hope in drawing a distinction between secondary meaning, "metaphor" (*gauṇa*), and error.

Silence does indeed befit a fully-accomplished Advaitin, and without a true audience (an other) and a need to speak, we might expect an Advaitin in touch with the ground of selfhood, knowing (imagining) himself to be the one great self (*ātman*), to remain silent, renouncing ordinary, referential language. And yet, since the Advaita literature is so vast, we can also assume there is some opening for speech to occur. Thus, Śaṅkara, foremost among composers of so-called Advaita philosophy,[3] must sustain a split of sorts, by virtue of which communication and writing (for Śaṅkara is a writer) can manifest in reality.

Śaṅkara seems to have been privy to a rare experience—touching as it were the ground of the soul, unfathomable in its difference from anything else in the world. The vision or realization of the irreducible difference between seer (*viṣayin*) and seen (*viṣaya*) is what Śaṅkara calls *viveka*; and one who is capable of *viveka* is a *vivekin*. What follows from this is a state of double consciouness wherein Śaṅkara recognizes himself to be *ātman* (in accordance with the Upaniṣadic vision) yet denies any sort of objective reality for *ātman*, the one true self (or even the physical body). But Śaṅkara then asserts that the Viveka-Vedāntin speaks "metaphorically" rather than erroneously, by means of a *gauṇa*

[2] BSBh 1.1.4.

[3] Śaṅkara is, by definition, the arch-exponent of the school of Advaita-Vedānta. However, in our exposition of Śaṅkara's secret teaching based on the theory of *adhyāsa*, Śaṅkara is not truly an Advaitin; he would be more accurately called *viveka-vedāntin*. See below.

or secondary mode of speech in a playful "as-if" attitude made possible by the distinction of self from non-self. In Upaniṣadic style, we would say: the author speaks, yet he does not speak. The difference between the author himself and the creatures of his mind (*siddhāntins* and *pūrva-pakṣins*) is thus a difference between secondary and primary speech. The *siddhāntins*' voices articulate primary meaning, while the author, aware of the irreducible difference between subject and object, speaks by *gauṇa*. The author's metaphorical state of mind is marked by tension and complexity due to his recognition of both *ātman* (the oneness of the "impersonal" self) and an objective universe that is completely dissociated from the self. Living in the void between self and non-self is difficult, nay, impossible (as suggested above). The surprising discourse of the allegedly silent and disembodied self or *ātman* and the mind (*manas*) in the *Upadeśa-sāhasrī* is most telling with respect to the nature of its author (see chapter 3). Who dares to make *ātman* speak in the first person and to represent the inherently unvoiced self through a talking and talkative agent while leaving the naturally restless mind in a state of stillness and silence? Reversing the roles of *ātman* and *manas* Śaṅkara experiments with an improbable dialogue between the two.

Śaṅkara's resistance to binding the self to objective reality sets him apart from the sacred tradition of the Upaniṣads. As he states in the introduction to the BSBh, in the true (*adhyāsa*-free) state of being, the usual authoritative means of knowledge no longer prevail (*na caitasmin sarvasminn asati asaṅgasyâtmanaḥ pramātṛtvam upapadyate*). Should any doubt arise in the reader's mind concerning the author's rejection of Upaniṣadic authority, Śaṅkara declares further that "...the recognized means of knowledge such as perception and sacred tradition (*śāstra*) are like other objects conceived by a false state of mind (*tasmād avidyāvad viṣayāṇy eva pratyakṣâdīni pramāṇāni śāstrāṇi ca*)." Reflecting on the Upaniṣadic theories of creation (which presuppose an inherent connection between self and world), he boldly asserts their falsehood (see below). While clearly indebted to the Upaniṣadic teaching of the oneness of *ātman*, Śaṅkara lives with the conceptual impossibility of correlating that oneness with objective reality. As he says in BSBh 1.1.2: *kiṃ brahmaṇā saṃbaddhaṃ kim anyena kenacit saṃbaddham iti na śakyaṃ niścetum*. This seemingly incidental remark is full of implications. A writer's intent is often ascertainable through such seemingly incidental remarks, as Wilhelm Halbfass observed.

Here and elsewhere in the BSBh, Śaṅkara does indeed reveal a coherent vision of truth and life.

The final chapter of this essay (the Epilogue) is devoted to what I have come to consider the core of Śaṅkara's reflections on his *viveka*-experience ("Śaṅkara's secret teaching").

To my way of reading, large portions of the *Brahmasūtrabhāṣya*—notably the *siddhānta*-positions that purport to offer definitive conclusions for debate—are excluded from the author's primary level of imagination (the voice of his "real self"). This may seem like a shortcoming, but it serves to augment the explanation. See, for example, the *siddhānta*-voices in favor of the Upaniṣadic theories of creation (plurality emerging from the one). These are, strictly speaking, incompatible with the principle of *adhyāsa*, "superimposition," the confusion of a metaphysical self (*ātman, viṣayin, sākṣin*) with worldly existence. Insisting on the irreducible difference between seer and seen, Śaṅkara, the Viveka Vedāntin, the *adhyāsa*-free author of the BSBh, must resist any theory of emanation of worldly (objective) existence from the one primordial seer. Indeed, that is what he does at the end of BSBh 2.1.33 when he asserts that Upaniṣadic theories of creation are not really true with respect to worldly existence; in fact, they form entirely illusory, ignorant perspectives. One must not forget, Śaṅkara says, that, the real teaching of the Upaniṣads concerns the oneness of *ātman* and Brahman (and nothing else) (*na ceyaṃ paramârtha-viṣayā sṛṣṭi-śrutiḥ avidyā-kalpita-nāma-rūpa-vyavahāra-gocaratvāt, brahmâtma-bhāva-pratipādana-paratvāc cety etad api naiva vismartavyam*).

The *viveka*-experience is hard to maintain. The unending thirst for life, unity, integration, and fusion of subject and object is always there, even for our Viveka-Vedāntin. In between the two separate poles of being (self and non-self), he keeps resisting an imminent fall, as it were (into *adhyāsa*, the confluence of subject and object). Responding to the irreducible void, the field composed of the disconnectedness of self from the world—out of which freedom of imagination emerges—Śaṅkara goes on speaking in many voices; among these, as we suggest in the Epilogue, only one is the pristine, real self, as it were. Except for the Epilogue, the bulk of this essay is devoted to a search for subtle distinctions between the author and his *siddhāntins*.

In the absence of such distinctions, Śaṅkara scholars have treated the author as essentially invisible, with no discrete existence apart from that of his exponent. The existence of a different, normally inaudible voice is the notion I use to explain the 'inner-split' in the intellectual make-up of the Śaṅkara Advaita. What I mean to suggest here is that Advaita messages are embedded in, even fostered by, moods of doubt, wonder, recognition of true opposition, and perhaps even pain. Sensing the presence of opposition and living in true dialogue with others who do not share his arch-exponent's (*siddhāntin*'s) views, Śaṅkara is fully human in his diversity of being and moods. The Advaita vision of a consciousness-generated self, insistent on the unity and oneness of everything is undoubtedly attractive. Śaṅkara's version however, (Viveka-Vedānta) invites opposition and doubt; it is an unbelievable truth. Yet the invisible composer of the BSBh lives out this truth, however incredible it may be, as a lonely figure even among the creatures of his mind. He should not be identified with his exponents (*siddhāntins*).

A new hero, an original thinker, and a man of the spirit emerges; Śaṅkara produces a discourse that offers a glimpse of a primary mode of speaking that is embedded in large sections of "as-if" speech-acts. To be sure, the emergent *vivekin* does repeatedly side with his victorious *siddhāntin*, who is committed to the Upaniṣadic version of *ātman* and experience. And yet, as he re-enacts complexities of tone and message, he brings out a quality of consciousness manifestly different from that of his arch exponent.

What, then, is the quality of our author's voice? In the greater part of this essay, I have represented Śaṅkara as a man of changing boundaries of self; he is, therefore, a philosopher holding, however implicitly, to a "fluid metaphysics." Remembrance of things past, reunion with an allegedly older self, use of referential language (committed, as it were, to the existence of objects), making room for others' voices—all these imply a fluidity in the boundaries of self.

In the course of this study, I offer a number of indications or expressions of the difference between the author and the *siddhāntins*. These include explicit confessions of the author's doubt-filled, questioning moods; the exponent's apparent weaknesses and failures in answering the opponent's (*pūrva-pakṣin's*) challenges; the dialogical framework inherent to the *bhāṣya*-structure; Advaita contents playfully put into an opponent's mouth; the *ātman*'s first-person speech-acts according to the *Upadeśa-sāhasrī*; the ironical attitude toward a somewhat ridiculous arch-exponent; the aforementioned rejection of the *siddhāntins*' verbalization of Upaniṣadic theories of creation, and so forth.

Behind the entire composition is a playful writer. Śaṅkara is a true artist who often speaks independently of his primary protagonist (the *siddhāntin*). As M. Bakhtin says of Dostoevsky (whom he considers a true author capable of representing the voices and consciousness of others): "If the umbilical cord uniting the hero to his creator is not cut, then what we have is not a work of art but a personal document."[4] Śaṅkara's work is not a single-voiced "personal document." Rather, it is a work of art where other, alien voices are truly heard.

Let us articulate the relationship between the author and his creature in terms of our alleged author's own self-understanding. Śaṅkara *would say* (we argue in chapter 5) that the positions of both author and arch-exponent are characterized by omniscience (*sarva-jñatva*), comparable to Pāṇini and his grammar and to Brahman and the Veda. The author and his exponent are 'omniscient.' And yet, just as Pāṇini has superior knowledge (*adhikatara-vijñāna*) in relation to his composition, and as Brahman—in his capacity as 'author of the Veda'—is superior to his composition, so is the omniscient author of the BSBh superior to his message in the shape of the exponent's finalized doctrine. Thus Śaṅkara's perception of authorship (BSBh 1.1.3) is a near explicit and conscious expression of the difference between himself and his chosen exponents. Indeed, Śaṅkara must have been fully aware of the contradictions between his own Viveka-Vedānta version of the Upaniṣadic wisdom (fully explicated in the introduction to the BSBh but finding expression elsewhere) and the *siddhānta*-positions expressed under certain circumstances in various intellectual environments.

Śaṅkara is held by the vast majority of Western and Indian scholars alike to have given the most elevated, pristine expression to Hindu spirit and thought. Mādhava (14th century) in his encyclopedia of Indian schools of thought (*sarva-darśana-saṅgraha*) places Śaṅkara's school of Advaita-Vedānta at the very summit of the philosophical and spiritual traditions of India (including Buddhist traditions). Mādhava's assessment of Advaita as the supreme vision of reality is accepted to this day among Hindu intellectuals and reformers, and scholars of Hinduism (see, for example, Rammohan Roy, 1772–1833). In short, Advaita is Śaṅkara's Advaita. And yet to my mind, a primary distinction is called for with respect to the scope of oneness implied

---

[4] Bakhtin 1993: 51.

in the concept of Advaita. In my exposition of Śaṅkara's teachings, the concept of Advaita is of two kinds: the greater and lesser Advaita. The first (greater) Advaita focuses on the consciousness-made oneness of the self which is everything. The lesser Advaita is the vision of the oneness of the self in its ontological difference from objective reality (which is real). Committed to the oneness of *ātman* yet also to the reality of worldly, objective existence, Śaṅkara is, in my view, a "lesser Advaitin." Challenged by the Upaniṣadic vision of greater Advaita, Śaṅkara develops his own secret teaching. The identity of self with Brahman (the "absolute") is in Śaṅkara's experience the ultimate reality of the oneness of self but this (experience) in no way nullifies or negates any reality other than that of the self. Thus, Śaṅkara shares the vision of the *pūrva-pakṣin* who considers light, *jyoyis*, to be real, namely, meant by the Veda, while the *siddhāntin* insists that the word "light" invariably signifies *ātman* or Brahman, leaving no space for anything other than that.

The doubt-ridden question underlying Śaṅkara's thought is this: how is this world possible? It is made possible, he answers, by the superimposition of the (real) self upon the (real) object and vice versa. Thus, Śaṅkara the lesser Advaitin tends toward the view of the *pūrva-pakṣin* who is aware that light (*jyotis*), space, and life-breath may have a separate existence. He occupies a position half-way between the greater-Advaita-*siddhāntin* and the *pūrva-pakṣin* in the *bhāṣya*s devoted to the meaning of certain Upaniṣadic words. Although neither an exponent nor an opponent, the author incorporates them both. It is this inherently in-between position that makes Śaṅkara what he is.

What, then, is Śaṅkara's greatest contribution to civilization? What has made his philosophy and commentary of the Upaniṣads and the *Brahma-sūtra* so resonant for millions of Hindus (and scholars and others in the West)? Whence comes this extraordinary recognition of the man's greatness? It would seem to be related to what he says about freedom, a state of mind conditioned by mankind's self-understanding. In Śaṅkara's vision, freedom and imagination of self go together. His articulation of the subtle connection between the imagined self and freedom seems to empower and enhance the presence of freedom half-hidden, as it were, beneath the surface of experience. For as a matter of fact everyone finds something resonant in the "idea of freedom." Given this datum of experience, as true and real as the (undeniable) sense of I, the question is how is freedom possible? Freedom, *mokṣa*, is the horizon towards which Śaṅkara's attention is drawn. The oneness of self (*ātman*) and the separation of self from non-self, he says, are implied by the very possibility of an intense openness called *mokṣa*. And the possibility of freedom, he would say, is real and invaluable; it is the essence of the nature of man and woman. In this context, Śaṅkara offers a telling comparison between human beings and beasts. Like beasts, human beings (however superior in intelligence) are afflicted by *adhyāsa*; they are by nature not free and incapable of imagining a true self. Only the enlightened, poet-like sage lives freely by his capacity for "metaphor," *gauṇa*. In short, *mokṣa* becomes possible for men and women by virtue of *viveka*.

Some twenty something years ago I was sitting with David Shulman on the lawn of the Givat-Ram campus of the Hebrew University. I told him of my fascination with the notion of different levels of truth and reality, a notion I believed to underlie Śaṅkara's BSBh. You should write a book about that, he answered. For me this was a moment of birth (in the spirit of healthy debt).

This slim volume is a payment of that debt to Shulman who, with his broad perspectives and the many disciplines and voices that gave rise to them (languages, poetry, grammars, philosophy, psychology) stands foremost among scholarly lovers of India in our age. In my case, it is Shulman's love for flesh-and-blood textuality expressive of moods, emotions and metaphysics that has made me approach literature and philosophy in a new way.

I also dedicate this volume to the memory of Wilhelm Halbfass, my mentor at the University of Pennsylvania. One day, as I expressed misgivings about myself engaged as I was in interpretation rather than solid, respectable research, he suddenly said: "Interpretation, that's what we want". For me, this statement of Halbfass made a big difference.

A re-reading of the entire BSBh as "multi-voiced Advaita-Vedānta" (no doubt a worthy project) is beyond the scope of this book. Moreover, my awareness of the distinction between the author and his Advaita protagonist requires constant alertness and resistance to the usual conflation of the two. It is a difficult endeavour. In my own terms, I am often a fallen reader, failing to differentiate the author from the creature of his mind. Thus, if reading the BSBh in its full-bodied textuality would be considered payment of my debt to Shulman, a sense of debt as yet remains.

I am grateful to Gadia Scott, my editor, who, overcoming motherly preoccupation with a child and a new baby, delved into a tradition opposite in values and spirit to her motherly circumstances. Alex Cherniak edited the Sanskrit and put the diacritical signs in place. Naphtali Meshel, a committed Sanskritist and scholar of ritual and the "grammar of sacrifice" in the Bible, made invaluable corrections and intellectual suggestions of many kinds. Absorbed in his PhD thesis on Upaniṣadic ritualized texts as workshops of death, Tzakhi (Yitzhak) Freedman made substantial contributions to the final form of this book, particularly in cutting off repetitive, redundant passages. Betsie Rosenberg, a poet and true lover of old India, made valuable comments on inner contradictions in my presentation of the differences between author and *siddhāntin*. Finally, my wife Rivka made me realize the need to let this book go, and be finished. I, for my part, would go on and on.

CHAPTER ONE

ON THE CHALLENGE OF LISTENING TO ŚAṄKARA'S VOICES: DIALOGUE AND MONOLOGUE IN ŚAṄKARA'S WRITING

Śaṅkara, author of the BSBh, is present in his work. The nature and quality of his voice and imagination are suggested in his writing. Does he make room for truly other voices? Are Śaṅkara's *bhāṣya*s "monologues" or "dialogues"?[1] The so-called conflating paradigm in reading Śaṅkara presupposes a quality of a single-voice monologue. The dialogical appearance of the text is merely an as-if dialogue, they say, but is inherently a monologue (an author's monologue). We offer, in contrast, a reading grounded in the assumption that the dialogical framework in Śaṅkara is genuine. We also argue that the way this framework is displayed in the BSBh necessarily implies a distinction between composer and *siddhānta*-hero. Thus, in our view, the author's re-enactment of his opponents' vision is thought-in-process, never reaching an organic stop. In a sense, the exponent's weaknesses (or indecisive victories) of sorts are inherent throughout.

Indeed, major propositions of Advaita-Vedānta are articulated with opposite ideas in view. Liberation is opposite to bondage; individual souls (*jīva*) are numerous, *ātman* is one; disembodiment is opposite to embodiment (self-identification with *ātman* is opposite to self-identification with a body); Vedic imperatives are contrasted with freedom from imperatives (*mokṣa*); pain in *saṃsāra* is opposed to *ānanda*, the irreversible relief of pain; a universe of instrumentality (cause-and-effect existence—*sādhya-sādhana-bhava*) is contrasted with the domain of total openness (*mokṣa*); action is opposed to renunciation of action; the reality of *ātman* is contrasted with illusory (worldly) phenomena. The world of multiplicity is illusory; Brahman is one and real. And so on. That is how the author of the BSBh heeds incessant opposition and lives in constant dialogue and doubt. For in Śaṅkara's life opposition seems to live on and on; its never-ending presence fuels the composition

[1] A dialogue preserves a sense of otherness respected. There is a true space in the author's consciousness for a voice different from his own.

of the BSBh. That is why we see the exchange with opponents as inherently, truly dialogical in nature. Given the importance, weight and disturbing presence of opposition of various kinds, the dialogical mood is also a token of doubt.

Doubt is inherent in the vivekin's life. For the author attending to the unabridgeable gap between self and non-self cannot but be acutely aware of the riddle of being "alive in the body," a living embodiment of contradiction, as it were. The appearance of the dialogical framework in Śaṅkara's work implies true dialogue rather than a mere literary device.

As noted in the preface, Śaṅkara is a true writer, like Dostoevsky according to Bakhtin's *Problems of Dostoevsky's Poetics*. Dialogue, says Bakhtin, is a primary vehicle in the creative process of formation of ideas and thought.

> The idea begins to live, that is to take shape, to develop, to find and renew its verbal expression, to give birth to new ideas, only when it enters into genuine dialogic relationships with other ideas, with the ideas of *others*. Human thought becomes genuine thought, that is, an idea, only under conditions of living contact with another and alien thought, a thought embodied in someone else's voice, that is, in someone else's consciousness expressed in discourse. At that point of contact between voice-consciousness the idea is born and lives.[2]

We take the dialogical framework of the BSBh in earnest; as suggested above, talk of Advaita doctrine is somewhat misleading. Rather than a solid, congealed theory, there is Advaita discourse, searching and, surely, also a horizon of attractive contact with the true self (*ātman*), one and only. Advaita doctrines such as the theory of the one *ātman* made of consciousness stand out in the field of Advaita discourse, but there is opposition as well as various philosophical experiments with the truth of the one *ātman*. Above all, recognition of recalcitrant objectivity makes the author of the BSBh speak and experiment. As suggested above, his own living in the face of its impossibility drives the philosopher.

The vast scholarly production on Śaṅkara's Advaita regularly relates to his work as marked with a sense of coherence, incompatible with the dialogical framework essential to Śaṅkara's writing and consciousness. There is, to be sure, an Advaita doctrine of the one self, without qualities (*nirguṇa*), eternal, the true existence, the contact and identification

[2] Bakhtin 1984: 88.

with which makes everything else mere appearance, illusion—as it were. But given the reality of dialogue and consequent sense of doubt, Advaita discourse is inherently multi-vocal, searching, ever watchful of opposition. Keenly heeding the "Advaita doctrine" of the one self, speaking Advaitins like Śaṅkara, author of the BSBh, preserve a recalcitrant recognition of true opponents and voices of otherness.

Given this presupposition of Śaṅkara's dialogical process of thinking, there is a need to adopt a compatible strategy of reading or re-writing the BSBh. I assume reconstruction of Śaṅkara's *bhāṣya* is advisable in order to expose his ways of thought and speech and the nature of his presence as author of the BSBh. Reconstruction in this context means re-writing the *bhāṣyas* in explicit dialogical form, which means, in my view, the addition of implied opponents (partners to dialogue).[3] Thus, an ideal reconstruction of a Śaṅkara *bhāṣya* entails the articulation of thought-in-opposition displayed in dialogues with overt and implied opponents. The presupposition informing such an apparently bold procedure (namely, introducing non-existing, as it were, opponents) is the following: Advaita-Vedānta invites intense opposition of which referential language is but the most conspicuous dimension. Built-in opposition is an integral component or presence in the very process of an Advaitin's thought.

The following is my reconstruction of BSBh 2.3.43–46 (to be discussed from a different perspective in chapter 3). In this section of the BSBh we notice a fluidity characteristic of the living Advaita discourse. A *siddhāntin* changes his mind (or is replaced by another). The opponent seems assured of an Advaita truth (of the oneness of *jīva* and *ātman*). Communication (dialogue) is true and real, leading to a conclusive statement which is not as conclusive and self-assured as one would imagine. The sublime truth of the *jīva*/*ātman* unity is said to be of value also for ordinary people (*laukikasyâpi*), or is of no negative impact (*ānarthakya*). In the context of this dialogue, as in others, the *siddhānta*-statement has a somewhat defensive, inconclusive tone.

Author: The individual soul and Īśvara are related as something which is acted upon (*upakārya*) and something which makes it (the individual soul) act (*upakāraka*). We see in the world that such entities are connected as master and servant or fire and sparks.

[3] I borrow and adapt this term from Wayne Booth's concept of implied author; Booth 1993: 71–76.

Implied Opponent: So what is the problem? It is obvious, as proposed above (BSBh 2.3.40–42) that Īśvara makes the soul act and that the soul is acted upon.

Author: But there is this doubt: is Īśvara master-like and the soul its servant, or is Īśvara like fire and the souls its sparks, as it were?

Opponent: There is indeed doubt here. I think there are two options; either this matter is inherently undecided, or that Īśvara stands in relation to the soul as master and servant; for such a relation is compatible with concepts of *upakāraka* and *upakārya*.

Siddhāntin: The *jīva* should be taken as part (*aṃśa*) of Īśvara as sparks are part of fire (*jīva īśvarasyâṃśo bhavitum arhati yathâgner visphuliṇgaḥ*).

Implied Opponent: Can the *jīva* be truly said to be part of Īśvara?

Siddhāntin: Of course not. *Jīva* is (merely), as it were, part of Īśvara (*aṃśa ivâṃśaḥ*).

Implied Opponent: Why do you hide behind an as-if position?

Siddhāntin: Because there is no part in the primary sense for the one without parts (Īśvara) (*na hi niravayavasya mukhyo 'ṃśaḥ saṃbhavati*).

Opponent: So why not simply assert that he is without any parts (and therefore the *jīva* is one with it) (*kasmāt punar niravayavatvāt sa eva bhavati*)?

Siddhāntin: Because there is instruction which asserts multiplicity (!) (namely, a difference of Īśvara and the *jīva*) (*nānā-vyapadeśāt*).

Opponent: Where do you find teachings of Vedānta about the difference of Īśvara and the *jīva*?

Siddhāntin: Chāndogya Upaniṣad 8.7: He (*ātman*) should be sought, must be known (*so 'nveṣṭavyaḥ sa vijijñāsitavyaḥ*).

Implied Opponent: You assert that *ātman* is different from the individual soul!

Siddhāntin: Yes, indeed. And there is more evidence for it.

Implied Opponent: What do you mean?

Siddhāntin: The *Bṛhadāraṇyaka* says: whoever knows him becomes a true sage (*etam eva viditvā munir bhavati*). And also 3.7.23: That which is within the self moves the self (*ya ātmani tiṣṭhann ātmānam antaro yamayati*).

Implied Opponent: And what do all these references come to?

Siddhāntin: If there were no difference (between *ātman* and *jīva*), the teaching of difference would not hold (*câivaṃ-jātīyako bheda-nirdeśo nâsati bhede yujyate*).

Opponent: Thus, if the soul is part of Īśvara (or *ātman*) (in the established difference of *ātman* and the soul), the relation of *ātman* and the *jīva* should be understood as similar to that of master and servant.

Siddhāntin: No. For there are other Vedic passages that refer to the soul as identical with *ātman*.

Implied Opponent: Are such references compatible with your conception of the soul as part of *ātman*?

Siddhāntin: Yes, indeed. For the teaching of the soul being part of *ātman* is not a consequence of references to the doctrine of the difference (of *ātman* and soul) (*na ca nānā-vyapadeśād eva kevalād aṃśatva-pratipattiḥ*).

Implied Opponent: What kind of references (with respect to the oneness of *ātman* and the individual soul) do you have in mind?

Siddhāntin: It is said in the *Atharva-Veda*: Fishermen, slaves, and gamblers are all Brahman.

Implied Opponent: But such people are lowly indeed!

Siddhāntin: Yes, they depend upon their masters as the soul depends upon Īśvara and is part of him.

Implied Opponent: But then everything is Brahman!

Siddhāntin: Indeed. The individual souls made of aggregates of components, implicated in a universe of causality and instrumentality, are all Brahman.

And there are other Vedic statements to the same effect.

Implied Opponent: Do you have some quotations from major Upaniṣads?

Siddhāntin: Yes, I do. See for example a passage from the *Śvetâśvatara Upaniṣad* 4.3: you are woman; you are man; you are youth; you are maiden; you are an old man...." And of course, a statement such as BU 3.7.23: He is the only seer; there is no other... (*nânyo 'to 'sti draṣṭā*).

Implied Opponent: What, then, is the connection between the contradictory statements on the difference and non-difference of the soul with *ātman* (or Īśvara) and the assertion that the soul is part of *ātman*?

Siddhāntin: Consciousness (*caitanya*) is common to Īśvara and the individual soul as heat (is common) to fire and its sparks (*caitanyaṃ câviśiṣṭam jivêśvarayor yathâgni-visphuliṅgayor auṣṇyam*).

Implied Opponent: But then the *jīva* and Īśvara are identical and also different!

Implied *Siddhāntin*: Yes, indeed.

Implied Opponent: How is such a theory compatible with the idea that *jīva* is part of Īśvara?

Siddhāntin: The theory of *jīva* being part of Īśvara is grounded in the conception of difference and non-difference (of *jīva* and Īśvara) (*bhedâbhedâvagamābhyām aṃśatvâvagamaḥ*).

(Here begins BSBh 2.3.45)

Implied Opponent: The idea of the *jīva* as part of Īśvara (or *ātman*) is in need of more evidence.

Siddhāntin: That the individual soul is part of Brahman is also known from *Smṛti*.

Implied Opponent: Where is it?

Siddhāntin: The *Bhagavad-Gītā* 15.7 says: An eternal part of myself is the *jīva* in this living world (*mamâivaṃśo jīva-loke jīva-bhūtaḥ sanātanaḥ*).

Implied Opponent: But in the case of Lord Kṛṣṇa the relationship of the Lord and the individual soul is that of master and servant, not of fire and sparks.

Siddhāntin: In this world, the relation of master and servant may not go together with the relation of part and whole. However, the Veda asserts that such relations might co-exist.

Opponent: Let it be so. But then listen to the following argument: if the soul is connected with Īśvara or the *ātman* as part and whole, then any pain experienced by the soul would be felt by Īśvara or *ātman* as well! Grim and miserable Īśvara or *ātman* would be.

Implied *Siddhāntin*: What do you mean?

Opponent: As the whole of Devadatta suffers and feels pain when his hand or leg are cut or injured, so would Īśvara or *ātman* be afflicted by any pain experienced by any part of theirs.

Implied *Siddhāntin*: What do you mean?

Opponent: In your view of the soul being part of Īśvara, it would be much better to live in *saṃsāra* than in *mokṣa*! For *ātman*'s suffering would in this case be endless!
(Here begins BSBh 2.3.46)

Siddhāntin: Īśvara does not experience pain in *saṃsāra* as the *jīva* does (*yathā jīvaḥ saṃsāra-duḥkham anubhavati nâivam para īśvaro 'nubhavatîti pratijānīmahe*).

Implied Opponent: How does the soul experience pain?

Siddhāntin: The *jīva* identifying itself with the body due to the power of misconception becomes afflicted with suffering by the thought "I suffer"; thus does one feel pain produced by misconception (*jīvo hy avidyâveśa-vaśād dehâdy-ātma-bhāvam iva gatvā tat-kṛtena duḥkhena duḥkhy aham ity avidyāyā kṛtaṃ duḥkhôpabhogam abhimanyate*).

Implied Exponent: How does Īśvara become free of pain?

Siddhāntin: Īśvara does not perceive his self to be in the body (*nâivaṃ paramêśvarasya dehâdy-ātma-bhāvaḥ*); neither does he imagine himself to be in pain (*duḥkhâbhimāno vâsti*).

Implied Opponent: But then the individual self (*jīva*) is different than [from] Īśvara, since it experiences pain or suffering.

Siddhāntin: No. The imagination of pain on the part of the soul is also unreal; such imagination originates by [in] the confusion consisting in lack of discrimination towards the nature of the entities bound by connection to the senses and so forth, objects created by virtue of misconception (*jīvasyâpy avidyā-kṛta-nāma-rūpa-nirvṛtta-dehêndriyâdy-upādhy-aviveka-bhrama-nimitta eva duḥkhâbhimāno na tu paramârthiko 'sti*).

Implied Opponent: And yet, I do feel many kinds of pain; I suffer when my son and friend suffer; it is plain pain, as real as the pain I feel in my own body.

Implied *Siddhāntin*: Bodily pain is as unreal as pain caused by self-identification with others. In both cases the cause is false understanding of the self.

Implied Opponent: But then correct metaphysics is the remedy for any and every type of pain!

Implied *Siddhāntin*: Indeed.

Implied Opponent: I love my son and friends. Even if I could let go of my own body, I could not forsake (renounce) my son and friends.

Siddhāntin: As in the case of one who experiences pain caused by burns and cuts in one's own body, so is pain caused by false identification with others such as sons and friends; one experiences pain insofar as one thinks by the power of love (*sneha-vaśa*) "I am really my son", "I am really my friend" (*yathā ca sva-deha-gata-dāha-cchedâdi-nimittaṃ duḥkhaṃ tad-abhimāna-bhrāntyânubhavati tathā putra-mitrâdi-gocaram api duḥkhaṃ tad-abhimāna-bhrāntyâivânubhavaty aham eva putro 'ham eva mitram ity evaṃ sneha-vaśena putra-mitrâdiṣv abhiniviśamānaḥ*).

Implied Opponent: If renunciation of one's identification with one's body is truly possible, then everything is possible!

Siddhāntin: Thus, by virtue of this consideration, the matter is finally settled (*tataś ca niścitam etad avagamyate*).

Implied Opponent: What precisely is the conclusion established by your argument?

Siddhāntin: That one suffers because of confusion and false sense of self (*mithyâbhimāna-bhrama-nimitta eva duḥkhânubhava iti*).

Implied Opponent: Is this the only cause of suffering?

Siddhāntin: Yes. Confusion and wrong sense of self is the exclusive cause of suffering (*....nimitta eva*).

Implied Opponent: Can you illustrate by examples how true knowledge eliminates suffering?

Siddhāntin: Yes. From the mutual exclusion of knowledge and pain I can show you how they differ (*vyatireka-darśanāc câivam avagamyate*).

Implied Opponent: Please show me directly, in a clear-cut way, as one points to a cow by holding its horns.

Siddhāntin: It is like that: Suppose that among the many people who have sons and friends, some of them identify themselves as such, and others (who do not see sons and friends as their own) do not. As a message comes through—"(Your) son is dead"; "(your) friend is dead"—there rises sorrow for those who identify their sons and friends as their own whereas there is no sorrow for wandering ascetics who do not consider son and friends their own (*tathā hi—putra-mitrâdimatsu bahuṣûpaviṣṭeṣu tat- sambandhâbhimāniṣv itareṣu ca putro mṛto mitraṃ mṛtam ity evam-ādy-udghoṣite yeṣām eva putra-mitrâdimattvâbhimānas teṣām eva tan-nimittaṃ duḥkham utpadyate nâbhimāna-hīnānāṃ parivrajakâdīnām*).

Implied Opponent: You are truly fond of drama. Carried away by excessive imagination, you seem to forget about Vedic authority.

Implied *Siddhāntin*: I only say what the author makes me say. And mind you, I did not say anything about the oneness of *jīva* and *ātman*; such a teaching is truly beyond me.

Implied Opponent: So what did you mean to say by way of your imaginary experiment of householders and *saṃnyāsins* whose sons and friends die?

Siddhāntin: Even for a worldly man true knowledge (of the self) is most useful (*ataś ca laukikasyâpi puṃsaḥ samyag-darśanârthavattvam dṛṣṭam*).

Implied Opponent: And yet, if the individual souls (*jīva*) are part (*aṃśa*) of Īśvara, then Īśvara (nonetheless) feels the pain of those householders caring for their sons and friends.

Siddhāntin: No. For the self, whose nature consists of mere consciousness, does not recognize anything other (than himself) (*kim uta* *viṣaya-śūnyād ātmano 'nyad vastv-antaram apaśyato nitya-caitanya-mātra-sva-rūpasyêti*).

Implied Opponent: But what about man and woman "in the world", individual souls as they are, being parts (*aṃśa*) of Īśvara?

Implied *Siddhāntin*: You are right. The *jīva* is not part of Īśvara or *ātman*. The individual soul is an as-if part of *ātman*, not truly part of Īśvara.

Implied Opponent: In your position, there is no difference at all between man and woman and *ātman*. They all are but one.

Implied *Siddhāntin*: That is indeed true knowledge.

Implied Opponent: And yet, the alleged true knowledge of the oneness of *jīva* and *ātman* is of no use for ordinary people unless they cease to be ordinary people (householders).

Siddhāntin: Therefore there is no negative use of true knowledge (*tasmān nâsti samyag-darśanânarthakya-prasaṅgaḥ*).

We see how complex Advaita discourse is. A preliminary protagonist (holding that the *jīva* is part—*aṃśa*—of Īśvara or *ātman*) is replaced by another (who asserts full identity of the two, thus implying non-existence of *jīva*); an opponent asserts the finalized Advaita proposition (that complete identity [oneness] of *ātman* and *jīva* (*siddhānta*-Advaita) is more reasonable than partial identity); a victorious protagonist advocates ultimate truth in a subdued voice (a metaphysics useful for householders who seek alleviation of sorrow); an imagined drama is brought in (terrible news reach the arena of debate). Thus, an author's creative presence is apparent. At the very least, a reader begins to wonder: who was the author of the BSBh, *Bṛhadāraṇyakôpaniṣad-bhāṣya, Bhagavad-gītā-bhāṣya, Upadeśa-sāhasrī*? A somewhat fluid sense of coherence (or underlying consciousness) is in need of articulation. Advaita discourse provokes thoughts of the sage who stitches voices of many kinds among which, of course, the Advaita doctrine of the one self (and only reality) stands out—but is not the only one.

By the methodology of *bhāṣya*-reconstruction, we can sense the reality of discourse within which the apparently final articulation of *siddhānta*-Advaita is but one (however important) moment. The metaphysics of discourse (and true dialogue) are different from those of an overt *siddhānta*-Advaita. Therefore, we say, the author approves of a continuum of reality-in-existence rather than a dichotomy of reality (*ātman*, Brahman) and illusion (*saṃsāra, vyavahāra, māyā*). Moreover, the author of Advaita-discourse should be distinguished from his exponent who holds the theory considered the exclusive doctrine of Advaita Vedānta. Śaṅkara's art of writing betokens a metaphysical truth other than his protagonist's.

CHAPTER TWO

ON DOUBT AND WONDER IN ADVAITA-VEDĀNTA: TOWARDS PERCEIVING A ŚAṄKARA AND A ŚAṄKARĀCĀRYA

Intimacy is dull without doubt.[1]

We have referred above to the nature of Śaṅkara's work as the creation of an Advaita-discourse informed by moods of doubt and dialogue. There emerges, we say, an author's consciousness more complex than that of his main protagonist's. Such complexity reveals itself in questions, doubt, and a dialogical framework. Thus, Śaṅkara, renowned author of the BSBh confesses to questions and doubt as he delves into the Upaniṣads, the sacred sources for true knowledge of the self (*ātman*); does the word *ākāśa* in Chāndogya Upaniṣad 1.9 mean ether or Brahman?[2] Does the word *prāṇa* in 1.2.4–5 mean ordinary breath or Brahman?[3] Does the word *jyotis* in Chāndogya Upaniṣad 3.13.7 denote light or Brahman?[4] Does the word *prāṇa* in Kauśītakī Upaniṣad 3.2 and 3.8 mean breath, the self of a deity (*devatâtmā*), the individual self (*jīva*), or the ultimate Brahman (*paraṃ brahma*)?[5]

Following these explicit acknowledgements of uncertainty, the author of the BSBh sets up a dialogical pendulum consisting of a *pūrvapakṣa* view (to be rejected) and a winning, *siddhānta* understanding of the respective Upaniṣadic passages. Sometimes, even the legitimacy of doubt is discussed. Thus, for example, the author articulates his doubt (*tatra saṃśayaḥ*) in the opening paragraphs of BSBh 1.1.28; in a counter move, an opponent denies any possibility for uncertainty, sounding a rhetorical question: how can doubt re-emerge (if the meaning of the word in question—*prāṇa*—has already been settled) (*katham iha punaḥ saṃśayaḥ sambhavati*)? But the author insists: since there are various—apparently conflicting—signs of the entity denoted by the word *prāṇa*,

[1] Annamaya 2005: 5.
[2] BSBh1.1.22.
[3] BSBh1.1.23.
[4] BSBh1.1.24.
[5] BSBh1.1.28.

doubt prevails (*ata upapannaḥ saṃśayaḥ*). However, at the end of each doubt-episode in the BSBh, there is a moment of alleged resolution, and the exponent of *siddhānta*-Advaita is declared victorious. The author seems to know the result of the debate in advance and imagines all sorts of opponents for the sake of persuasive articulation. There was, it seems, no question of doubt from the very start. No wonder the winner wins, and the loser loses.

But suppose for a moment that the author confesses to doubt in earnest; suppose that a sort of natural (*suprasiddha*) or immediate (*śīghram*)[6] interpretation of the sacred text (different from the *siddhānta's*) does arise in the author's mind, creating thereby an occasion for uncertainty, as he (the author) claims. We have then a situation of an author-in-doubt, imagining (or conceiving of) a doubt-free agent (the *siddhāntin*). What would such a textual strategy represent?

There are three possible articulations of the doubt function that unfolds in Śaṅkara's *bhāṣyas* in contexts informed by Veda affirmation: A) the author's doubt is true and is finally resolved (declaration of the *siddhānta*); B) the author's confession of doubt is spurious, a mere literary device bound to persuade an actual or imaginary audience; C) the author's confession of doubt is true but its resolution is often spurious.

According to articulations A and C, the author's voice is distinguished from his *siddhāntin*'s. Proposition A means that the voices of the author and his exponent differ in the beginning (the author oscillates between a *pūrva-pakṣa* and a *siddhānta* view of apparently equal merit), but the *bhāṣya* ends with full concordance; in other words, the author finds truth in his *siddhāntin*'s position. Proposition C asserts that since doubt is a prevailing stance in the BSBh, it should be taken in earnest as a true expression of the author's being; the author-in-doubt is aware of a deeper reality than his exponent; thus, he is inherently different from his doubt-free *siddhāntin*. The author is energized by recurring doubts while the *siddhāntin* is 'crippled by certainty.'

In contradistinction to A and C, proposition B implies full conflation of the author and his *siddhāntin*. The author, according to B, does not truly present *pūrva-pakṣa* and *siddhānta* views on the same par (as a constant or preliminary condition of doubt); rather he playfully

[6] These are terms used by the opponent to recommend the interpretation of *ākāśa* as 'space' rather than *ātman* (BSBh 1.1.22).

introduces opposing voices in order to assert the *siddhānta* view from the very beginning, in a unified author/*siddhāntin*'s voice. The author's confessions of doubt must not be taken 'in earnest.'

The entire tradition and scholarship on Śaṅkara's Advaita are grounded in the B paradigm, which implies (perhaps unconscious) conflation of the voices of the author and *siddhāntin*. Indeed, *every single scholarly statement* on Advaita conflates Śaṅkara the author of the BSBh with the Advaita-*siddhāntin* articulated therein. Every mention of 'Śaṅkara,' Śaṅkarācārya or 'Ādi-Śaṅkarācārya' has been bound to conflate the author and his exponent. Of course, such readings (which I label "confluent") are not implausible; they have proved fertile, exciting, and invaluable. However, to explore the distinction between author and exponent is to free up a space for further speculation about the moods and variations of Advaita-Vedānta.

This commonly held conflation of author and exponenet is consequential to descriptions of Śaṅkara's philosophy or metaphysics. If, as I propose, the denomination 'Śaṅkara' as a unified source of vision or metaphysics is indeed unwarranted, the respective presentation of his metaphysics would be somewhat unwarranted (distorted) as well. If we accept the separation of author and *siddhāntin*, we must inevitably allow for two types of metaphysics (author's and exponent's); the difference between the two voices would imply differences of vision and metaphysics.[7]

In fact, some rather significant differences of metaphysics are already apparent; the most important is the two respective perceptions of the relationship between Brahman and worldly plurality, briefly discussed in the preface to this book. The *siddhāntin* is often a pure monist since he ascerts that the self or Brahman is the only unchangeable true reality; everything else is illusionary. Once we realize that the snake is a rope, it vanishes from existence altogether; there is nothing in-between the real and the unreal. In terms of the exponent's Advaita meta-psychology, there is no place for doubt or ambivalence in the encounter between worldly phenomena and Brahman or *ātman*. The author, on the other hand, maintains his sense of wonder grounded in the resistence to (or negation of) any possible relation (or connection) of Brahman and the world. The sense of wonder emerges from a successful, ice-cold

[7] Explication of the author's and the exponent's respective metaphysics is beyond the scope of the present study.

refusal to project selfhood on the world and vice versa (to superimpose objectivity onto the self). The *adhyāsa*-free author recognizes the existence and relevance of the world, and sees a measure of truth and reality in worldly phenomena. Such truth and reality are perhaps inferior to those of Brahman and the self, but they are nonetheless undeniable. Śaṅkara is an author driven by wonder and doubt, deeply familiar with *ātman*'s existence yet somewhat insecure in expressing its relationship with worldly plurality as revealed by sense-perception (*pratyakṣa*). According to the introduction of the BSBh he is prone to negate any such relationship altogether. How then can he talk and move his body? As suggested above, Śaṅkara asserts that ordinary, voluntary motions of the body are impossible without projection of self on the body. How then is speech and life possible? There is of course an answer; the *adhyāsa*-free author, aware of the unabridgeable void between *viṣayin* and *viṣaya* speaks as if there is a connection of sorts (for the author of the BSBh is alive). And yet, since life goes on for the *adhyāsa*-free sage, wonder and doubt prevail.

As an example, we might refer to his cry of wonder, as it resounds succinctly in BSBh 1.1.2: "Is this perceptible world connected with Brahman? Is it connected with anything else? It is indeed impossible to know" (*kiṃ brahmaṇā sambaddhaṃ, kim anyena kenacit sambaddham iti na śakyaṃ niścetum*). The statement that "it is indeed impossible to know" is, in my reading, either an expression of true doubt or wonder or negation of any relation of self and the world. It is the author's voice, one of the glimpses of Śaṅkara's secret teaching. The *siddhāntin* never admits doubt and is forever victorious; he is one who thinks that he knows.

Resisting the conflation of author and exponent invites a split within the reader. This is somewhat painful, for one has to re-read Śaṅkara's *bhāṣya*s with a double sense of doubt or suspicion; the apparent *siddhānta*-contents may not be shared by the author (the "real Śaṅkara") and the voluminous, rich scholarly output on Śaṅkara's Advaita must now also be re-assessed.

Let us choose a few incidental examples of good confluent reading. Surendranath Dasgupta succinctly sums up some major principles of conflated Śaṅkara's Advaita-Vedānta:

> Śaṅkara does not try to prove philosophically the existence of the pure self as distinct from all other things, for he is satisfied in showing that the Upaniṣads describe the pure self unattached to any kind of impurity as the ultimate truth. This with him is a matter to which no exception can

> be taken, for it is so revealed in the Upaniṣads. This point being granted, the next point is that our experience is always based upon an identification of the self with the body, the senses, etc. and the imposition of all phenomenal qualities of pleasure, pain, etc. upon the self; and this with Śaṅkara is a beginningless illusion.[8]

Dasgupta offers a sober presentation of common knowledge regarding Śaṅkara's Advaita. It is indeed a standard, reliable version of conflated Advaita.[9] Moreover, as far as the role and presence of the Upaniṣads in the mind of both author and *siddhāntin*, Dasgupta may be right (although an exploration of the relationship of revelation and reason could supply some points of difference). Both a conflated and a non-conflated reading of author and exponent with respect to Vedic authority are potentially correct, or at least adequate; for, as suggested above, the intimacy of author and *siddhāntin* is founded on acceptance of the Upaniṣads as *pramāṇa*, in particular the proposition of the oneness of the self. Now, even with respect to the primary principle of Śaṅkara's meta-psychology, namely, imposition (*adhyāsa*) of self on object and vice versa, conflation of author and *siddhāntin* seems legitimate or valuable. However, Dasgupta's excellent articulation of Śaṅkara's philosophy of *adhyāsa*-inflicted experience does not incorporate the distinction between the author committed to the reality of objective, worldly phenomena and the Upaniṣadic *siddhāntin* who conceives of the object as illusion. Considering the strong dualism of the introduction to the BSBh, together with the minimal logical force of the numerous *dṛṣṭānta*s as well as the vivid imagination of rival positions and numerous introductory confessions of doubt, etc., Dasgupta's posited dichotomy between the reality of Brahman and the world as utter illusion may be an integral aspect of the *siddhāntin*'s, not the author's, metaphysics. The author of the BSBh maintains doubt and wonder in regard to the relationship between pure subject and object, (or of the

---

[8] Dasgupta 1997, v. 1: 435.

[9] See, for example, T.J. Hopkins' articulation of the dichotomy between Brahman's ultimate reality and the illusionary world: Śaṅkara argued that the entire Vedānta, in which he included the *Gītā* as well as the Upaniṣads and the Brahma Sūtras, taught the sole reality of the impersonal Brahman devoid of all qualities (*nirguṇa*). The assumption of qualities and of name and form is a result of ignorance (*avidyā*) resulting from *māyā* ('illusion," as Śaṅkara interprets it). The entire phenomenal world is thus ultimately illusory, since its existence results from the false imposition of qualities on Brahman. It is not unreal in a practical sense, but in comparison with *nirguṇa* Brahman it has no real existence. Hopkins 1971: 119.

possibility of such a relationship between self and body, as distinct from one another as light and darkness), and between Brahman and the plurality of worldly phenomena.

A characteristic hallmark of conflated Advaita is it's being naturally grounded in a certain sense of strict coherence superimposed on the Advaitin's texts. An underlying presupposition of Dasgupta's presentation is that Śaṅkara says one thing, in one voice. Coherence is, of course, very important for our *siddhāntin*; he asserts, in fact, that the Upaniṣads are coherent in that they assert one and only one proposition, namely, that *ātman* and Brahman are one and everything. I do not mean to say that Śaṅkara contradicts himself; such a statement would again be informed by conflation of author and exponent. The *siddhāntin* does not contradict himself; his teaching is inherently coherent (and, one may even add, reasonably cogent). And yet, again, the author is not necessarily his exponent. Professional philosophers and scholars striving for coherence tend to overlook the possibility that a multiplicity of voices may exist.

Another example of a scholarly endeavour based on such a conflation is Halbfass' presentation of Śaṅkara's complex view on the relationship of revelation and reasoning in Advaita-Vedānta. See how attractive, well-integrated and coherent Halbfass' Śaṅkara seems to be:

> Śaṅkara says that in all the Upaniṣads ultimate unity is first presented as a thesis and then explicated or illustrated in the sense that the world, "by means of examples and reasons," is explained as a modification or part of the absolute self; finally, unity appears again as a conclusion or summary: *sarvāsu hy upaniṣatsu pūrvam ekatvam pratijñāya dṛṣṭāntair hetubhiś ca paramâtmano vikārâṃśâditvaṃ jagataḥ pratipadya punar ekatvam upasaṃharati.*[10] Śaṅkara adds that the cosmological passages dealing with the origination, continuation and dissolution of the world appear generally between "introductions" (*upakrama*) and summarizing "conclusions" (*upasaṃhāra*) concerning the unity of the individual and the absolute self.[11]

Halbfass allows for multiple dimensions in Śaṅkara's writing. He identifies educational impulses (of persuasion, instruction, etc.) in Śaṅkara's writing. Thus, according to Halbfass, Śaṅkara the author of the BSBh is a personality with goals other than the mere coherence of overt contents.

---

[10] BUBh 2.1.20.

[11] Halbfass 1971: 157.

> The terminology which Śaṅkara uses in this context is in part identical with the terminology of the classical theory of inference. But it is also a terminology of persuasion and instruction, and its "logical" connotations cannot be separated from its "pedagogical" implications.[12]

And yet, Halbfass' scholarly energies are blocked by the presupposition of the author/*siddhāntin*'s identity. However much depth, coherence and clarity are evident in Halbfass' presentation, it allows no space for the emergence of doubt and wonder on the author's part. But, an opponent would say, there is no need to assume a significant distinction between the voices (ultimately, it does not make a real difference!). And yet, the separation of author and *siddhāntin* does make a difference; it creates the opportunity for discovering Śaṅkara's inaudibly articulated Advaita and his exponent's (Śaṅkarācārya's) overt Advaita.

Moreover, however forceful, complex and reliable his presentation of Śaṅkara's composition, Halbfass is bound to ignore the opponents (*pūrva-pakṣins*) and their role in Śaṅkara's *bhāṣyas*. In Bakhtin's terminology, Halbfass considers Śaṅkara's BSBh a single-voice verbalization (controlled by a strict sense of coherence), and thus not a work of art but rather a "personal document." In general, confluent readings of Śaṅkara's Advaita tend to relegate *pūrva-pakṣa* views and positions to the distant background, while potentially challenging alternatives (which allow for uncertainty) are denied significance. Consequently, the dialogical quality of Śaṅkara's thought is also ignored.

In his own way, D.D.H. Ingalls also unconsciously conflates author and *siddhāntin*, beautifully moving from consideration of an inherently conflated text to the identity of its author:

> In all these passages one sees that Śaṅkara never admits either horn of the dilemma. Avidyā is never said to be real. It is never said to be unreal. But no new modality is set up to solve the difficulty. One may even state that it is likely that Śaṅkara disapproved the postulation of a third truth-value. This is only a guess. But the concept is certainly as old as the time of Śaṅkara and one may hazard a second guess as to why he rejected it. If the characterizing of the phenomenal world as *anirvacanīya* makes the world no more real than it is in Śaṅkara's doctrine, it makes it a great deal less unreal. Such a characterization may well have seemed unsound to Śaṅkara's intuition.[13]

---

[12] Ibid.
[13] Ingalls 1953: 69–72.

Since the text does not show commitment to either the reality of Avidyā or to its unreality, Ingalls thinks that coherence is not as important to the author of the BSBh, BUBh, BGBh as other things are.

> What Śaṅkara does is to avoid the difficulty. He concentrates on what he considers the heart of the matter, the teaching that is necessary for the attainment of *mokṣa*. The teaching is that Avidyā, whatever its modality, is never truly connected with the self. Here, as in other differences that may be noticed between Śaṅkara and his disciples, one may say that Śaṅkara's approach to truth is psychological and religious. His interest in metaphysics and logic is always subordinated to the center of his attention.[14]

As suggested above, the outcome of the intense quest for coherence, a quest rooted in deciphering the overt meanings of the *siddhāntin*, is that the dialogical quality of Śaṅkara's voice (and its respective metaphysics) is neglected. Conflation of author and exponent makes the presence of opponents imperceptible; they are merely an excuse for the convincing speech of the exponent. However, a close reading reveals that the presence of opponents in the BSBh may hardly be denied meaning. Most significant in this respect are opponents who accept the Upaniṣads as a true means of knowledge (primarily of *ātman*, the self) yet offer a contrasting view to the exponent's radical sense of coherence based on his monolithic perception of the Veda.

The presence of opponents—conspicuously articulate in scholarly literature—is expressive of deeply rooted doubts and wonder on the part of the author and commentator. Indeed, notions of doubt are not lacking in ancient Indian tradition. Controversy lies at the core of speculation in ancient India, and it is accompanied by doubt. As Phyllis Granoff has demonsrated, this doubt reveals itself in the use of supra-natural means in determining the winner in a debate.[15] In Vidyāraṇya's *Śaṅkara-dig-vijaya*, Ubhaya-Bhāratī, Maṇḍana's wife, the incarnation of Sarasvatī, goddess of wisdom, adorns the head of her husband and Śaṅkara with garlands in order to decide the winner; a garland that withers signifies a loser. The narrative is thus skeptical about the entire verbal discourse between the *siddhāntin* (Śaṅkara) and his opponent (Maṇḍana). Like Vidyāraṇya, the author of the BSBh doubts whether reasoning is in itself a sufficient means to realize a philosophical or religious truth, such as the *siddhānta*-truth of his

---

[14] Ibid., p. 72.
[15] Granoff 1985.

exponent. Śaṅkara's potent uncertainty betokens a different metaphysical perspective to that of the exponent; it is, as suggested above, an Advaita vision that is under-explored in the scholarly tradition of the past and the present.

Let us briefly review Granoff's close reading of hagiographies such as the *dig-vijaya*. Granoff highlights doubt in Advaita (as well as in other traditions of thought) from a different perspective. She says:

> ...these texts all reveal a deep-seated suspicion of the ability of debate to determine the truth and convince people of the validity of any given philosophical doctrine.[16]

Granoff offers a potentially illuminating point of view with respect to the nature of the BSBh itself (not only in regard to the doubts which underlie hagiographic traditions). Granoff uses the notion of *śruti* to highlight a tradition of doubt vis-à-vis the power of reasoning to determine truth:

> Debate and rigorous argument had always formed the backbone of Indian philosophical texts from the time of their earliest composition. Nonetheless, Indian religious scholars who engaged in these debates had also always been consistent in emphasizing the primacy of *śruti*, or revealed doctrine, over human reasoning. Within the Vedānta tradition itself, classical thinkers, regardless of their particular scholastic affiliation, agreed in confining human reasoning unsupported by textual authority to the sphere of the mundane. By this they meant to imply that no religious truth could be determined by human intellectual activity alone. The source of such truth must ultimately remain the authoritative texts.[17]

Granoff seems to imply that, functionally, addressing the unnatural in hagiographical literature and philosophical approaches to *śruti* are similar; resolution of doubt is common to both. However, in our reading of the BSBh, discussion of *śruti* is often a primary occasion for the arising of doubt rather than an occasion for certainty. The theme articulated in Śaṅkara's introduction to the BSBh may thus contain a clue for a strategy for reading the entire BSBh. According to such a strategy, the author suspects his exponent's reasoning especially when the *siddhāntin* offers interpretations of *śruti* (Upaniṣads). The exponent's encounter with the Upaniṣadic intention is most often inherently weak. In this regard, we might recall, for example, the opponent's claim in BSBh 1.1.22, stating that the word *ākāśa* as designating ether (rather

[16] Ibid.
[17] Ibid.

than as a designation of Brahman) comes naturally (*suprasiddha*) and quickly (*śīghram*) to the mind.

In accordance with his coherent world-view, the *siddhāntin* is, strictly speaking, certainty-bound; the author, as suggested above, is certainty-free. His exponent's expressions of certainty are often somewhat grotesque, suggesting the opposite of a well-established sense of security. (In other words, the *siddhāntin*'s certainty is concomitant with the author's insecurity or doubt). In this respect, my hypothesis is this: the closer we read the *bhāṣya*, the more capable we are of noticing the difference between the author's and exponent's voices. True competence in reading the *bhāṣya* using this 'way of distinction' would amount to re-reading the entire BSBh.

As a start we can attempt to read some of the more obvious illustrations. See for example the *siddhāntin*'s expression of certainty at the end of the discourse of BSBh 3.3.17. He says that his interpretation of the meanings and connections between four Upaniṣadic passages is as incontrovertible as the meaning of sentences such as 'bring the pot' and 'the pot, bring it' (*āhara pātraṃ pātram āharêty evam-ādiṣv artha-sāmye 'pi tad-darśanāt*). But of course, the exponent's triumphant declaration is a striking banalization of the most important issue of Vedic interpretation, namely, the relationship of conventional meanings (*artha*) and the force of context, etc. While the *siddhāntin* is right that *āhara pātram* and *pātram ahara* have the same meaning (this is trivially true), the overly simplistic argument leaves the reader wondering about the commentator's intentions. Could he really let the winner win this way? Looking closely into the controversy, we can't help but acknowledge the difference between the certainty-bound exponent and his doubt-charged creator. The level of certainty with respect to *āhara pātram* and *pātram āhara* is patently different from, and incompatible with, the alleged sense of certainty attributed to the *siddhāntin*'s interpretation of the respective Upaniṣadic source. Such incompatibility does not seem congruent with the witty, sophisticated, gifted perspective of the author.

Let us view more closely the flavors of spurious certainty and underlying doubt as these are present in the 'pot-illustration' mentioned above. The debate starts at BSBh 3.3.16, which focuses on creation and the one primordial cause, and then moves on to issues of intertextuality, pivotal in the field of Vedic interpretation. With respect to the order of creation, the exponent (whose position is somewhat precarious) says that it really does not matter, since the detailed narrative of creation is of no use for man's (highest) good (*tat-pratipattau puruṣârthâbhāvāt*).[18] At this point, the discourse focuses on coherence as a dimension of intertextual relations. A question is raised about passages of central importance from the two classical Upaniṣads, the *Bṛhadāraṇyaka* and the *Chāndogya*. Do the Upaniṣads speak of one and the same object (or subject) even though they differ in terms of apparent meaning (*artha*)? Or, more specifically, do certain passages in the BU and ChU speak of *ātman* even in cases where no mention is made thereof? The author articulates a doubt and asks: are these passages—though allegedly different in meaning—of the same import (*tulyârtha*) or not (*tatra saṃśayaḥ—tulyârthatvaṃ kim anayor āmnānayoḥ syād atulyârthatvam vêti*)?

The author of BSBh 3.3.16-17 considers passages from BU 4.3.7, 4.4.25, and ChU 6.2.1 and 6.8.7 (which contains *tat tvam asi*) and discusses fundamental issues of Vedic interpretation. Suppose, says the author, some passages refer explicitly to *ātman* or Brahman, and others do not. May one connect the respective passages so that the ones which do not mention *ātman* or Brahman are interpreted in order to refer to *ātman* or Brahman? This is, as suggested above (in the opening paragraphs of this chapter) the theme underlying all the core-*bhāṣya*s in the BSBh. More specifically, are conventional word-meanings (*artha*) or context (*prakṛta, prakaraṇa, vākya-śeṣa*) more forceful in illuminating correct interpretation of Vedic intention (*tātparya*)? The author of the BSBh presents a *siddhānta*-Advaita which submits the following hermeneutics: whenever a passage mentions *ātman* or Brahman it means—by the force of meaning and context—*ātman* or Brahman. Whenever it refers to apparently other entities (such as ether, breath, light, etc.) it refers to *ātman* or Brahman (by force of context). The opponent, as we have seen before, is attentive to *artha* rather than context. He says: difference of denotation reflects difference of meaning (intention) in the Veda. Interpretation of the Veda depends, after all, on meanings; if the meanings of (two) Vedic passages are different it is illegitimate to read them as if their meaning were the same (*atulyârthatvam iti tāvat prāptam atulyatvād āmnānayoḥ. na hy āmnāna-vaiṣamye saty artha-sāmyaṃ yuktaṃ pratipattum āmnāna-tantratvād artha-parigrahasya*).

---

[18] *na hy ayaṃ sakalaḥ kathā-prabandho vivakṣita iti śakyate vaktuṃ, tat-pratipattau puruṣârthâbhāvāt. Brahmâtmatvaṃ tv iha vivakṣitam.*

Thus, the crux of BSBh 3.3.17 is the sameness or oneness of Vedic references, an issue that repeats itself throughout the so-called core-*bhāṣyas*. The exponent and opponent accept the authority of the Veda in its power to determine existence or reality. *Siddhānta*-Advaita asserts that only the one *ātman* exists and—therefore—must necessarily be the only reference of the Veda. Thus, even in passages where *ātman* is not mentioned by virtue of word-meanings (*artha*), it is referred to all the same. The discourse presented in BSBh 3.3.17 reveals a pattern visible in all the core-*bhāṣya*s of the BSBh. The passages from the BU, says the author, speak of *ātman* and its nature. The self is within the heart, made of understanding (*vijñāna-maya*), a person made of inner light (*antar-jyoti*) (BU 4.3.7). By the same token, BU 4.4.25 summarizes the Upaniṣadic teaching of the self as follows: *ātman* is great, unborn, never old, undying, immortal, of no trace of fear, and is Brahman (*sa va eṣa mahān aja ātmâjaro 'maro 'mṛto 'bhayo brahma*). In the famous passage from ChU 6.2.1 Uddālaka Āruṇi tells his son Śvetaketu about the origin of everything; in the beginning, he says, there was existence (*sat*), only one without a second (*sad eva somyêdam agra āsīd ekam evâdvitīyam*). Does the passage from the ChU—which does not mention *ātman* –refer to it as do the passages from the BU?

Giving due respect to what the Veda says by means of word-meanings, the opponent claims that BU teaches about the *ātman*, whereas the ChU must be understood to be different (*vājasaneyake câtma-śabdôpakramād ātma-tattvôpadeśa iti gamyate. chāndogye tûpakrama-viparyayād upadeśa-viparyayaḥ*). But no, says the *siddhāntin*. The difference in apparent meaning does not necessarily imply difference in intention (*āmnāna-vaiṣamyam api nâvaśyam artha-vaiṣamyam āvahati*). Thus though 'bring the pot' and 'the pot, bring it', are apparently different statements, they express the very same intention (*āhara pātraṃ pātram āharêty evam-ādiṣv artha-sāmye 'pi tad-darśanam*). By the same token, in other cases where there are apparent differences in particular contexts of Vedic speech, the intention must not be taken as different. This is the final conclusion of the debate (*tasmād evaṃ-jātīyakeṣu vākyeṣu pratipādana-prakāra-bhede 'pi pratipādyârthâbheda iti siddham*).

The question is: was the author of BSBh 3.3.17 aware of the staggeringly inappropriate nature of his victorious "bring the pot, the pot, bring it" illustration at the end of BSBh 3.3.17? To reduce the all-important, foundational controversy concerning the interpretation of the Upaniṣads as *śabda-pramāṇa* to the 'pot-illustration' seems like a joke. The *siddhāntin*'s weakness in this case is too palpable to ignore.

Can we identify the author's voice with his exponent's in this instance? The author, so it seems, must have been aware of his exponent's improper complacency. In this context, one should exercise the principle of charity and make a distinction between the gifted, profound, playful author and his certainty-crippled, self-assured *siddhāntin* who dares to use the pot-illustration with respect to the meaning of texts like ChU 6.2.1 ('In the beginning, my dear, there was existence only, one without a second'), BU 4.4.25 ('This *ātman*....immortal, is Brahman') and other such passages.

Here lies an existential choice for the reader; if he senses, as we do, the grotesque quality of the simplistic pot-illustration, then he must resist the author/exponent conflation. The author capable of doubt presents a hero incapable thereof; the exponent's pot-illustration can hardly be considered the author's creation 'in earnest' (in his own voice). But what then does the author offer (which his *siddhāntin* does not)? It seems that the author's main focus of interest is the type of coherence that exists within the Upaniṣads (or the *jñāna-kāṇḍa*) of the Veda.

The author of the BSBh investigates the nature of Vedic coherence. His chosen exponent articulates the strictest options in the domain of reference and meaning; whatever the meanings, the Upaniṣads have one inherent reference. Vedic presence points to the one *ātman*. This is the proposition and ideology informing the core-debates of the BSBh through the *siddhāntin*'s voice. Perhaps other references to so-called individuals and other conventionally conceived entities exist. However, such references do not carry ontological commitment; they are used for didactic or pedagogical reasons. When the Veda speaks in earnest it refers to one and only one thing: *ātman* or Brahman. The structure of inner-circle debates with opponents who think otherwise, namely, who propose, for example, that when the Upaniṣad says 'light' it refers to light, are invariably defeated; when the Upaniṣad says 'light' it means or refers to *ātman*.[19]

[19] The programmatic statement in the opening paragraph of BSBh 1.1.4 comes to mind. This Brahman which is omniscient, omnipotent, the cause of the creation, continuity, and dissolution of the world is known exclusively by means of the Veda. How is that possible? By virtue of strict coherence or commensurability (*samanvaya*). For *all* the statements of the Veda cohere with the one intention (purpose) of teaching about this (*tad brahma sarva-jñaṃ sarva-śakti jagad-utpatti-sthiti-laya-kāraṇaṃ Vedānta-śāstrād evâvagamyate. kathaṃ samanvayāt. sarveṣu hi vedānteṣu vākyāni tātparyeṇâitasyârthasya pratipādakatvena samanugatāni*).

But the author does not seem completely satisfied with the *siddhāntin*'s position of extreme coherence. Thus, he confesses to doubts, raises questions, and imagines other perspectives and views. At the end of BSBh 3.3.17 he playfully articulates his exponent's total, dense sense of certainty; whatever the apparent meanings, everything the Upaniṣads say boils down to or is equal to *mahāvākya*s such as *tat tvam asi* (I am that) or *ahaṃ brahmâsmi* (I am Brahman). It is as absolute as the significance of reference expressed by statements such as 'bring the pot' and 'the pot, bring it.' Such a sense of certainty is foreign to our gifted, playful author capable of doubt and wonder.

CHAPTER THREE

ĀTMAN DISTURBED: SELF AND MIND AS ITS OTHER IN THE *UPADEŚA-SĀHASRĪ*

In an unexpected twist in Śaṅkara's *Upadeśa-sāhasrī* ("A Thousand Teachings"), the inherently silent *ātman* (Advaitin's "new self"), which is the one, all-encompassing self, paradoxically becomes a speaker who addresses the mind (*manas*) (the "old self"). Who is behind both *ātman* and the mind? Śaṅkara, the alleged author of the *Upadeśa-sāhasrī* (Upad) creates the self's speeches, aware of the disturbing presence of *manas*. Like the commentator on the *Brahma-sūtra* who invents the *siddhāntin* and his opponents (the *pūrva-pakṣins*), the author of the Upad seems to invent the mind as *ātman*'s recalcitrant, disturbing opponent.

There is, however, a difference in the encounter of *ātman* and mind; for according to the Upad, the latter remains silent. Unlike the numerous, vocal *pūrva-pakṣins* portrayed in the BSBh and Śaṅkara's other works, the mind in its role as *ātman*'s opponent (*pūrva-pakṣin*) in the Upad never says a word. And yet *manas* is definitely present, disturbing the self, unsettling the great, unchanging, immortal, eternal *ātman*. The author of the Upad makes a paradoxical, costly move: the inherently silent *ātman* unburdened by the presence of others, speaks in the first person, the language of I and me.

Such a move is so unlikely (and rare), that in view of the style and contents of the BSBh, the author of the BSBh and the composer of the Upad may not be identified. And yet, the difference may not be as crucial as it seems. The exponent portrayed in the BSBh, as well as *ātman* as presented in the Upad, are vulnerable to certain modes of otherness; they seem moved to speech by virtue of a common vulnerability. Both *ātman* and the exponent of *siddhānta*-Advaita violate the silence inherent in their being, and speak out. Or, better, they are made to speak by the author (or authors) of the BSBh and the Upad. The two authors are familiar with the body of Advaita-truths of the one *ātman* or Brahman, which is, in a sense—paradoxically—an impersonal self, as it were. The commentator on the BS and the composer of "A Thousand Teachings" thus express their knowledge of

Advaita in what might be called structurally similar ways. Dialogues of pure subjectivity lie at the core of both texts. This unlikely imaginative move (letting *ātman* speak) provides us with a clue to the nature of the unknown, almost unknowable author of the Upad (or perhaps even the nature of the author of the BSBh). What is Śaṅkara's "state of mind" in this context?

The Upad is an exceptional work of art and philosophy composed in two parts, one in prose, and the other in metrical verse. Many regard it as an author's independent composition, not a commentary. The mind (*manas*) is *ātman*'s interlocutor, as it were, or audience, in the majority of the latter's references to itself in the course of the Upad.

Ātman's speech in the first-person cannot be regarded as an aberration in the Upad. I counted more than 80 occurrences of 'I' and 'me' in the metrical section. *Ātman*'s voice, as we shall see, is complex and marked by two apparently opposite moods: complete self-sufficiency in the consciousness of its oneness, and poignant recognition of another (beyond *ātman*'s boundaries). See the following samples: 'Since I am not constructed (*avikriya*) and I am conscious of true reality, you do not confuse me by your incessant motions' (*na me 'sti mohas tava ceṣṭitena prabuddha-tattvas tv asito hy avikriyaḥ*);[1] 'I am everything, one without a second (*advaya*), omnipresent (*sarva-ga*), consisting of mere consciousness (*cin-mātra*)';[2] 'I am always free (*ahaṃ satataṃ vimuktaḥ*);[3] 'I am pure, mere seeing, unborn, inherently without any trace of objectivity (*dṛṣṭis tu śuddho 'ham avikriyâtmako, na me 'sti kaś cid viṣayaḥ svabhāvataḥ*).[4] 'I am the fourth (*turīya*) state of consciousness';[5] 'I am eternal, and nothing else. Lack of eternity belongs to differentiation in the domain of construction and change. I am always shining and non-dual. That which is constructed (*vikalpita*) is definitely unreal (*asat*).'[6] All these phrases are markedly different in nature to statements such as: 'Oh, my mind, your very nature is non-existence… (*abhāva-rūpaṃ tvam asîha he manaḥ*…).[7]

Thus Advaita metaphysics of the one pure consciousness, without attributes, all-encompassing, is embedded within the first-person

[1] Upad 2.19.6.
[2] Upad 2.9.3.
[3] Upad 2.10.1.
[4] Upad 2.10.2.
[5] Upad 2.10.4.
[6] Upad 2.19.7.
[7] Upad 2.19.8.

speech-act. Does this act of embedding mean anything? Does it signify metaphysics different in essence from an ordinary (exponent's) Advaita? If we take *ātman*'s unprecedented first-person speech in earnest as the frame within which Advaita truth of the one impersonal Brahman is embedded, we begin to consider a level of reality from which speech originates, a level deeper than the respective impersonal truth.

In other words, the enhanced reality of the commentator on the BS and the author of the Upad imply metaphysics significantly different from (or foreign to) the one announced by *ātman* (in the Upad) or the *siddhāntin* (of the BSBh). In view of the I-nature of *ātman* or Brahman this is not completely absurd. And yet, knowledge of the *ātman*, devoid of personal identity, voiced by an as-if-personal frame in the stimulating presence of the mind (*manas*), is hard to contain. The paradox is obvious and forceful. Indeed, *ātman* itself, if we may use the phrase, rebukes the mind for this very weakness, concomitantly committing the same error! See for example Upad 2.19.2:

> You employ the language of 'I' and 'me' in vain; others as well think that you act only for another (and not for yourself).[8] You do not have true consciousness of things, and I do not entertain any desire whatsoever. Therefore, mind, silence is appropriate for you (*ahaṃ mamêti tvam anartham īhase, parârtham icchanti tavânya īhitam/ na te 'rtha-bodho na hi me 'sti cârthitas. tataś ca yuktaḥ śama eva te manaḥ*).

As is well known, liberation, according to ordinary (orthodox) Advaita theory, means cessation of (individual) I-consciousness or mine-consciousness. Thus, for example, we find the following statement in the Upad 2.15.54:

> If a man, having completely excluded "I" and "my" notions, has a firm belief in that ether-like state destitute of the body, which has been declared according to well-studied scripture and inference, he is released (*mamâham ity etad apohya sarvato vimukta-dehaṃ padam ambarôpamam/sudṛṣṭa-śāstrânumitibhya īritaṃ vimucyate 'smin yadi niścito naraḥ//*).[9]

[8] The others meant here are apparently the Sānkhya philosophers, who distinguish the *puruṣa*—which exists for its own (*svârtha*) and the *prakṛti*, which exists (or acts) for another (*parârtha*). The mind (*manas*) is part of *prakṛti*, and thus, existing for another.

[9] Mayeda's translation, p. 147.

How to interpret the embedding of standard Advaita theory or ideology within the—apparently self-contradictory—voice of an individualized *ātman*? Like the author of the BSBh, who embeds a *siddhānta*-Advaita within his individual commentator's voice, the author of the Upad embeds *ātman*'s voice within his own.

Suppose for a moment that the author of the BSBh and the BUBh is also the composer of the Upad. What can we learn of Śaṅkara the author of the BSBh? The paradigmatic conflation of the voices of Śaṅkara and his exponent would make a presupposition concerning Śaṅkara's authorship of *ātman*'s first-person language most unlikely. We would imagine that the *ātman* as envisioned by Śaṅkara, if left to itself, would not speak at all. If, however, we distinguish between the voice of Śaṅkara and his *siddhāntin*, we may comfortably find an expression of the commentator's being in *ātman*'s first-person language in the Upad. While the doubt-free *siddhāntin* in the BSBh could never contain such a feat of imagination (*ātman* saying I in the face of a stubborn mind [*manas*]), the questioning commentator who entertains doubt and wonder could.

Let us assume then, in accordance with modern scholarly tradition, that Śaṅkara the author of the Upad is also the author of the BSBh. Do the two respective texts shed light on their common author? In order to answer this question we might turn to the dualistic metaphysics of Sāṅkhya-Yoga. Adopting it's terminology we would say that the author of the Upad accepts *manas* in its disturbing presence as an integral part of *prakṛti*, objectivity. Though *manas* is a product of the process of *avidyā* and triggered by the inconceivable contact of *puruṣa* and *prakṛti* (and thus capable of thinking and talking), it still retains an unconscious quality. As seen above (Upad 2.15.54), *ātman* views it as "existing for another" (*parârtha*), in accordance with a major tenet of classical Sāṅkhya-Yoga.[10] Thus, *ātman* in this case, in his diagnosis of *manas*'s condition, speaks Sāṅkhya language, a specific dualistic declamation of the author's voice. It is evidently not a light matter to let *ātman* speak Dvaita Sāṅkhya-Yoga language in such a context.

The mind's silence, perhaps somewhat eerie and unlikely for persons unfamiliar with Sāṅkhya conceptualization of the mind as an object, is most natural for a principle or mode of being exclusively objective and inherently unconscious (*acetana*). Thus, the mind's silence in the

---

[10] See Īśvarakṛṣṇa's Sāṅkhya-Kārikā, Patañjali's Yoga-sūtra 3.35.

so-called discourse (*saṃvāda*) with *ātman* expresses a noticeable flavor in our author's dualistic perspective. Sāṅkhya-Yoga metaphysics informs the author's voice in the metrical part of the Upad.

The same is true in regards to Śaṅkara's introduction to the BSBh. Indeed, scholars have noticed that 'Śaṅkara cannot be said to have been really hostile to Yoga. In fact, he refers to the Yoga-śāstra at several places in the BSBh respectfully.'[11] The author of the BSBh succinctly expresses the same voiced dualism in the seminal opening phrases of his introduction to the BSBh:

> The object (*viṣaya*) and the seer of it (*viṣayin*), manifested respectively in the ideas of 'you' (*yuṣmat*) and 'me', are different from each other like darkness and light, and thus may never be identified. Likewise, the respective qualities of the subject whose essence is consciousness cannot be attributed to the object, and vice versa, the qualities of objectivity cannot be imposed on the subject; and thus, the mutual illegitimate superimposition of the seen and seer is inappropriate, and is a wrong perception.[12]

The adaptation, at least to some extent, of Sāṅkhya-Yoga metaphysics is thus a common feature in the authorship of both the BSBh and the Upad.

Now, keeping in mind the dualistic undertones implied in Śaṅkara's (the commentator's or author's) discourse, let us reflect for a moment on some expressions of paradigmatic conflation of author and exponent as such conflation is assumed and entrenched in the practice of current scholarship. See, for example, Paul Hacker's fascinating hypothesis about Śaṅkara's conversion from Yoga to Advaita. Following the publication (1952) of the alleged commentary by Śaṅkara (*Yoga-sūtra-bhāṣya-vivaraṇa*) on Vyāsa's commentary on the *Yoga-sūtra*, Paul Hacker proposes that Śaṅkara was first a Yogin and then converted to Advaita.[13] H. Nakamura supports such a thesis. W. Halbfass is skeptical;[14] T.S. Rukmani proves that Śaṅkara the author of the

---

[11] Pande 1998: 111.

[12] *yuṣmad-asmat-pratyaya-gocarayor viṣaya-viṣayiṇos tamaḥ-prakāśavad viruddha-svabhāvayor itarêtara-bhāvânupapattau siddhāyāṃ tad-dharmāṇām api sutarām itarêtara-bhāvânupapattir ity to 'smat-pratyaya-gocare viṣayiṇi cid-ātmake yuṣmat-pratyaya-gocarasya viṣayasya tad-dharmāṇāṃ câdhyāsaḥ, tad-viparyayeṇa viṣayiṇas tad-dharmāṇāṃ ca viṣaye 'dhyāso mithyêti bhavituṃ yuktam.*

[13] Hacker 1968: 119–148.

[14] Halbfass 1991.

BSBh could not have been the author of the Vivaraṇa.[15] However well argued, such scholarly arguments are grounded in what I consider a simplistic identification of the author with his chosen exponent.

Even if we accept Śaṅkara's authorship of the Vivaraṇa, what could it mean? Authorship of the Vivaraṇa, as well as of the BSBh, does not imply any essential features. The author of the *Yoga-sūtra-bhāṣya-vivaraṇa* could have been the author of the BSBh; an eloquent, scholarly sage charged with doubt and curiosity, deeply connected with the subject of his study yet somewhat free, aware of his distinction from his exponent's position. See, for example, the author of the Vivaraṇa commenting on Vyāsa's *Yoga-sūtra-bhāṣya* 3.26. Vyāsa explains how meditation (*saṃyama*) on the sun brings about "knowledge of the universe" (*bhuvana-jñānaṃ sūrye saṃyamāt*). Vyāsa explicates in detail the features of the universe to be known (oceans, continents, flavors, etc.) by virtue of yogic meditation. The author of the Vivaraṇa makes the following comment: all these details might be known as well from other sources (such as the *Purāṇas*). Such an expression betokens doubt and a measure of freedom on the author's part. It could even be read as an expression of doubt and suspicion with respect to the very reality and power of yogic meditation.

The Upad is perhaps the most telling and explicit among Advaita literary products in its references to disturbances and moods within the abstract, one *ātman* or Brahman, the ground and self of everything. We have already suggested that *ātman*'s standard, professed identity as an inherently indifferent totality is belied by his reaction to the mind's presence. The nature and condition of *ātman* resembles, in our description, that of the doubt-charged author of the Upad (and also of the commentator on the BS). Thought-provoking in this respect is the fifth verse of the eighth chapter, in which the author says, or makes *ātman* say, that he composed (*ahaṃ…praklptavān imaṃ saṃvādam*) the discourse between itself (*ātman*) and the mind in order to release mankind from bondage and ignorance. Is such a speech-act significant? Can it be taken seriously as a token of the author's metaphysics and self-understanding?

Let us examine this statement, one of the most puzzling among the many first-person statements in the metrical portion of this work, in some detail.

---

[15] Rukmani 1998.

> Considering that people are attached to (the notions, paradigm) of cause and effect, I have composed this dialogue, which makes (these people) awake to their true nature, in order to free them (from the attachment to cause and effect).[16]

The question is: who is the one who says "I" in this statement? Or, who, according to Upad 2.8.5, composed the dialogue between *ātman* and the mind? Naturally, we would ascribe such a statement to Śaṅkara, the narrator of the Upad. However, first-person singular references to oneself are extremely rare in Śaṅkara's writings, and if we pay heed to the statements that precede Upad 2.8.5, the preliminary answer to the question about voice in 2.8.5 may be different: the pure self, absolute *ātman*, speaks here.

In order to reflect upon Śaṅkara's intention with respect to the speaker's identity in Upad 2.8.5, let us translate in full the four opening verses of Upad 2.8 (those preceding Upad 2.8.5).

> 2.8.1: Being consciousness only, oh mind, my connection with sensations such as taste etc. is due to your confusion. Therefore, since I have no distinctive attributes (*viśeṣa*), I have no benefit whatsoever from your efforts (*ato na kiṃcit tava ceṣṭitena me phalaṃ bhavet sarva-viśeṣa-hānataḥ*).
> 2.8.2: Give up, here and now, your activity rooted in illusion, and come to rest from your quest after the wrong; for I am the ultimate Brahman (*ahaṃ paraṃ brahma*), always as if released, unborn, one only, free of duality (*dvaya-varjita*).
> 2.8.3: I am the same in all beings, alone (*kevala*), the highest Brahman am I, all-pervading like space, imperishable, benevolent (*śiva*), without parts (*niṣkala*), uninterrupted, without action (*akriya*). Therefore, I have no use (benefit, fruit—*phala*) for your efforts (*tato na me 'stîha phalaṃ tavêhitaiḥ*).
> 2.8.4: I am one, and there is no other whom I desire to be mine (*ahaṃ mamâiko na tad anyad iṣyate*). And thus I, being unattached, do not belong to anybody (*na kasyâpy aham asmy asaṃgataḥ*). Being by nature unattached, I have no use for your doings since I am not of any duality (*asaṅga-rūpo 'ham ato na me tvayā kṛtena kāryaṃ tava câdvayatvataḥ*).
> 2.8.5: Considering that people are attached to (the notions, paradigm of) cause and effect, I have composed this dialogue which makes (these people) awake to their true nature, in order to free them (from the attachment to cause and effect).

[16] *phale ca hetau ca jano visaktavān iti pracintyâham ato vimokṣane/janasya saṃvādam imaṃ prakḷptavān sva-rūpa-tattvârtha-vibodha-kāraṇam.*

If the speaker in Upad 2.8.5 is the same as the one speaking in first-person singular in Upad 2.8.1–4—the reading implied in this case—it is the absolute itself that is meant (by Śaṅkara) to be the author of this dialogue with the mind. However, we know that Śaṅkara knows he is the author of the dialogue. Thus, verse 2.8.5 signifies either conflation of Śaṅkara's and *ātman*'s voice, or a transition from *ātman*'s voice (2.8.1–4) to "Śaṅkara's own voice" (as different, in Śaṅkara's experience, from *ātman*). Indeed, the concluding verse of this chapter (Upad 2.8.6) seems to be in line with the impersonal tone characteristic of Śaṅkara's voice throughout works such as the BSBh etc.; it does not contain any first-person expression, glossing impersonally over the value of the preceding discourse:

> 2.8.6: If man ponders this dialogue, he will be released from the root of fear, which is ignorance (*ajñāna*). Such a man is a knower of *ātman* (*ātma-vid*), happy, free of desire, always the same, moving around with no suffering (*aśoka*) (*saṃvādam etaṃ yadi cintayen naro vimucyate 'jñāna-mahā-bhayâgamāt/vimukta-kāmaś ca tathā janaḥ sadā caraty aśokaḥ sama ātma-vit sukhī//*).

The metaphysics of flexible, shifting boundaries between self and other is thus common to the author of the Upad and the commentator on Bādarāyaṇa's *Brahma-sūtra*. The commentator's *siddhāntin* as well as the pure, singular *ātman* articulated in the metrical part of the Upad are inherently responsive to the presence of the other. In the case of the BSBh, the various *pūrva-pakṣins* make the exponent speak; in the case of *ātman* as it is revealed in the Upad, it is the mind (*manas*) which triggers the pure inactive self to action. Here we come across a familiar theme in Indian literature. The poet Kālidāsa imagines Śiva's vulnerability in the presence of Pārvatī by the same tokens. In the first canto of *The Kumāra-sambhava*, he asserts (in the narrator's voice) that only those whose consciousness is undisturbed in the presence of triggers of inner distortions are truly established in wisdom (*vikāra-hetau sati vikriyante yeṣāṃ na cetāṃsi ta eva dhīrāḥ*).[17]

An author who imagines *ātman* speaking and, moreover, *ātman* composing a discourse with the mind, sustains a contradiction in terms of ordinary Advaita. A contradiction of such magnitude could hardly be composed unawares. The author of the Upad must have been conscious of the paradoxical, striking move of allowing *ātman*

[17] Kumāra-sambhava, 1.59.

speak in the first person. *Ātman* addressing the mind in the metrical part of the Upad breaks completely new ground for Advaita-Vedānta. The dialogical framework that confronts these two selves—one real and alone in its oneness, the other confined within a body, individual, resisting disappearance—seems familiar but also, many would argue, foreign to the spirit of Advaita-Vedānta. This framework is, on the one hand, familiar, since so much of Advaita is articulated in the dialogical mood; the *siddhāntin* portrayed in the BSBh speaks Advaita in the presence of all sorts of *pūrva-pakṣins*. Thus, the structural affinity of the BSBh and *ātman*'s first-person language in the Upad is obvious. On the other hand, of course, the *siddhāntin* displayed in the BSBh never speaks for *ātman* itself in the first person. The author of the BSBh is never as bold as that of the Upad.

As suggested above, the vulnerability of *ātman* articulated in the Upad corresponds with the vulnerability of the exponent in the BSBh. The commentator who creates the BSBh, who recognizes the *siddhāntin*'s weaknesses, and the author of the Upad who lets *ātman* 'contradict itself' by speaking in the first-person in the presence of another share a common metaphysics that can be distinguished from what might be called standard Advaita. The author of the Upad as well as the commentator on the BS necessarily holds different Advaita metaphysics from the *siddhāntin* portrayed in the BSBh.

On the one hand, a somewhat tense co-existence (and intimacy) of old and new selves is suggested here; indeed, the prevailing, recurrent message from *ātman* to the mind is simple: shut up, do not disturb, stop your pretensions to existence! On the other hand, there is a more intimate tone as well, as *ātman* embraces the mind, as it were ("you are myself!"). Metaphysics based on reciprocity, co-existence, love and hate is thus contrasted with a metaphysics based on the experience of indifference (the real *ātman* does not bother about the unreal, shadowy mind).

In general, the lives of the Advaitins are assumed to "follow" or embody Advaita doctrine. This assumption is somewhat unwarranted; for if Advaitins are actualizations of Upaniṣadic norms (or of the inherently indifferent, never-changing *ātman*), whence the speaking, voluminous verbal output, and the need for persuading others? *ātman*'s encounter with the mind is the most obvious expression of the difference between Upaniṣadic norm and an Advaitin's experience merged with creative authorship and imagination (for the act of making *nirguṇa* Brahman speak seems a very costly move). However,

Śaṅkara's own verbal activity bespeaks the same costly and paradoxical move (if he too is considered as the never-changing *ātman*).

Śaṅkara the author of the BSBh (and also perhaps of the Upad) is capable of daring imagination, intense reasoning, controlled articulation, and cognitive empathy with others. *Ātman* as portrayed in the Upad is composed in his creator's image; a vulnerable being, yearning to be himself, concomitantly saying 'Yes' and 'No' to the Upaniṣadic truth. Thus, like '*ātman* himself,' the author of the BSBh is not an otherness-free agent, and his works of art, philosophy, and imagination are nourished by what might be called "Dvaita moods," with their solid boundaries between self and others.

CHAPTER FOUR

INDIVIDUAL LOSSES AND ADVAITIC CONSCIOUSNESS: A NOTE ON ĪŚVARA'S, ŚAṄKARA'S AND ŚAṄKARĀCĀRYA'S SORROW

Is the author of the BSBh free of sorrow? A fully successful Advaitin who knows himself as the one *ātman* would not, by definition, experience pain. Śaṅkara's main protagonist, the *siddhāntin*, asserts that suffering (*duḥkha*) of body and soul originates in ignorance of one's true self. Can our *siddhānta*-Advaitin become his old self again (even momentarily)? Śaṅkara's exponent, who knows *ātman* or Brahman, does not experience pain. His capacity to know of others' pain is questionable as well. For a pre-*mokṣa* presence of the old self is apparently a prerequisite for access to all kinds of suffering, whether one's own or someone else's.

The question arises with respect to our author: Does his exponent's alleged renunciation of wrong metaphysics (*mithyā-jñāna*) imply the author's forgetfulness of his own and others' suffering (embedded as such suffering is in mistaken self-identification)? Such questions are made possible by the distinction of author and hero; the latter is inherently indifferent to losses of close relatives and friends; the former knows something about depression and pain. Pain caused by cuts and burns is real, says the disciple. But no, says the master, cuts and burns are felt in different locations in the body, not in the perceiver. Without self-identification with the body, bodily pains do not exist.

Śaṅkara the author of the BSBh points to the death of sons, friends and the like (*putra-mitrâdi*) as paradigmatic losses in *saṃsāra*. Is this an incidental choice? Or is omitting explicit reference to a father's or mother's death meaningful?

Suffering and pain are tangible tokens of *saṃsāric* existence, manifestations of the primary misconception (*avidyā*). The following is a brief study of two contexts of *saṃsāric* loss and types of memory; loss and memory of a friend or a son according to BSBh 2.3.46, and loss and memory of a father (implied by one's desire for re-union) according to BSBh 4.4.13–14. Loss of sons and friends (*putra-mitrâdi*) is presented in BSBh 2.3.46 as unreal and as such pain-free (from the *mukta*'s perspective); a father who is a liberated mendicant (*parivrājaka*) is unaffected by the news of his son's death. (Similarly, cold and aloof Īśvara, had he friends or sons, would not be moved by their deaths.) Other people present at the experiment (or trial) designed by Śaṅkara according to BSBh 2.3.46 are deeply troubled in these same circumstances. They are householders who live by an old self, a mistaken metaphysics, and a vision whereby their connection with sons and friends is really an aspect of their selves ("I am my property," "I am my son," etc.). Their self is inherently "old," bleeding at the news.

What is Śaṅkara's location in this field of existential testing? How would the author of the BSBh respond to messages of individual losses such as the death of sons, friends (and we add to this implied losses of a father and mother)? We know, of course, how the author conceives of his exponent's consciousness. Like Īśvara, he would remain calm and indifferent, a living manifestation of the truth of Advaita. If fused with Śaṅkarācārya, his *siddhānta*-exponent, the author Śaṅkara would apparently be stationed among the "new-self group" (which includes Īśvara, *parivrājaka*s, and their like). But the author of the BSBh seems to know the sorrow of losing friends and sons. He might share with his hero a certain measure of indifference over such losses; perhaps he did not have a son or friends. But perhaps there are other losses (such as of a father and a mother) to which he is not as indifferent as his hero. Omitting references to such losses could mean, if one insists on this type of psychological speculation, a distance between the voices of protagonist and author; the latter expresses a somewhat more complex—and possibly richer—perspective than his exponent's, Īśvara's or the *parivrājaka*s' (differing too from the ordinary householders who are present at the experiment). Yet in the experiment, according to BSBh 2.3.46, a Śaṅkarācārya would take his seat with Īśvara, *parivrajaka*s, and other kinds of fulfilled *saṃnyāsin*s; he would reject his friends and sons, denying any connection with them. And perhaps, incapable of re-enacting a wrong metaphysics (based on the veracity of the ordinary, individual self), he would not remember his relationship with friends and sons. The author, however, also present (as the rest of humanity is) in the field of trial, would be different. Loss of father in early childhood and a complex separation from his mother have perhaps left their mark.[1]

[1] There may be a trace of truth in the *Dig-vijaya* tradition; Śaṅkara's father's death and the boy's difficult separation from his mother are episodes narrated in all the versions of the *Dig-vijaya* type.

Speculating on the author's subtle, invisible presence in the so-called field of trial leads us to integrate our vision of the author's being in terms of sorrow and freedom thereof. In our highly speculative conception, the author maintains access to an old *Saṃsāric* self, as it were; his choice of losses such as of sons and friends (rather than of a father and mother) is not purely incidental. By his Viveka-Vedānta standpoint he is capable of complexity of mind unavailable to his *siddhāntin* (or Īśvara).

But how can the old and new selves co-exist? The old one, immersed in wrong vision (*avidyā*) and incessant lamentation, has apparently vanished. Belonging to an inferior order of reality, it is like a lifeless shadow incapable of resurrection. Śaṅkara's protagonist is emphatic on the irreversibility of the liberating Advaitic transformation. Once the insight of the true (new) self emerges, previous metaphysics is doomed to inferiority or oblivion *forever*. In BSBh 1.1.4 Śaṅkara says: By the established insight of unity, the destroyed vision of duality does not rise again (*na hy ekatva-vijñānenônmathitasya dvaita-vijñānasya punaḥ sambhavo 'sti*). The underlying pattern of such conceptualization of the old/new-self field is that of dissociation; the new self is bright, free of old afflictions, newly born, inherently forgetful of the old.

However, memories do exist, inviting a question as to the whereabouts of the old self. Miraculously, this self has not evaporated; it still lives somewhere. Even though he has become Brahman, our mature Śaṅkara author of the BSBh remembers, or—at least—speaks as if he remembers. He speaks of people, teachers and disciples, masters and servants, of property, suffering, of bowls, carpenters, magicians, wooden dolls, etc. Whence all this talk? These are Śaṅkara's things past, old-self things, old ontology and boundaries made present, retrieved—we imagine—through an as-if attitude, as if real or as if significant against the voracious, ever-hungry background of the new self (*ātman*). The author's *gauṇa* state of mind, resisting superimposition of *viṣayin* and *viṣaya*, based upon the separation of seer and seen makes it possible for the incorporation of worldly existence in the philosopher's mind. We shall embark on a discussion of this "as-if" attitude of Śaṅkara later on.

Thus, a measure of continuity or co-existence (of the old and new selves) is implied in the Advaitin's speech. Indeed, commenting on BS 4.1.15, Śaṅkara suggests that the old self lives on even in *mokṣa*, as long as the body continues. Actions begun before the rise of perfect knowledge do have their impact by the force of subliminal impressions (*saṃskāra-vaśa*). Thus, Śaṅkara's BSBh 4.1.15 'remembrance of things past' is a reflection on the old self's post-liberation mode of being. The old self continues, like a potter's wheel (*kulāla-cakra*), until its motion stops of itself. Likewise, says Śaṅkara (in the author's voice) in BSBh 4.1.15, even wrong knowledge (*mithyā-jñāna*) continues to live after the rise of perfect knowledge, similarly to a defective vision such as of two moons (which, Śaṅkara suggests, goes on for sometime after correct vision is restored). Images of oil that sticks to the vessel even when the jug has been emptied[2] are part of the "continuity-pattern" underlying the relationship of the old and new selves. As suggested above, co-existence of old and new selves signifies our author's wonder, doubt, and the metaphorical as-if mood. The recognition of worldly existence concomitant with the viveka-insight of the void between the seer (*viṣayin*) and the seen (*viṣaya*), provide the condition of the tense co-existence of the old and new selves.

The psychological and spiritual reality implied in the conversion to Advaita-existence is necessarily complex. The successful Viveka-Vedāntin (such as Śaṅkara)—significantly different from the purely monist one—lives by two occasionally competing selves, oscillating between metaphysics and values. The Advaitin's imagery mentioned above (potter's wheel, sticky oil, lingering eye-disease) points to an extant, perceptible, continuous old self. And yet, the incompatibility of the two selves is of course a primary tenet of Viveka-Vedānta, the essence of its theory of conversion. Śaṅkara says: If someone argues that the real force of the remaining *karma* obstructs liberation, then such an argument is misplaced; for the Veda tells us that perfect knowledge annihilates *karma* altogether (*śeṣa-karma sad-bhāve 'nirmokṣa-prasaṅga ity ayam apy asthāne sambhramaḥ. saṃyag-darśanād aśeṣa-karma-kṣaya-śruteḥ*).[3]

Thus, two modes of relationship between the two selves find expression in Śaṅkara's writings: dissociation and co-existence. The old self (*adhyāsa*-inflicted) may not exist at all, being irreversibly subdued, erased; this is the condition embodied by Īśvara and "pure Advaitins." And the old self may co-exist (in varying vitality) with the new one, making for a somewhat more differentiated, changing innerness. The constructed field of trial is an occasion to explore some complexities

---

[2] See BSBh 3.1.8.
[3] BSBh 4.4.15.

implied by the conversion to Advaita-existence, and also Śaṅkara's location in this field.

Let us now look at Śaṅkara's experiment in BSBh 2.3.46, designed to demonstrate the difference between *saṃnyāsins* free of *saṃsāra* (and pain) and worldly people afflicted by grievances such as loss of sons and friends.

> Let us consider the case of many men, each of whom possesses sons, friends, etc., sitting together, some of them erroneously imagining that they are connected with their sons, friends, etc., while others do not. If then somebody calls out 'the son has died,' 'the friend has died,' grief is produced in the minds of those who are under the imagination of being connected with sons and friends, but not in the minds of religious mendicants who have freed themselves from that imagination. From this it appears that perfect knowledge is of use even to an ordinary man; of how much greater use then will it be to him (i.e. the Lord) whose nature is eternal pure intelligence, who sees nothing beside the Self for which there are no objects.[4]

Three preliminary presences—classes—are discernible in Śaṅkara's grim experiment: ordinary (*laukika*) people, liberated people (*parivrājakas* and the like), and an invisible third—God (Īśvara). This one, Īśvara, is largely similar to the liberated ones—both types being in possession of true vision—but also perceptibly different. Īśvara cannot, by definition, undergo suffering or pain, for these derive from *avidyā*, *adhyāsa* (superimposition), or *abhimāna* ("false identification"), and Īśvara is inherently—eternally—free from such mistaken metaphysical modes. He is, of course, different from ordinary people afflicted by attachment and pain, but also different from all sorts of successful Advaitins potentially in touch with their old selves. God did not undergo an Advaitic transformation as others have. From time immemorial he has been omniscient, free of attachment and error.

There is apparently another presence at the experiment, that of the observer (Śaṅkara). The author of the BSBh is neither a worldly (*laukika*) man tormented by the news of the death of a son or a friend, nor a completely dissociated *saṃnyāsin* or *parivrajāka*. By the speech-act describing the experiment, he establishes a domain in this world of *saṃsāra* capable of reflecting the differences between those assembled in the field of trial. Recalling relationships to friends and

---

[4] Thibaut 1962: v. 2, p. 64.

sons, he uses old-self language, referring to suffering others in their ignorance, relating to his unhappy brethren through an involvement with his old self.

Thus there are various stations and spiritual personalities present at the experiment, each representing characteristic responses and the inner complexity stimulated by the emerging trial. At one end of the continuum there are Īśvara and *parivrājaka*s and their like, epitomes of the ultimate and indifferent. Their new self is totally, irreversibly dissociated from the old. On the other end there is the ordinary (*laukika*) person, overwhelmed by grief over sons and friends. Śaṅkara, though a successful Advaitin, is very close to the ultimate and indifferent, yet he can still relate efficiently to his past self.

As the participants in Śaṅkara's experiment increase in number and variety, including four types at this point (Īśvara and Śaṅkara not explicitly included by Śaṅkara in the BSBh 2.3.46 experiment), the way is open for further additions of personnel. Many candidates (if not all humanity) may participate in the experiment of loss. However, some are more likely to draw our attention, expressing in their lives or stories significant variants of the experiment. Two such persons are Vyāsa and his son Śuka, according to a story from the Mahābhārata.[5]

Vyāsa, Śuka's father, has programmed his son to sit among the *parivrājaka*s and the like in Śaṅkara's experiment, namely, to become a *saṃnyāsin* and actually disappear as an empirical person (and a son). However, when the time comes for the son to dissolve in *mokṣa*, the father cannot bear it. Pathetically, he beseeches his son to stay one more day. But Śuka, surpassing his father in yogic power (and insight), is beyond Vyāsa's supplications; converted to Advaita or yoga, he is by now profoundly different from his father. Naked girls bathing in a pond ignore Śuka's presence, but become anxious and embarrassed when they recognize Vyāsa flying above. Rejecting his old self and bond with his father, Śuka would thus stand firmly among the *saṃnyāsin*s (*parivrājaka*s) present at the experiment (along with Śaṅkara's Īśvara). His father, however, though very learned and recognized as a competent teacher of renunciation and *mokṣa*, stands somewhere in between (perhaps closer to Śaṅkara, author of the BSBh).

David Shulman sees in the Śuka story "the most trenchant narrative expression in the Hindu tradition of the actual emotional price inher-

---

[5] Mahābhārata (Southern Recension) 12.309.

ent in the cultural ideals of renunciation and release."[6] Though a great teacher of yoga and *mokṣa*, under the circumstances of the experiment Vyāsa finds himself in a worldly crowd incapable of rejecting their sons and friends, remembering, thinking of them as their own. Seated at the experiment's arena, he is deeply moved, shattered, as the news arrives. When the moment of separation from his son comes, his suffering is unbearable. And Vyāsa is apparently as prepared for this moment as one can be. He too cannot but think of his son as his own.[7]

A somewhat disturbing presence in this gathering remains that of Īśvara. How indeed did he—bereft of ancestors, sons, or even friends—get there? Indirectly, indeed, he illustrates the nature and value of knowledge. He, apparently the most susceptible (by virtue of his omniscience) to experiencing the pain of all creation, emerges in the experiment as the most invulnerable in the universe. Rather than making Him the most sensitive observer of human suffering (necessarily sharing human suffering), knowledge (omniscience) grants him absolute freedom from pain. Innocent of pain, he is thus different from all the others gathered at the experiment.

The use of knowledge of Brahman by man and God (Īśvara) is the explicit theme of the entire experiment-discourse. The exponent's Advaita-knowledge implies the dissociation of old and new selves. (The crux of such knowledge is forgetting pain as one's own.) However, the transition from the use of knowledge by man to the use of knowledge by Īśvara invites questions. Is Īśvara's always a new self? What is Īśvara's affliction corresponding to one's loss of a son? The answer is most obvious: Īśvara possesses perfect knowledge from time immemorial (*anādi*) and thus, according to Śaṅkara, is *always* indifferent to His sons' and friends' fates (death). Like losses of earrings and property, losses of sons and friends are rooted in false identification (*abhimāna*). Participating in Śaṅkara's experiment, sitting amidst people informed of the deaths of sons and friends, He does not move. Śaṅkara's Īśvara is evidently a *parivrājaka*; playful,[8] omniscient, and somewhat cold.

---

[6] Shulman 1993: 117.

[7] Traditionally, the son is his father's self. See P. Olivelle's translation of Aitareya Brāhmaṇa 7.13: "The husband enters the wife/Becoming an embryo he enters the mother/In her he becomes a new man again/He is born in the tenth month." Olivelle 1992: 26.

[8] See for example BSBh 2.3.31.

The underlying, implicit theme of this passage from BSBh 2.3.46 is the potential suffering of God by virtue of his relationship with man. The subject of God's pain is raised in BSBh 2.3.45, which deals with the hazards of God's omniscience (knowledge of pain may make for the knower's pain). Śaṅkara asserts that man is both part (*aṃśa*) of Īśvara and his servant (*bhṛtya*). He quotes in this context Bhagavad-Gītā 15.7 ("an eternal part of me becomes the *jīva* in this world"). Responding to this possibility of man's being part (*aṃśatva*) of God, the opponent suggests that God is thus all the worse for this kind of relationship with man:

> If we admit that the souls are parts of the Lord, it follows that the Lord also, whose part the soul is, will be afflicted by the pain caused to the soul by its experience of the *saṃsāra*-state; as we see in ordinary life that the entire Devadatta suffers from the pain affecting his hand or foot or some other limb. Herefrom it would follow that they who obtain Brahman obtain a greater pain; so that the former *saṃsāra*-condition would be preferable and complete knowledge be devoid of purpose.[9]

Thus, better to be without *mokṣa* and knowledge of Brahman, since it brings so much suffering,[10] says the opponent. Śaṅkara's experiment outlined in BSBh 2.3.46 is a response to this suggestion of the opponent. Īśvara is not made unhappy by his omniscience, and neither are virtuous, pure Advaitins. Advaita consciousness, Śaṅkara says, annihilates pain-producing dynamics, uprooting the cause of all suffering. Physical pain—such as that caused by burns or cuts—is due to wrong identification with the body; psychological suffering—such as follows the loss of a son or a friend—is due to wrong identification with one's son or friend (*yathā ca sva-deha-gata-dāha-cchedâdi-nimittaṃ duḥkhaṃ tad-abhimāna-bhrantyânubhavati, tathā putra-mitrâdi-gocaram api duḥkhaṃ tad-abhimāna-bhrāntyâivânubhavati*). False identification finds its expression in the experience or thought, "I myself am my son," "I myself am my friend" (*aham eva putro 'ham eva mitram*). By the force of affection (*sneha-vaśena*) one enters into, identifies oneself with sons, friends, and so on (*evaṃ sneha-vaśena putra-mitrâdiṣv abhiniviśamānaḥ*). Advaita knowledge—a particular type of

---

[9] Thibaut's translation of BSBh 2.3.45 in Thibaut 1962: v. 2, p. 63. One recalls Ecclesiastes 1:18.

[10] There are many stories of saints' exceptional sensitivity to others' (including animals' and even plants') pain. Tamar Bental reminded me of many stories about Ramakrishna's extreme openness to others' pain.

forgetting—destroys all such possible worldly attachments and wrong identifications, and thus makes one inherently free of pain. Īśvara is a prime illustration of such freedom. However, he cannot forget if (and what) he cannot remember. Indeed, he cannot know what *avidyā* is.

The nature and place of Īśvara in Śaṅkara's thought and experience is complex and not always unambiguous. Īśvara is the creator of the world and thus is active. Though somewhat impersonal in his identity as the entire cosmos, he is, mysteriously, also a person. Īśvara is not the absolute yet very close to it, as if standing in-between man and Brahman. He is superior to man, endowed with superior excellent qualities (*atiśayôpādhi-sampanna*). It is thus natural, Śaṅkara says in BSBh 2.3.45, that such a God commands men endowed with inferior (*nihīna*) qualities. On the other hand, as suggested above, being a person, Īśvara is not the *nirguṇa-brahman*, the qualityless *ātman*. Seated at the experiment, Īśvara remains distant. In principle—one might hope—being omnipotent, Īśvara could have done something for the ordinary person overwhelmed by suffering.

However, Īśvara *cannot* identify himself with afflicted people, and consequently does not feel their physical and mental pains. Indeed, this is disappointing for some newly added witnesses to the experiment. Thus, for example, G. Thibaut, who thinks very highly of Śaṅkara's efforts at making the Upaniṣadic doctrines coherent and cogent, who even justifies Śaṅkara's distinction between an inferior Īśvara and the absolute self, expresses—though indirectly and through a voice he identifies as that of the "masses of India"—some reservations about Śaṅkara's conception of the personal God and his relationship with humanity:

> But although this form of doctrine has ever since Śaṅkara's time been the one most generally accepted by Brahminic students of philosophy, it has never had any wide-reaching influence on the masses of India. It is too little in sympathy with the wants of the human heart, which, after all, are not so very different in India from what they are elsewhere. Comparatively few, even in India, are those who rejoice in the idea of a universal non-personal essence in which their own individuality is to be merged and lost for ever, who think it sweet 'to be wrecked on the ocean of the Infinite.'[11]

[11] Thibaut 1962: cxxvii. Thibaut's quotation is from Leopardi.

Thibaut is a man longing for expressions of God's benevolence, and is thus—while seated at the experiment—somewhat disappointed. Surrounded by people's sorrow for sons and friends, Śaṅkara's Īśvara remains unmoved and unchanged. But can he be moved? Devoid of old self—for Śaṅkara's Īśvara has always been omniscient and a sort of Advaitin—Īśvara *may not know* of the suffering around him, as an old self to remember is not available for him. But Śaṅkara the author of the BSBh is not an Īśvara; he remembers, he knows. For Śaṅkara, the old self is the prerequisite condition for pain, and suffering is its hallmark. Lacking an old self, how can Īśvara *know* of (or be in) pain? Śaṅkara's own attention to the pain of others is part of his re-enactment of pre-transformation metaphysics and self. In this sense, the author of the BSBh is superior to his God, for he writes and can teach. Capable of sorrow and doubt, of old-self-remembrance, the author of the BSBh as we portray him is complex, truthful, and fully humane.

Indeed, Śaṅkara *conspicuously rarely* refers to Īśvara's grace (*prasāda*) or benevolence. Exceptionally, in BSBh 3.2.5, he says that ordinary people do have the potential to become omniscient and omnipotent like Īśvara, but this potential is covered, concealed (*tirohita*). For some people who do devote themselves with much effort to God he grants—by his grace (*prasādāt*)—knowledge, vision. As medicine *sometimes* has the power to cure eye-disease (*timira*), so by Īśvara's grace some people materialize their innate nature (to be like Īśvara himself). As fire is buried, concealed in wood (as yet not burning), so Īśvara's potency and knowledge are veiled in ordinary people's lives.[12] However, such promotion to an Īśvara-state is most uncommon in Śaṅkara's writings; Īśvara's grace is definitely and conspicuously a negligible expression of His being.

But is not Īśvara cruel (allowing so much sorrow around him)? No, Śaṅkara would say; Īśvara is bound by considerations of *dharma* and *adharma* (manifested in the lives of miserable or happy people). There is thus no blaming Īśvara (*īśvarasyâparādha*) for the uneven lot of living creatures.[13] During the experiment, Īśvara (bereft of an old self) may not understand what is going on. (And apparently, even if he knew, he could have done very little.)

---

[12] See BSBh 3.2.6.
[13] BSBh 2.1.34.

Another possible guest in Śaṅkara's disturbing experiment is S. Radhakrishnan. Deeply interested in the nature of Īśvara, he makes many references to God in Śaṅkara's thought (not insignificantly, I think, he does not address the issue of "Īśvara at the Experiment"—BSBh 2.3.45–6). Some of Radhakrishnan's remarks about Īśvara are profound and important, particularly his perceptive notes on the relationship between Fichte's conception of the subject and its other and Śaṅkara's view of Īśvara. However, similarly to Thibaut, Radhakrishnan seeks something for the heart, namely love, possibly found in Śaṅkara's Īśvara:

> For Īśvara, changelessness and inactivity are impossible. As real in the empirical sense, he must be ever acting, losing himself to find himself, going out to the universe and returning to himself through the universe. He who does nothing and stands aloof from the world is not God, not at any rate a God of love. Love lives in the life of its objects....[14]

And yet, Īśvara does "stand aloof from the world", and he is Śaṅkara's God. Whether making excuses for his God as "bound by considerations of *dharma* and *adharma*", or by avoiding reference to Īśvara's *prasāda* (BSBh 3.2.5 is exceptional), or in his insistence of Īśvara's indifference to human suffering, Śaṅkara does not conceive Īśvara as a warm, loving God. Nor is He very powerful. Śaṅkara's Īśvara is vaguely omniscient, playful but inherently impotent.

Let us return to the experiment. Śaṅkara's answer in BSBh 2.3.46 to the opponent's suggestion in BSBh 2.3.45 is puzzling; if man has the quality of "being a part" (*aṃśatva*) of Īśvara, then Śaṅkara's experiment proves that man is *not* a part of God, since unlike Devadatta's parts (which make the entire Devadatta ache), the suffering of man does not touch Īśvara at all. In other words, the experiment, apparently originating in the presupposition of man's being part of Īśvara, undermines this very presupposition. Accepting the ineluctable logic of the opponent's argument, yet breaking the boundaries of the discourse, Śaṅkara has produced an experiment that establishes the power of perfect knowledge.

Of course, by introducing the rejection of one's sons as a *parivrājaka*'s ultimate test, Śaṅkara recognizes the immensity of love for sons (*putra-sneha*) and friends. Love for one's son epitomizes everyday

---

[14] Radhakrishnan 1929: 557.

life. Śaṅkara's old self in this regard is visibly present, expressed, for example, in BSBh 2.2.29: "When, for instance, a man remembers his absent son, he does not directly perceive him, but merely wishes so to perceive him."[15]

The logic of rejection or renunciation of sons applies as well to the denial of one's connection with one's father. Relationships with relatives (more external than one's relation with one's body)[16] are many and varied, including one's relation with one's father, as we see, for example, in BSBh 2.2.17:

> Devadatta although being one only forms the object of many different names and notions according as he is considered in himself or in his relations to others; thus he is thought and spoken of as man, Brāhmaṇa, learned in the Veda, generous, boy, young man, old man, father, son, grandson, brother, son-in-law, etc.[17]

Now let us extend the original experiment of BSBh 2.3.46 to include the news of one's father's death. Śuka, Īśvara, Śaṅkara, Śaṅkarācārya, Vyāsa, Thibaut, and Radhakrishnan all participate in the Universal Experiment. Like Job, they receive various messages of loss. Different announcements are heard: "Your property is lost," "Your earrings are lost," "Your friend is dead," "Your son is dead," "Your father is dead," "Your mother is dead," and so forth. Some of those gathered at the experiment, the worldly ones, would tremble at the news of their loss of earrings or property. By the force of *abhimāna*, experiencing their connection with such things, these people would cry in lamentation at their losses.[18] Śaṅkara, Vyāsa, Śuka, Īśvara, and others are unmoved; they have forgotten their connection with such assets. Yet as messages of woe become incrementally harsher, the congregation becomes fur-

---

[15] BSBh 2,2.29. Thibaut's translation. v. 1, p. 425.

[16] See, for example, BSBh 4.1.2 "For we clearly observe that when the body is cut or burned a wrong notion springs up, 'I am being cut,' 'I am being burned;' and similarly we observe that when sons, friends, etc.—who are even more external to the Self than one's own body—suffer affliction, that affliction is wrongly attributed to the Self." (G. Thibaut's translation, v. 2, p. 336).

[17] G. Thibaut's translation (v. 1, p. 397). In his programmatic introduction to the BSBh, Śaṅkara associates the primary dynamics of *avidyā*—superimposition, *adhyāsa*—with identification with sons and wife (*putra-bhāryā*): "Extra-personal attributes are superimposed on the Self, if a man considers himself sound and entire, or the contrary, as long as his wife, children and so on are sound and entire or not." (Thibaut 1962: 8).

[18] See BSBh 1.1.4 for Śaṅkara's description of the working of *abhimāna* with respect to earrings and property.

ther differentiated. Like fish in a net, Vyāsa's heart and old self tremble, violently palpitating as news of his son's death reaches him. Reflecting on his sorrow, he may also feel his incompetence as a guru and successful renouncer. Śuka, the *siddhāntin* (Śaṅkarācārya) and Īśvara remain calm. Śuka and Īśvara are thoroughly immobile. Fortunately or unfortunately, Śuka has an underdeveloped old self; ever-young, he remains a "crazy fool of God."[19] Likewise, Īśvara, lacking the resources to know the pain of others, is indifferent.

I assume that Śaṅkara's decision to present the worldly people and others (*parivrājakas* and the like) with deaths of sons and friends at the experiment is significant. He, after all, designs an experiment which exposes the merits of knowledge in overcoming suffering, highlighting thereby Īśvara's invulnerability to pain. I assume that the deaths of intimates are losses not unbearable in Śaṅkara's mind, otherwise he would not have designed the experiment as he did. However, he does seem acutely aware of others' agony.

As noted in the beginning of this chapter, conspicuously missing among the messages reaching the gathering at the experiment according to BSBh 2.3.46 is news of one's father's death. Suppose such a message came. Īśvara would not know about it. Bereft of an old self, He cannot know what it means; He would reasonably suspect that nobody is addressing him by the announcement. Śuka, of course, would remain indifferent (let us assume he does not recognize his father at the experiment). Vyāsa would most probably lament his father's death, sharpening his awareness of the culturally sanctioned debt to ancestors in the Vedic tradition. What about Śaṅkara the author of the BSBh, and what about Śaṅkarācārya, his *siddhānta*-exponent? In Advaita Vedānta, of course, with its background of the One Brahman, the renunciation of one's father is necessarily equivalent to that of one's son; both renunciations signify the force of forgetting, or success in overcoming the binding, pain-producing force of affection or love (*sneha-vaśa*). And both kinds of forgetting—of sons and fathers—attest to the value of perfect knowledge, according to the narrative of BSBh 2.3.46.

However, standing in the field of experiment, Śaṅkara, a successful Advaitin in his own way, may not be quite so composed with respect to news of his father's death. It is noteworthy that the occasion for

[19] D. Shulman's expression. Shulman 1993: 123. Shulman adds a warning to fathers such as Vyāsa: "Fathers, and prospective fathers, should watch their words." (124).

father-renunciation does not arise at all in the experiment; fathers (and mothers) are not included in the range of significant *saṃsāric* losses in this context. Does Śaṅkara inadvertently forget about father and mother in the course of his choice of losses paradigmatic in their power to provoke pain? Or was he somewhat reluctant to be in conflict with the *dharma* concerning the obligation and respect to dead ancestors? Did he thus forget his father, or was his father's loss too painful at this moment (of designing the experiment)? It is hardly possible to guess well in such matters. However, there may be more vitality to Śaṅkara's old self in this case relating to the absence of his father and mother.

According to BSBh 4.4.13–14, sons maintain relentless affection for their (absent) fathers, well beyond the boundary of *saṃsāra* and *mokṣa*. In (qualified) *mokṣa*, whether bodiless or embodied, sons think and dream of their fathers. Thus according to BSBh 4.4.13:

> When the physical body along with its sense-organs does not exist, then, like in the condition of dream (in which the senses are inactive and objects of the senses do not appear) the longings for a father and such objects (*pitrâdi-kāma*) are made of mere perception (i.e. mental only), so also in the condition of liberation (*mokṣe 'pi*) such longings would be (mental only), made of mere perception (*upalabdhi-mātra*).[20]

Thus, as far as the old self consists of attachment to one's father, the bond of father and son continues into the condition of qualified *mokṣa*. Though this type of *mokṣa* is clearly different from the exponent's version of ultimate liberation grounded in the identity of one with the absolute, Śaṅkara—most significantly—calls it *mokṣa*, expressing its highly elevated mode of being. Śaṅkara's *bhāṣya* on the following sūtra completes the basic meanings manifest in BSBh 4.4.13. Affection for one's father and so on does not contradict the nature and essence of qualified liberation; on the contrary, if perchance one becomes liberated in an embodied condition, the desire for the father continues in such a condition:

---

[20] *yadā tanoḥ sêndriyasyâbhāvaḥ, tadā yathā saṃdhye sthāne śarīrêndriya-viṣayeṣv avidyāmāneṣv apy upalabdhi-mātra eva pitrâdi-kāmā bhavanti, evaṃ mokṣe 'pi syur, evaṃ hy etad upapadyate.*

> In the case of the existence (in *mokṣa*) of the physical body, if longings for father and so on exist in a wakeful state, they also exist (embodied) in liberation.[21]

Are commentaries such as BSBh 4.4.13–14 voiced by the same author of the trial (BSBh 2.3.46)? The spirit, vision, and mood of the two contexts are perceptibly different. And obviously, there is a striking contradiction between the theory of Advaitic consciousness and *saṃsāric* losses implied by the two references to the latter (according to BSBh 2.3.46 and BSBh 4.4.13–14). The transformation into a *mokṣa*-condition described in BSBh 4.4.13–14 implies a mode of existence and remembrance of the old self totally different from the mode implied in the description of the experiment (BSBh 2.3.46). Certain old-self experiences, desires, losses, and memories move into the new-self condition; the old self seems to be transformed rather than rejected and denied reality. Under the circumstances implied in BSBh 4.4.13–14, Śaṅkara's old self would respond violent, would come back to life in agony if a message such as his father's death were delivered in the experiment.

Śaṅkara's choice of the desire for (re-union) with one's father or ancestors and the like as his illustration of the continuity of *saṃsāra* and (qualified) *mokṣa* is striking. The desire for the company of one's father or ancestors seems strangely positive. In order to make his point, Śaṅkara has to pick up as an illustration something necessarily continuous in every state, in dream and wakefulness, in *saṃsāra* and in *mokṣa*. He chooses yearning for one's father (apparently absent, missing, or dead).

Śaṅkara's commentary is very close to the overt meaning of the sūtras he comments upon. BS 4.4.13 (*tanv-abhāve saṃdhyavad upapatteḥ*—in the non-existence of the body, by virtue of the possibility of existing [like in dreams]) and BS 4.4.14 (*bhāve jāgradvat*) provide the core of Śaṅkara's vocabulary in his commentaries on these two sūtras. Śaṅkara's major addition and contribution consist of the illustration he gives of the entity desired in all states: the father. Similar theme and imagery appear in BSBh 4.4.8.

BSBh 4.4.8 deals with the power of will in the condition of (qualified) *mokṣa* for one who meditates "on the heart." Is the mere wish

---

[21] BSBh 4.4.14: *bhave punas tanor yathā jāgarite vidyamāna eva pitrâdi-kāmā bhavanty, evaṃ muktasyâpy upapadyate.*

to bring about "rising of fathers and so on" (*pitrâdi-samutthāna*) sufficient for such rising to occur? Śaṅkara reflects in BSBh 4.4.8 on the meaning of ChU 8.2.1, which says: "If he wishes for the world of the fathers (ancestors), his fathers rise by his mere wish" (*sa yadi pitṛ-loka-kāmo bhavati saṃkalpād evâsya pitaraḥ samutiṣṭhante*). The Upaniṣad refers to many desires, mostly pertaining to relatives (desire for mother, brother, sister). Is mere willing enough to materialize such wishes? And who are the "fathers"? In the Upaniṣadic source, fathers (in plural, *pitaraḥ*) may signify ancestors rather than the single biological father. However, Śaṅkara's presentation of the *pūrva-pakṣin*'s position points to the nature of the father or ancestors in this context. The opponent thinks that "as in the world" (*lokavat*), a father's presence is materialized by actual going (*gamana*) (towards him), so also in the condition of *mokṣa* (*yathā loke 'smad-ādīnāṃ saṃkalpād gamanâdibhyaś ca hetubhyaḥ pitrâdi-sampattir bhavaty, evaṃ muktasyâpi syāt*). Mere will is thus insufficient for meeting with a father and so on, for the liberated as well as for the ordinary person. Obviously, the opponent means meeting with one's *living* father (rather than with dead ancestors), an appointment achieved by actually going to him. In his response, Śaṅkara does not contest this suggestion of the *pūrva-pakṣin* but bases his opinion on the difference between a liberated and an ordinary person; the former's wish (such as to see his father) is inherently different in force from the latter's (*prakṛta-saṃkalpa-vilakṣaṇatvān mukta-saṃkalpasya*). The comparison between the will of a liberated person and that of an ordinary one is grounded in the similarity of their objects. In both cases, the biological father is meant.

Thus, BSBh 4.4.8 is very similar in its basic import and imagery to BSBh 4.4.13–14. The son is devoted to his father, dreams of him and wishes to see him, in *saṃsāra* as well as in *mokṣa*. Recalling the absence (or omission) of any reference to one's father's death in the field of trial, and the devotion to one's father underlying BSBh 4.4.13–14, Śaṅkara's old self seems very present in the BSBh 2.3.46 experiment. His father's memory lingers on, like a defective vision of two moons, his Advaita-awareness not overwhelming enough to eradicate the action of some *saṃskāra*s or *vāsanā*s born long ago.

We may now return to the congregation at the field of trial, with it's various participants, differentiated by incoming messages of fathers' deaths. Again, Śuka hears, understands, and stays indifferent, ever-young. His Advaita-consciousness is whole, complete, overwhelming, new, dissociated. Īśvara may watch, but understands nothing. His Advaita-consciousness is—like Śuka's—whole and secure. Śaṅkarācārya (the author's exponent) stands with Īśvara and Śuka; he is whole, coherent, self-assured. There are many others, infinitely varied.

Presiding supreme over the assembly gathered at the experiment is Śaṅkara himself, the author. Relentlessly resisting the powerfully attractive, voracious *ātman* (new self), thus saving a little new life for the old one, holding fast to memories of mud and water, carpenters and wooden dolls, attached to his father, Śaṅkara keeps a balance most precarious, even painful. Under the force of this unstable balance, he composes the *Brahma-sūtra-bhāṣya*.

CHAPTER FIVE

ON DOUBT AND SELF-UNDERSTANDING: THE OMNISCIENCE OF AN AUTHOR AND HIS ARCH-EXPONENT

Who was Śaṅkara, the author of the BSBh? This is the question we keep asking in this essay. Prudent scholarship requires that we acknowledge the paucity of external sources in giving a true picture of Śaṅkara's life and circumstances.[1] Thus, we resist the temptation to draw conclusions about the man in accordance with later traditional scholarship and hagiographies (of the *dig-vijaya* type). Let us assume that we only have definitive, authorized texts at our disposal. Thus, limiting our investigation of Śaṅkara to the authorship of the BSBh we ask: who was he?

Śaṅkara's text pits his exponent (the *siddhāntin*) against all sorts of opponents (*pūrva-pakṣins*) such as yogins, Buddhists, Jainas, or inner-circle thinkers who disagree with the exponent on the meaning of certain Upaniṣadic words. The exponent wins, the opponents lose. What can we know of the author of texts such as these (structured as dialogues between a winner and various losers)? The author allegedly expresses his thoughts and vision through the exponent's words. But the following textual inconsistencies, if we are to call them that, indicate that something else may be happening: sometimes the *siddhāntin* fails, his arguments patently weak; opponents voice *siddhānta* contents; there are striking contradictions in the exponent's position with respect to the connection between Brahman and the world, etc.; the *siddhāntin* engages in the critically flawed strategy of interpreting Upaniṣadic statements according to their primary meaning (*abhidhā, mukhya*) whenever it suits him, and relegates other statements to their secondary meaning (*lakṣanā, gauṇa, upacāra*); the author richly evokes the *siddhāntin*'s opponents (with an imaginativeness which the *siddhāntin* lacks); the author boldly envisages Brahman speaking in the first-person; and he confesses to doubts which are wholly his own

[1] "Today there are no extant materials from which to reconstruct his (Śaṅkara's) life with certainty." Mayeda 1992: 3.

(never to be shared with his *siddhāntin*); the author allows his self-awareness as author to emerge in textual play (like imagining Brahman as the composer of the Veda or Pāṇini as the composer of the *Aṣṭādhyāyī*). All these are meaningful in terms of Śaṅkara's authorship, but what do these textual eccentricities actually mean?

In my view, textual phenomena such as the above invite resistance to the notion of conflating author and exponent. An author of Śaṅkara's caliber is entitled to a measure of charity on our part—namely, the charity to see him as conscious of the distinction between himself and an often-quixotic *siddhāntin*. Thus, we visualize a scholarly artist who peruses manuscripts, reads widely, confesses to doubt in his own voice; a man of humor and wit, curious about the thoughts of others, who enjoys what he does; one who is perhaps not a *saṃnyāsin* but a city-dweller with the leisure to write using his palm-leaves and ink. Now, such a man might be different from his staunch *siddhāntin* ('crippled by certainty' as we describe him). The latter, as we have seen above, reduces notions of coherence and congruity of Upaniṣadic speech to the trivial tautology of *āhara pātram* and *pātram āhara*. In short, as we saw in the previous chapters of this essay, the conflation of author and exponent does not do justice to the great Śaṅkara, author of the BSBh.

And yet, others might argue, although a writer is necessarily different from his spiritual hero—as Plato was distinct from Socrates—more direct evidence should be provided to justify our argument. Otherwise, it might be claimed that the distinction offered here is not persuasive—a mere intellectual exercise of no consequence. In view of the appeal of conflation manifested in traditional and other scholarly literature there is no sufficient reason, as our interlocutor says, to resist such conflation. If our author (Śaṅkara) was conscious, even dimly aware of the distinction between himself and his hero (Śaṅkarācārya), he must be shown to express it more directly.

Is there any direct reference to the author's consciousness of himself as the creator of his *siddhāntin*? Since Indian philosophy is traditionally strictly impersonal, there may not be such an explicit reference. However, there may be indirect references to authorship and composition which could shed light on what we call the author's self-awareness.

Let us speculate about the author's notion (or consciousness) of his authorship. Our challenge is to understand what we see as the intimacy shared between the author and his *siddhānta*-hero. The author may not be identified with his hero, but—on the other hand—he does choose a victorious exponent; the author's familiarity with his *siddhāntin* is thorough and more creative than his familiarity with the other creations of his mind. Moreover, there is an aspect of spontaneous closeness between author and hero. Therefore, we view the author as an intimate friend (even a devotee) of his exponent. However, further evidence such as conscious recognition—on the author's part—of a clear distinction between author and hero is also required.

Suppose Śaṅkara endows Brahman with authorship of the Veda; suppose also that he compares Brahman's level of knowledge with that of the Veda; suppose also that he compares the level of knowledge of a human being (such as Pāṇini) with the level of knowledge expressed in his creation (the *Aṣṭādhyāyī*). Is it not reasonable to assume that a similar relationship of authorship exists in our author's mind with respect to his own relationship with his exponent? Brahman is omniscient; the Veda is omniscient; Pāṇini is omniscient; Pāṇini's grammar is omniscient; the exponent's (Śaṅkarācārya's) *siddhānta*-Advaita is omniscient; Śaṅkara, the author of the BSBh is omniscient.

As Brahman authors the Veda, and Pāṇini the *Aṣṭādhyāyī*, so the author of the BSBh spontaneously provides the words spoken by his exponent. And yet, in our exposition, the creator of *siddhānta*-Advaita is different from his *siddhāntin* as Brahman is to be distinguished from the Veda and Pāṇini from his grammar. (The author of the BSBh is full of doubts and his exponent is 'crippled by certainty').

We base our reconstruction of Śaṅkara's thought (or chain of associations) on BSBh 1.1.3, where Śaṅkara touches upon two types (or levels) of knowledge, which he refers to as an "author's omniscience" (*sarva-jñatva*) and the omniscience manifested in his work. An omniscient author, Śaṅkara says, works from a higher level of knowledge (*adhikatara-vijñāna*) than the level of the composed text he composes (the text is a manifestation of a lesser omniscience, as it were). Thus, Pāṇini, the author the *Aṣṭādhyāyī* is omniscient, and so is his work on grammar.

Bādarāyaṇa's BS 1.1.3 (*śāstra-yonitvāt*) *sūtra* is somewhat enigmatic or ambiguous, as most of the *sūtra*s are. It asserts either that the Veda (*śāstra*) is the origin of something else (such as knowledge of Brahman), or that the Veda has its origin in something else (such as Brahman). Thibaut goes for the latter option; he paraphrases the *sūtra* thus: (The omniscience of Brahman follows) from its being the source of

Scripture.[2] Here is Thibaut's translation of the opening paragraph of BSBh 1.1.3:

> Brahman is the source, i.e. the cause of the great body of Scripture, consisting of the Ṛg Veda and other branches, which is supported by various disciplines (such as grammar, *nyāya, Purāṇa*, etc.); which lamp-like illuminates all things; which is itself all-knowing as it were. For the origin of a body of Scripture possessing the quality of omniscience cannot be sought elsewhere but in omniscience itself. *It is generally understood that the man from whom some special body of doctrine referring to one province of knowledge only originates, as, for instance, grammar from Pāṇini, possesses a more extensive knowledge* (*adhikatara-vijñāna*) *than his work*, comprehensive though it be;[3] what idea, then, shall we have to form of the supreme omniscience and omnipotence of that great Being, which in sport as it were, easily as a man sends forth his breath, has produced the vast mass of holy texts known as the Ṛg Veda etc., the mine of all knowledge, consisting of manifold branches, the cause of the distinction of all the different classes and conditions of gods, animals, and men![4]

In the comparison of Brahman and Pāṇini, we notice an uncanny note. Brahman is of course not a speaker.[5] Thus, the association of Brahman as the source (*yoni*) of the Veda is somewhat loose, metaphorical as it were. Pāṇini, on the other hand, is the author of the science of grammar in a primary sense. How indeed did it occur to Śaṅkara to associate Brahman as the cause of the Veda with Pāṇini as the author of the *Aṣṭādhyāyī*? Is there a link between Brahman and Pāṇini? What could this link be?

Brahman the absolute is radically different from Pāṇini the person who produced an exhaustive descriptive grammar of the Sanskrit language of his day. How indeed could the author of the BSBh compare the 'beyond human' (*apauruṣeya*) Brahman with the man Pāṇini? The association of Brahman's *yonitva* of the Veda with Pāṇini's *Aṣṭādhyāyī* would be somewhat more explicable if we assume a third, invisible

---

[2] Thibaut 1962: 17.

[3] *yad yad vistarârtha śāstraṃ yasmāt puruṣa-viśeṣāt sambhavati yathā vyākaraṇâdi Pāṇiny-āder jñeyâikadeśârtham api sa tato 'py adhikatara-vijñāna iti prasiddhaṃ loke.*

[4] Thibaut 1962: 20 (my italics).

[5] See for example BSBh 1.2.2: although in the Veda, which is not the work of man, no wish in the strict sense can be expressed, there being no speaker, still such phrases as 'desired to be expressed' may be figuratively used on account of the result, viz., (mental) comprehension." (*yady apy apauruṣeye vede vaktur abhāvān nêcchârthaḥ sambhavati tathâpy upādānena phalenôpacaryate*).

entity connecting the two. This entity could be a person naturally associated with Vedic knowledge; he would be a person and a speaker like Pāṇini, and also an exponent of Vedic truth (like Brahman). Śaṅkara, the author of the BSBh is a likely though imperceptible candidate for the missing link between Brahman and Pāṇini. As Brahman is intimate with the Veda (its source) and Pāṇini is intimate with his grammar, so does the author of the BSBh maintain intimacy with his chosen exponent. They share omniscience but they differ in their level of knowledge. The author evokes his authorized speaker and in the process expresses his doubts. He imagines a victorious hero but also imagines others whose arguments and modes of perception are not foreign to his own consciousness.

Author and *siddhāntin* are thus intimate colleagues as well as distinct voices. Both are omniscient, but their respective levels of knowledge are different, and they exist separately. Śaṅkara's inner being is inherently divided; the two levels of knowledge collide; the BSBh dialogues are an inner debate of the scale and significance displayed in the hagiographic literature of the debates.

Tensions between the two are revealed in a leap of imagination which calls for interpretations in the spirit of dissociation of author and exponent. Śaṅkara's presentation of Uṣasta's sarcastic challenge to Yājñavalkya (BUBh 3.4.2) is telling and bold: Why all this excessive talk? Man, stop your tricks generated by your desire for cows, and show us Brahman tangibly (*kiṃ bahunā? tyaktvā go-tṛṣṇā-nimittaṃ vyājaṃ, yad eva sākṣād aparokṣād brahma ya ātmā sarvântaras taṃ me vyācakṣvêti*). Thus, Uṣasta accuses Yājñavalkya of lowly, egocentric motivation, hypocrisy, greed, malice, etc. Such accusations are unexpected and inventive on the author's part; they are charged with a somewhat unusual, almost personal, idiosyncratic interpretation. For of course, one could view Uṣasta's challenge to Yājñavalkya in other ways. One also recalls *ātman* speaking in the first-person to the *manas*. "Since I am free of any particular quality, your actions are of no benefit to me."[6] "Your efforts are useless." "You'd better be silent" (...*praśamāya te hitam*).[7]

Who then is the author who puts such a bitter, sarcastic accusation in Uṣasta's mouth? How can such a leap of imagination on the

[6] Upad 2.8.1, etc.
[7] Upad 2.19.3.

author's part be explained? Of course, it may be an expression of talent. But, it could also be an expression of deeply rooted doubt, the core of Advaita doubt-psychology found in the transition from Upaniṣadic verbalization to true self-understanding and spiritual transformation.

Considering evidence such as the *siddhāntin*'s apparent weaknesses, and the explicit expressions of doubt on the author's part, how is a reading that conflates author and *siddhāntin* possible? We assume that a subtle desire for integration and coherence is probably at work. Underlying a confluent reading of the BSBh is the following presupposition: the author/*siddhāntin* of the BSBh is eager to win and persuade using all means at his disposal. In his eagerness to win he seems forgetful of his hero's apparent weaknesses. Such a presupposition diminishes, I think, our author's mastery. Through our author's divided allegiance—his innermost sense of the absolute (the one *ātman*, which is the self of everything), on the one hand, and his experience (of multiplicity) on the other—our author expresses one of the most significant frustrations of a philosopher's life.

In order to answer questions pertinent to the so-called discovery of an author's metaphysics (as distinct from the *siddhāntin*'s), a re-reading of the entire BSBh is called for. For the distinction between author and exponent makes a difference with respect to every single aspect of scholarly research of Advaita. Principles of metaphysics, concepts of truth and truth-values, revelation and reasoning, coherence, etc. should be rethought on the basis of this distinction. If it is justified, then current and traditional expositions of Śaṅkara's Advaita—all of them somewhat blurred due to conflation—should be clarified by splitting the two respective Advaitas. Such research and re-writing of the two (or even three) *Brahma-sūtra-bhāṣya*s are beyond the scope of this volume.

In our view, Śaṅkara's discussions of inner-circle debates of Vedic meanings constitute the core of the BSBh. The kernel-*bhāṣya*s of the BSBh integrate Advaita-Vedānta in terms of epistemology (the exclusive *pramāṇatva* of the Veda), ontology (the existence of Brahman or *ātman*), and soteriology (correct understanding of the Veda being a necessary and sufficient cause of *mokṣa*, or *mokṣa* itself). The status of the Upaniṣads as the only means of knowledge (*pramāṇa*) of the self (*ātman*) is primary, definitive in any version of Advaita-Vedānta. It is, I believe, the basis of the intimacy between author and *siddhāntin*. The difference between the *siddhāntin* and his creator is grounded in their accord on this fundamental issue.

However, while Śaṅkara and Śaṅkarācārya share the assumption that the Veda is the exclusive authority with respect to the nature of the one self (*ātman*), the *bhāṣya-kāra*'s fundamental motif is 'doubt' (wonder),[8] while his *siddhāntin*'s is the expression of certainty. Indeed, as seen above, inner-circle discussions invariably begin with expressions of doubt regarding the meaning of words in certain Upaniṣdic passages, and they end with the author's assertion of the arch-exponent's victory. However, as opponents (*pūrva-pakṣins*) are essential within the framework of our author's condition of doubt, they are also, in a sense, exponents. (I refer to the *siddhāntin* as arch-exponent; the opponents might be called sub-exponents). Most significant among the sub-exponents are those committed to the Upaniṣads as the source of truth. As repeatedly suggested above, Śaṅkara the author of the BSBh expresses doubt exclusively in the presence of such sub-exponents; no reference to doubt is available in the author's voice when he is introducing debates with opponents who deny Vedic authority (such as Buddhists, Jainas, etc.).

In my view, the depth of the author's doubt, or the nature of his wonder are the most interesting issues in the study of Advaita-Vedānta. The choice the author has made—to use doubt and the questioning mode as the vehicle of his thought—is an indication of his self-awareness as author. Assertion of doubt is legitimate in Śaṅkara's Advaita-Vedānta. At other periods in Indian thought, expressing doubt may not have been legitimate even as a rhetorical option (for example, expressions of doubt [*saṃśaya, saṃdeha, cintā*] are generally absent in Upaniṣadic literature). But here, in Śaṅkara's writings of the eighth century, doubt prevails as a privileged mode of self-assertion. One should not, however, belittle the significance of the author's choice of arch-exponent. Neither should the author's choice of doubt-episodes as a major vehicle for introducing intellectual debates be ignored.

Śaṅkara's Advaita-doubt is a fertile disease of the soul, as it were, consisting of two contradictory motions. On the one hand, the author is deeply familiar with Upaniṣadic and other Advaita sources, and recognizes that Upaniṣadic propositions are the ultimate truth. On the other hand, there seems to be a sense of failure in the recognition of

[8] There are over 80 explicit references to doubt in the BSBh, including verbal combinations such as *saṃśaya-kāraṇa* (1.2.24); *saṃśaya-jñāna* (2.2.33); *saṃśaya-nirṇaya; saṃśaya-mātra* (3.3.54); *saṃśayâdi-vṛttikam* (2.3.32); saṃśayānā (3.2.10); *saṃśayānâtivṛtti* (2.3.24); *saṃśayânupapatti* (1.1.23); *saṃśayâviṣayatva* (1.1.23).

oneself as the one *ātman*. The disciple's bitter complaints according to Śaṅkara in the prose-section of the Upad revolve around such a sense of failure. In a sense, the disciple's feeling of failure is more tangible (or lively) than the master's assertions of Upaniṣadic truth (mainly in the form of pronouncements or citations). I am one, says the disciple, and he is another. Cut or burnt I just feel pain, which is *my* pain. Such experiences are tokens of doubt, which also find expression in the dialogical framework of the BSBh. The author, in our view, brings to life mankind's primordial anxiety, namely, the tension between the Upaniṣadic requirement for truth and individual existence.

Committed readers of Śaṅkara's Advaita know that the reading and apparent understanding of every sentence, illustration, or quotation in Śaṅkara's writings does not generate "knowledge of self" or consequent joy. In this regard, the frustration of committed readers resembles Śaṅkara's own doubt, or discomfort of the soul. (Such distress of the spirit is experienced by the truly committed, not by mere readers of the uncommitted type).

Sufficiently close readings of Śaṅkara's core-*bhāṣya*s are hard to find. Enormous cultural differences manifest themselves at each attempt. In our view, a sufficiently close reading means finding faults with the *siddhāntin*'s arguments as well as with his inherently doubt-free and uniform mode of Advaita. We suspect that such faults, fully conscious on the author's part, are to be found in each and every core-*bhāṣya*. Dissociation of author and arch-exponent contributes to a clearer sense of the author's mastery as well as to his ability to give expression to one of mankind's innermost predicaments, namely, the gap or dissonance between experience and the belief in an absolute truth. In the context of reading the Upaniṣads as the exclusive source of truth about the self, or of the only one that truly matters, the arch-exponent invariably faces opponents (or sub-exponents) expressive of the truth of multiplicity and experience. The author knows that his *siddhāntin* knows the truth of the one and only *ātman* and yet, like Uṣasta and Kahola, he experiences the aforementioned distress of the soul as rooted in the dissociation of truth and experience. Discussions regarding the meaning and reference of Upaniṣadic words reflect the dynamics of the doubt process and its apparent resolution.

At the end of BSBh 1.1.22 the author makes the *siddhāntin* say that the word *ākāśa* ("ether") in Chāndogya Upaniṣad 1.9 denotes Brahman in the same way as the word *agni* denotes a boy in a sentence such as *agnir adhīte 'nuvākyam* ("Agni studies a passage"). As a reader replaces, or transcends, as it were, the meaning of *agni* (fire) in favor of a boy's personal name, so one transcends the ordinary meaning of *ākāśa* (ether) in ChU 1.9 in favor of Brahman. This is a curious and somewhat ambiguous statement. For, as we shall see, the two cases are patently different.

The Chāndogya Upaniṣad asserts that all creatures emerge from *ākāśa* and merge in *ākāśa* as they die. The Upaniṣadic intention in this case is indeed doubtful, says the author. Ether is the more natural, established meaning (*suprasiddha*), arising naturally and immediately (*śīghram*) in one's mind. Moreover, he says, *ākāśa* denotes ether in Vedic contexts as well as in conventional language. And yet, sometimes *ākāśa* seems to denote Brahman, and it is also a well-known Upaniṣadic proposition that everything comes out of Brahman and dissolves into Brahman. So, where do all the creatures go as they die, according to ChU 1.9? Is it ether or Brahman? Having expressed his doubts about it, the author proceeds to present a *pūrva-pakṣa* and a *siddhānta*. The *pūrva-pakṣin* argues for the elemental ether; the *siddhāntin* argues for Brahman. The exponent's major theme is context (*prakaraṇa*), characteristic marks (*liṅga*), and primary subject (*prakṛta*) of the ChU 1.9. The apparent meaning of *ākāśa* is rejected for the powerfully implied notion of Brahman. On a triumphant note which signifies the resolution of doubt, the *siddhāntin* asserts that just as the meaning of '*agni*' (fire) must be rejected in the case of "Agni studies a passage", so the notion of *ākāśa* as elemental ether must be rejected in ChU 1.9 for the notion of Brahman. The teacher's suggestion here is, of course, that just as doubt about *ākāśa* in Chāndogya Upaniṣad 1.9 dissolves, so in the course of BSBh 1.1.22 the doubt about the nature of the denotation of '*agni*' in *agnir adhīte 'nuvākyam*, is dissolved.

But the *siddhāntin*'s comparison seems inappropriate; there is doubt about *ākāśa* in ChU 1.9 whereas there is none in "Agni studies a passage"! Agni is a personal name, and thus completely appropriate in "Agni studies a passage"; there is hardly a noticeable transition from *agni* ("fire") to Agni (the personal name). The process of interpretation which commences with doubt and the need for its resolution does not exist in the case of "Agni studies a passage." Moreover, the notion of Agni as a boy's personal name is well-established (*suprasiddha*) and arises naturally (*śīghram*) in the mind—in congruence with the *pūrva-pakṣin*'s way of interpreting *ākāśa* in ChU 1.9 as ether. Applied to ether in ChU 1.9 the principle implied by "Agni studies a passage" would yield ether rather than Brahman.

One suspects that the author's underlying idea is that *ākāśa* in ChU 1.9 is *unlike* "Agni studies a passage." Since the *siddhāntin*'s illustration seems inappropriate (there being no room for true doubt), we tend to assume that the author must have presented it as such. In such cases, where the exponent is patently unconvincing, one tends to separate author and *siddhāntin*. But this method, one might argue, would allow the author to say whatever came to mind even if it was in striking opposition to what the *siddhāntin* said! But no—in the author's presentation, there is doubt in the case of *ākāśa* in ChU 1.9, whereas there is none in the case of Agni, etc. The two cases are inherently dissimilar. Using Śaṅkara's language (actually, the *siddhāntin*'s), we could say that the true subject of BSBh 1.1.22 is doubt and its resolution, and the *siddhāntin*'s somewhat inappropriate, triumphant note at the end exposes a weakness inherent throughout the author's presentations of his doubt-free *siddhāntin*. Indeed, the *siddhāntin* does seek to experience ChU 1.9 as pointing to Brahman rather than to ether. This represents the inherently clear-cut, doubt-free *siddhānta*-Advaita of the exponent. However, its weakness is inherent in all cases of intimate discourse with *pūrva-pakṣin*s committed to Vedic *pramāṇatva*.

The infected-by-doubt author and the infected-by-certainty arch-exponent should be viewed with their differing sub-conscious perceptions of existence (metaphysics) in mind. Śaṅkara, the author of the BSBh, recognizes existence as a connected whole infused by different intensities of *ātman*'s presence; he refuses to deny existence or reality to its various levels. Thus, in my view, as repeatedly suggested above, Śaṅkara's intensely felt perception of rival positions has metaphysical implications. Śaṅkara seems to me keenly interested in what his imagined *pūrva-pakṣin*s have to say. Had he been totally preoccupied with *ātman*'s presence as the only reality or presence, he would not have been as open to alternative opinions, especially considering that the verbal exchanges he imagines have emerged from his own mind. Thus I claim that Śaṅkara probably recognizes an ultimate *ātman*-presence, a pure *ātman*, as it were; yet he recognizes the existence of other presences, however inferior to pure *ātman*, as also true.

The author voices explicit doubts (*saṃśaya, saṃdeha, cintā*) at the opening paragraphs of numerous *bhāṣyas* that express his refusal to deny the presence and existence of entities other than *ātman*. In the author's view or Advaita, as I see it, the snake does not completely disappear. It leaves its trace, lingering on, resurrected and potentially always there. The *siddhāntin*, on the other hand, accords truth and reality to *ātman* alone. His sense of totality, *ātman*'s oneness, is informed by neither doubt nor wonder at multiplicity. In this sense, I think that Śaṅkara the author of the BSBh shares the *pūrva-pakṣin*'s (Mīmāṃsaka's) view, expressed succinctly in BSBh 1.1.4. According to this view the Brahmin who is repeatedly exposed to knowledge of Brahman is still not transformed and remains in *saṃsāra* as before (*yathā-pūrvam*). The *siddhāntin*, on the other hand, asserts that once knowledge of Brahman or *ātman* is achieved, it is inherently transformational (and irreversible).

The arch-exponent of Śaṅkara's Advaita is awe-inspiring; in his assertion of the oneness of the self and all, he presents humanity with an irresistibly attractive and courageous vision. It is, however, a fatal attraction, as it were, for ordinary folks like ourselves, that is, ordinary readers of the Upaniṣads and the BSBh. Immersed in illusion and the petty individualism prescribed perhaps by nature, we keep Advaita at a distance. In our view, the author of the BSBh shares some traces of that distance with the rest of humanity. And yet, like *ātman* disturbed (see above, chapter 3), our author is deeply attached to the Advaita vision and is pained by the incessant, interminable call of his rivals, who expose his inner divisions and his gnawing sense of doubt.

CHAPTER SIX

ŚAṄKARA'S ŚAṄKARĀCĀRYA: THE INVISIBLE AUTHOR OF BSBH AND HIS BELOVED *SIDDHĀNTIN*

The author of the BSBh conceived of his spiritual hero—the Advaita-exponent—as an accomplished winner (*siddhāntin*) in the debates he composed for the BSBh. Though seemingly only a literary character and imaginary being (supposedly less real than the author), the figure of the *siddhāntin* incorporates an entire trajectory of traditional as well as modern scholarly learning. In fact, almost the whole tradition of Advaita-Vedānta is founded on the speeches of Śaṅkara's *siddhāntin*. This is not a critical weakness in the tradition. The *siddhāntin* is an enlightened, eloquent and thoughtful figure who articulates the deepest mysteries and meanings of life (such as the oneness, existence and identity of *ātman* and Brahman). The other, namely the author, is taken for granted. Although he is an intelligent and thoughtful commentator transmitting a body of knowledge, the author functions as a transparent channel of communication. Thus, just as it seems natural that Don Quixote is for most of the readers more attractive than his creator Cervantes, so Śaṅkara's *siddhāntin* is the focus of far more attention than that focused on his author, Śaṅkara, the author of the BSBh, Upad, *Bṛhadāraṇyakôpaniṣad-bhāsya* and *Bhagavadgītā-bhāṣya*.

Śaṅkara created an intimate friend or "human ideal" in the figure of his *siddhāntin*. The author loves his hero, the inherently vulnerable *siddhāntin* who defends the inconceivable truth of the one, all-inclusive self, formed of pure consciousness. An Advaita precept such as this is not easy to defend, and its prevalence within the elite Brahmanical Sanskrit culture for generations is possibly misleading. I think the *dig-vijaya* hagiographic tradition as well as the essential structure of Śaṅkara's *bhāṣya*s on the *Brahma-sūtra*s and the Upaniṣads contain more than a kernel of truth: opposition to Advaita was intense. Based on the ancient and often incoherent Upaniṣads composed about 1300 years before his time, the eighth-century sage imagined a hero who ceaselessly articulated an ineffable *nir-guṇa-brahman* never in sight, devoid of tangible godly presence, who was not to be found in temples or elsewhere. Maintaining such a philosophy required extra-ordinary resistance to ordinary, devotional, or scholarly learning (such as Buddhists logic) of that time. Śaṅkara's compassion for his imaginary being is thus understandable. Numerous capable exponents and opponents of many kinds were available. But among all the competitors vying for attention, victory and truth, the author chose one—the Advaita exponent—as his beloved *siddhāntin*, who—against all odds—wins all the debates. I am not aware of the author's own loneliness in the midst of adverse opposition—reflected, some would say, in his imaginary hero's. But the fact that Śaṅkara's imaginary *siddhāntin* has become accepted as the true winner over the course of time should not make us blind to the initial, essential Advaita position as a truth not easy to defend. In other words, familiarity with Advaita ideology and its subsequent dominance within Hindu scholarly community should not block a vision of its inherently incredible—though perhaps true—claims. The compassionate Śaṅkara is aware of this paradox; he is ambivalent, and numerous opponents co-exist in his mind along with the winner.[1]

Let us be less sentimental and more in conformity with scholarship focused on "impersonal philosophy", in regard to Śaṅkara's relationship (love, compassion) with his imaginary *siddhāntin*. Obviously, the author appreciates and is even committed to his *siddhāntin*'s Advaita positions, the chosen winner's stance in the debates with Sāṅkhya-Yoga opponents, Buddhists, Pūrva-Mīmāṃsakas, and others. In terms of philosophy or theology, the author, Śaṅkara, is evidently excited about Advaita. Though not necessarily an accomplished *saṃnyāsin* and knower of Brahman, the author of the BSBh[2] retrieves hundreds of Vedic propositions[3] and uses his logic and wit extensively to defeat the *siddhāntin*'s rivals. Thus, the author can be considered a genuine and resourceful Advaitin. Sometimes he even seems to make his exponent exaggerate his interpretation of Upaniṣadic coherence, saying, for example that *all* the Vedāntic statements (*sarveṣu hi vedānteṣu*...)[4]

[1] The major thesis of this chapter has already been implied: Śaṅkara the creator may not be identified with the *siddhāntin* of his imagination. Added to this are references to dimensions of the relationship between the two personalities to be distinguished. A moment of compassion for the lonely *siddhāntin* is the source of creativity for an author perhaps as lonely as his imaginary hero.

[2] I refer to the Brahma-sūtra-bhāṣya as Śaṅkara's definitive work; he is invariably seen by responsible scholars as (by definition) the author of the BSBh. The authenticity of his other works is judged with respect to this text.

[3] Śaṅkara's favorite authorities of the Veda are, of course, the Upaniṣads. The Bṛhadāraṇyaka and the Chāndogya are the most frequently quoted.

[4] BSBh 1.1.4.

speak of Brahman alone as the cause, subsistence and destruction of the world (this is an exaggeration since we can be sure that the Upaniṣads speak of other matters as well). Such exaggerations might sound pathetic, a kind of compensation for lurking traces of doubt. Nevertheless, heeding Śaṅkara's volume of creative expression, it is possible to re-assert that Śaṅkara is passionate about Advaita philosophy and vision or, at least, that on the level of his relationship with his hero, the *siddhāntin*, Śaṅkara loves his Advaitin more than he loves the other *pūrva-pakṣins* in the debates.

Thus, Śaṅkara's love or compassion for his chosen *siddhāntin* corresponds cognitively to his excitement about the Advaita vision or understanding of reality. How does one commit oneself to the incredible Advaita truth of the one *ātman*, formed of pure consciousness? Though the distinction between author and *siddhāntin* generates possible answers to such questions, only quasi-tautological statements present themselves to mind at this point. The author's excitement about Advaita is palpable in the particular intimacy he shares with his literary hero. Convinced of the Advaita truth, free of doubt, consistent, deeply familiar with the Upaniṣads, the *siddhāntin* expresses knowledge of Brahman; certainly he is a knower of *ātman*. As the Upaniṣad says: he knows Brahman, he becomes Brahman (...*brahma veda brahmâiva bhavati*).[5] The author, it seems, imagines himself as the *siddhāntin*, thinking perhaps "I myself am my *siddhāntin*" (or, "the *siddhānta* winner is my self"). The author loves his hero and is his *siddhāntin*'s devotee. There is always excitement of the deepest kind associated with the empathetic experience of emotion such as pain conceived (or imagined) as *my* pain, pleasure as *my* pleasure, thought as *my* thought. On the other hand, the literary hero in Śaṅkara's case is often grotesque; fighting unlikely opponents, he seems complacent about spurious victories and is equally complacent about spurious rhetorical coherence. In other words, the author's compassion is compatible with the situation. In short, neither identical with his *siddhānta*-hero nor totally different from him, the relationship between author and *siddhāntin* is that of intense intimacy. Thus, let us say that Śaṅkara's *siddhāntin* is the author's intimate companion; no more, no less.

Theoretically, I think, the idealized guru/philosopher, namely, the Advaita-*siddhāntin*, may be seen as more powerful (even more intelligent,

---

[5] Muṇḍaka Upaniṣad 3.2.9.

some would say) than his author. Fully grounded in his Advaita vision, free of doubt, in control of the debate, *ātman* itself as it were, the *siddhāntin* is truly great (or, some would say, as great as the author could make him). Thus, the *siddhānta* imaginary speaker is worthy of being recorded and studied. And yet, there is also scholarly merit in attending to the real yet invisible author of the BSBh, whose consciousness contains, as we have seen, traces of doubt, ambiguity, ambivalence, and complexities of reflection often beyond his characters' reach.

In addition, there is also the master's presence, the alleged flesh-and-blood guru/philosopher who once upon a time (prior to the composition of the BSBh)[6] had made an impact on the Indian mind. Distinct from *siddhāntin* and master alike, the author's presence *qua author* is new to us and worthy of curiosity and attention. Thus, by making a distinction between author and the *siddhānta*-exponent I seek to salvage some notion of the "inconceivable author," Śaṅkara, the agent behind the BSBh.

Identification of Śaṅkara the author of the BSBh with the *siddhāntin* (Śaṅkarācārya) is the paradigm that has prevailed unawares in the study and reading of the BSBh and Śaṅkara's other works up to this day. An additional identification is sometimes added; Śaṅkara the author of the BSBh as well as Śaṅkarācārya the intellectual winner in the debates presented therein are identified with a wanderer/master (henceforth Ādi-Śaṅkarācārya) who had supposedly traveled throughout the subcontinent of India, teaching Advaita, defeating rivals, and founding monasteries of research and knowledge. Thus, there are three theoretical entities that emerge in Śaṅkara studies (designated here as "Śaṅkara," "Śaṅkarācārya" and "Ādi-Śaṅkarācārya"). Some scholars have resisted identifying Śaṅkara and Ādi-Śaṅkarācārya.[7] However, the distinction between Śaṅkara and Śaṅkarācārya has invariably been ignored.

In order to illustrate the difference between Śaṅkara's voice—which expresses uncertainty—and the Advaita *siddhāntin*'s doubt-free

---

[6] Independently of the *dig-vijayas* (hagiographic stories of Ādi-Śaṅkarācārya, current in India over 700 years after the composition of the BSBh), there is no evidence of the wandering sage or guru/intellectual.

[7] See K. Potter's argument below. However, he bases his resistance to the identification of Śaṅkara and Ādi-Śaṅkarācārya on the identification of Śaṅkara with Śaṅkarācārya (see below).

expositions, let us closely explore the structure of a typical (or paradigmatic) *bhāṣya*. In BSBh 1.1.28 Śaṅkara (author, not *siddhāntin*) expresses uncertainty as he deals with the necessary choice between four interpretations of the word *prāṇa* in the *Kauśītakī Upaniṣad* 3.1–3. According to the story told in the third section of the Upaniṣad, Indra tells the warrior Pratardana the means whereby one may kill one's father and mother without becoming tainted. Look at me, he says. I am *prāṇa*, the inner conscious self (*pratyātman*); meditate on me as life and immortality, and so on. The author of BSBh 1.1.28 expresses his doubts: "With respect to this there is the following doubt (*tatra saṃśayaḥ)*: in this context, is simple breathing meant by the word *prāṇa*, or the self of a certain divinity, or the individual self (*jīva*), or the absolute Brahman (*kim iha prāṇa-śabdena vāyu-mātram abhidhīyata uta devatâtmêti jīvo 'thavā paraṃ brahmêti*)". This doubt on the part of the author is now challenged: But it has already been proved—in BS 1.1.21—that the word *prāṇa* means absolute Brahman (*athâiva prāṇa ity atra varṇitaṃ prāṇa-śabdasya brahma-paratvam*). And in this context as well, characteristic marks of Brahman are specified, namely "bliss, no aging, immortality" (*ihâpi ca brahma-liṇgam asty ānando 'jaro 'mṛtaḥ*).

Thus, the "preliminary *pūrva-pakṣin*" presented in BSBh 1.1.28 aims at suppressing doubt altogether; he ends his plea for certainty with the following question: How does doubt become an issue again in this context (after the meaning of the word *prāṇa* has already been established) (*katham iha punaḥ saṃśayaḥ sambhavati*)? But no, says the author. We say we are in doubt because there are many characteristic marks of Brahman (some of them possibly incompatible with the reference of "*prāṇa*" as Brahman in KauU 8.1–3) (*aneka-liṇga-darśanād brūmaḥ*). In our context (KaU 3), characteristic marks of Brahman are not the only ones mentioned (*na kevalam iha brahma-liṇgam evôpalabhyate*). There are other qualities as well (*santi hîtara-liṇgāny api*). Thus, for example, Indra's assertion "You should know me only" (KaU 3.1) expresses a quality of a god's self (*mām eva vijānīhîtîndrasya vacanaṃ devatâtma-liṇgam*). The Upaniṣadic saying "Holding this body, makes it rise up" (KaU 3.3) is characteristic of breathing (*prāṇa*) (*idaṃ śarīraṃ parigṛhyôtthāpayatîti prāṇa-liṇgam*). The Upaniṣadic statement "Let a person know the speaker rather than speaking" implies reference to the individual self (*jīva*). Thus, the author sums up his position on the legitimacy of doubt with the following statement:

"Therefore doubt is a worthwhile option in this context" (*ata upapannaḥ saṃśayaḥ*).[8]

In fact, the author is an exponent of doubt throughout the Veda-committed sections of the BSBh. As such, he is remarkably different from the preliminary opponent who rejects doubt (as in BSBh 1.1.28 above). By the same token, the author is not the Advaita-*siddhāntin* who wins the debate after the legitimacy of doubt has been recognized. Indeed, the *pūrva-pakṣin* who opposes the author-*siddhāntin* in the opening sections of the *bhāṣya*s is by no means the staunch Advaitin who wins the debate over the non-Advaita *pūrva-pakṣins*. Thus, the loser (*pūrva-pakṣin*) in the preliminary debate over the legitimacy of doubt becomes the winner (*siddhāntin*) in the latter debate focused on Vedic intention and the nature of Brahman or *ātman*. The author maintains distance from loser and winner alike.

The prevailing paradigm based upon integration of apparently separate personalities is fascinating (even if fanciful). As mentioned previously, it seems to express an innate drive towards coherence, richer Gestalts, fullness of being, etc. And unless forced, as it were, to resist integration, combination, and false plenitude, the reader is irresistibly drawn to the beauty of fullness and integration. The following is an illustration of my own articulation of a typical *bhāṣya* in the spirit of the Śaṅkara/Śaṅkarācārya/Ādi-Śaṅkarācārya combination. Integrating various forces and personalities in the *bhāṣya*-domain is enriching, attractive and valuable. The dialogical domain, charged by the combined, integrated personality of a spiritual master/guru, forceful logician, and gifted writer is rewarding, almost irresistible in its display of human greatness.

In the shade of a tree, seated among close disciples, persons of the inner-circle, the great master concedes doubt. The Upaniṣad tells of 'space' (*ākāśa*) as the origin of all beings and the final abode and resting place into which they merge as they die. Does '*ākāśa*' mean elemental space, or Brahman, "the absolute"? The audience, those disciples devoted to the Veda as *śabda-pramāṇa*, the source of Advaita insight and experience, who are familiar with knowledge of *ātman*

[8] Śaṅkara's state of mind of doubt is reminiscent of Yudhiṣṭhira's according to the famous Yakṣa's questions in MBh 3.313. Yudhiṣṭhira defines the human condition as follows: Reasoning has no foundation (*tarko 'pratiṣṭhitaḥ*); scriptures are self-contradictory (*śrutayo vibhinnāḥ*); there is no single sage whose thought is truly authoritative (*nâiko ṛṣir yasya mataṃ pramāṇam*).

or Brahman, are expectant and anxious; they wait for Vedic joy to emerge. Indeed, the uncertainty is important; re-enactment of the Advaita vision is at stake. The presence of another vision embedded in "ordinary experience" of "real" time and space, duality and trouble, of creatures and objects dissociated from Brahman, looms large; non-Advaita perception of reality is even 'natural' (*suprasiddha*), rising quickly and mechanically (*śīghram*) in the mind, as the teacher admits.[9] This, I assume, is the meaning of taking Vedic words such as '*ākāśa*' in Chāndogya Upaniṣad 1.9 in their more ordinary denotation. Rather than academic or intellectual luxury, the choice between ether and Brahman is one between duality and unity, or if you like, for the master's audience, between death and life. As the Veda constitutes the self of those open to its voice, the interpretation of Vedic words as pregnant with doubt is highly charged. The disturbing presence of the 'mind' (*manas*), as we shall see below, is another manifestation of doubt and its omnipresence, and of the consequent dissonance within the Advaita universe (characterized elsewhere as "*ātman* disturbed," or "*ātman* suppressed").[10]

The above is my articulation of the skeletal text of BSBh 1.1.22, which refers to the meaning of *ākāśa* in Chāndogya Upaniṣad 1.9.[11] I have added the expectant audience (close disciples), the existential flavor of Upaniṣadic semantics, the corresponding inner conflict present in the listeners' souls, and so on. In other words, I have done my best to make the typical BSBh 1.1.22 into a description of Advaita-reality in the midst of which stands (or sits) Śaṅkara/Śaṅkarācārya/Ādi-Śaṅkarācārya, the Advaita guru who is a philosopher as well as a theologian, writer, therapist, and mystic. My attention focused on the *siddhāntin*, the spiritual hero, arch-speaker in the BSBh, the most accessible entity in the dialogic domain: a seemingly perfect sage who knows Brahman. I have assumed the identification of the *siddhāntin* (Śaṅkarācārya) with the master attended by his disciples under the shade of a tree (Ādi-Śaṇkarācāya), and also with Śaṅkara, the dark, almost invisible author and writer of our seminal text, the BSBh. In accordance with the prevailing paradigm, I have not made an effort to refer to the author of the BSBh. As if he were a perfect, indistinguishable

[9] BSBh 1.1.22.
[10] See discussion of the mind's disturbing presence displayed in the dialogues of *ātman* with the mind.
[11] See previous chapter for a discussion of this section of the BSBh.

copy of his shadowy creator, the *siddhāntin* absorbs all the attention. Indeed, if the author and his *siddhāntin* are the same, how can one distinguish between the two? Questions with respect to the identity of the master/guru have often been raised. Issues related to the separation of author and *siddhāntin* have never been discussed.

The context of Śaṅkara's speech or writing and the nature of his voice are obviously clues to a good-enough reading of his works. Śaṅkara's audience and the cultural and historical setting of the period condition not only the tone and texture of the author's voice but also the meaning of the text. Was Śaṅkara—author of the BSBh—a scholar seeking certainty in times of unrest? Did he know the *ātman*, eagerly seeking to transmit his vision for the release of humanity from bondage and ignorance? How and to what extent was Śaṅkara committed to Vedic authority? Was he scared of the Buddhists? Was he a mere scholarly philosopher practicing his logic and talent and somewhat uncommitted to the Advaita vision and arguments? Did he resist popular practices at temples, like Rammohan Roy? What, indeed, did he want? Readers of Śaṅkara feel the urge to contextualize his speech and say something of the man; for much of the reading experience (and interpretation) depends upon the context and "nature of voice."

Whereas Śaṅkara, as we speak of him, is indeed—by definition—the author of the BSBh, the identification of author and *siddhāntin* is not quite as tautological. Indeed, the *siddhāntin* is—of course—an Advaitin. The author, however, might contain a consciousness significantly different—more complex, perhaps—than that of his hero's; theoretically, he *may not* be an Advaitin at all.

Since integrating the three Śaṅkara-personalities fulfils the need for meaning (and corresponding satisfaction), a sense of loss is felt when we split the Śaṅkara/Śaṅkarācārya/Ādi-Śaṅkarācārya hero. Such an integrated man-hero, if he ever existed, was great indeed; spiritually enlightened, scholarly informed, intent on playful, sophisticated writing yet also "active in the world," teaching, defeating rivals, conquering the quarters of the earth. Though silent in the presence of the ineffable Brahman, he is also voluble, hectic in his reasoning, as he argues for the benefit of mankind and creatively adjusts to the intellectual assumptions of his audience. Greatness, indeed, is often an aspect of a many-sided, multi-dimensional personality. Moreover, conviction of a spiritual truth such as the reality of *ātman* (in the presence of which the world is experienced as a mirage) exerts pressure from within. One who realizes such a truth would burst with exclamations of *mokṣa* ("awake, awake!)" The aforementioned conviction (in the actual being of a universe, formed of consciousness, where men and women are inherently playful and free), would generate inexhaustible energy. Eager to share with others such a liberating truth, a combined Śaṅkara/*siddhāntin*/master would ceaselessly speak, think, study and write. Such a man is great indeed. Why deprive such an integrated entity of writer/literary figure/guru-instructor of its greatness (by dissection and separation)? Why replace such greatness by a vision of a secluded scholar and writer inflicted with doubt and passion for its resolution, insisting on the feasibility of liberation yet allegedly removed from it? Loss of greatness seems to me a grave danger. And yet, greatness has many faces; the greatness underlying the composition of the BSBh could also be that of an invisible author, intensely alive, committed to logic and doubt, in quest of the full realization of *ātman*, listening with passion to Upaniṣadic voices, projecting onto the *siddhāntin* his hopes and desire for *mokṣa*.

The attractions and advantages of combination and integration are obvious. Every speech-act, every thought, every feeling is a moment of integration. Meaningfulness implies *gestalt* and integration, as do consciousness and "life itself." Unrestrained combination, however, might result in a fuzzy, blurred vision. Take for example our case of the combined Śaṅkara/Śaṅkarācārya/Ādi-Śaṅkarācārya. The author of the BSBh is a gifted artist, playful, often ironical and humorous in his references to everyday-life situations as illustrations of the most abstract and mystical references to the self and Brahman. Identifying with his hero-*siddhāntin*, he lets him win all the debates. And yet, we must not forget: the *siddhāntin* is—by definition—his invisible author's invention; and as such, he is different from his creator (as Ishmael is other than Herman Melville).

The core of the "autobiographical paradigm" which conflates author and *siddhāntin* (and sometimes master) consists of the author's invisibility turned into non-existence. The author *qua author* is invisible relative to the sensual objectivity of the speaking *siddhāntin* and the ghost-like reality or potential existence of the master, Ādi-Śaṅkarācārya. Paradoxically, the most real, so to speak, among the three entities referred to here as Śaṅkara, Śaṅkarācārya, and Ādi-Śaṅkarācārya becomes non-existent by virtue of his merger with the more tangible yet—in a sense—less real personalities of the triad.

In my view, the relation of the author to his imagined *siddhāntin* is a solid object of scholarly research. The scarcity of information regarding eighth-century Indian sages and wanderers, coupled with true thirst for knowledge of the man and his time, seems to generate a conflated, unified, attractive and yet somewhat incorrect and misleading vision. Here is an example provided by one of the most competent scholars of Śaṅkara in our age, S. Mayeda:

> Śaṅkara would not teach his doctrine to city dwellers. In cities the power of Buddhism was still strong, though already declining, and Jainism prevailed among the merchants and manufacturers. Popular Hinduism occupied the minds of ordinary people while city dwellers pursued ease and pleasure. There were also hedonists in cities, and it was difficult for Śaṅkara to communicate Vedānta philosophy to these people. Consequently he propagated his teachings chiefly among *saṃnyāsins*, who had renounced the world, and intellectuals in the villages, and he gradually won the respect of Brahmins and feudal lords. He made enthusiastic efforts to restore the orthodox Brahmanical tradition, without paying attention to the *bhakti* (devotional) movement, which had made a deep impression on ordinary Hindus in his age.[12]

Taking Śaṅkara, Śaṅkarācārya, and Ādi-Śaṅkara as the same personality is laudable yet costly. Working within the paradigm of Śaṅkara/Śaṅkarācārya/Ādi-Śaṅkarācārya as a single identity, Mayeda seeks to say something of an author who is inherently invisible, identical with a *siddhāntin* who is essentially a literary figure, and with a flesh-and-blood master who teaches Advaita to intellectuals in the village. Suppose the combination of these personalities is unreal or not true. The portrayal of the combined personality would necessarily be somewhat untruthful. Indeed, none of Mayeda's propositions concerning Śaṅkara's life are truly warranted. We simply do not know enough about these things. We do know, however, that the author of the BSBh is not necessarily the historical master or even the literary spiritual hero. However, as we shall see further, scholars have done their best to say something of the Śaṅkara/Śaṅkarācārya/Ādi-Śaṅkarācārya combination. Sometimes they distinguish Ādi-Śaṅkarācārya (as a semi-legendary hero) from Śaṅkara or Śaṅkarācārya, but as mentioned earlier, they never make the distinction between the author and his Advaita-exponent, the *siddhāntin*.

---

[12] Mayeda 1992: 5.

A strikingly different (yet similarly doubtful) vision of the combined Śaṅkara/Śaṅkarācārya/Ādi-Śaṅkarācārya's cultural circumstances is the following:

> The most celebrated Hindu intellectual of the early medieval age, Shankaracharya (788–820), made his name during his short life by developing a Sanskrit high-culture rendition of Tamil devotional poetry, by reconciling Shaivism and Vaishnavism through a non-dualist *Advaita* philosophy that drew on the Upaniṣads and incorporated elements from Buddhism, and by traveling from Kerala to Kashmir and back again to establish monastic centers. Shankara helped to absorb and normalize popular devotionalism in elite Brahman high culture.[13]

The traditional and scholarly fusion of the voice of the author and *siddhāntin* does contain a significant truth; Śaṅkara's identification with his spiritual hero was obviously deep and thorough, by far exceeding in intensity his cognitive empathy with non-Advaita rivals of many kinds. And yet, let us note that in the presence of rivals, the existential situation of author and *siddhāntin* is similar but also inherently different. Both author and *siddhāntin* recognize the opponents' presence and position. However, necessary asymmetries prevail; the author is free to look at the *siddhāntin* as one of the opponents (the victorious one); the *siddhāntin*, on the other hand, cannot see his creator. A measure of freedom is available to the author; he chooses the *pūrva-pakṣins* and *makes them speak*. At the most basic level, Śaṅkara's dialogical *bhāṣya*s signify the difference between the author and the intellectual rivals of his imagination. By activating the voices and positions of various opponents, the author is necessarily separated from every participant in the intellectual battles (Advaita-*siddhāntin* and *pūrva-pakṣin*). Such an underlying sub-textual presupposition is perhaps too obvious and simple to consider. But if heeded, the difference between the author and his imaginary companions would generate a vision of a new spiritual agent: an author who generates doubt but also seeks its resolution by choosing a dialogical textual structure.

Herein lies the difference: the Advaita exponent recognizes the presence and philosophical position of his opponent as given, and responds with this assumption in mind. Indeed, the *siddhāntin* is bound to answer his opponent's statements, establishing thereby a certain correspondence with his rival. The essential working presupposition of

---

[13] Ludden 2004: 55.

Indian philosophical training is accommodation to the assumptions of one's rivals.[14] By virtue of such philosophical training, a Vacaspati Miśra was possible. Such a presupposition of dialogue and legitimate communication generates connections and correspondences among the participants in philosophical or theological debates. But the author is free from such connections and correspondences; in making *ātman* and the mind speak in the Upad, he posits himself beyond them both, above them, as it were, a meta-participant in the universe of discourse and speech.

Committed to dialogue, and creatively negotiating other states of mind, the author of the BSBh is able to contain competing systems of thought and life perspectives. The author's mode of mind and speech is inherently open, complex and given to doubt. The mind of the Advaita *siddhāntin* offers a different perspective; hunting down rivals and enemies, he is focused on his target, and cannot entertain doubt and openness as his free-floating creator is at leisure to do. Although the author invents *siddhāntin* and *pūrva-pakṣin*s of many kinds and is thus significantly different from both winner and losers in the imaginary debates, he has remained elusive, hidden by the irresistible pull of reading, and unavailable to the reaches of thought and imagination.

In general, scholarly attention has focused on the distinction between Śaṅkara the "real man," namely, the historical Śaṅkara, and Śaṅkara as he is known from the *dig-vijayas*, the hagiographic accounts of his life.[15] In the quest for Ādi-Śaṅkarācārya, the distinction between author and *siddhāntin* becomes even more elusive. See, for example, K. Potter's criticism of identifying Śaṅkara the philosopher (author of the BSBh) with the mythological Śaṅkara who is believed to have founded the *maṭhas*. Potter describes the identification of Śaṅkara the philosopher with the mythological Śaṅkara as follows:

> According to Daśanāmī tradition.....their order was founded by the Advaita philosopher, a young but spiritually advanced person who spent a good part of his brief 32 years on this earth acquiring disciples and then, with them in attendance, traveling throughout India establishing monastic centers at which the foremost among the disciples were installed

[14] See Śaṅkara's statement in BSBh 2.1.1 about the need to refute others' positions without resorting to one's own assumptions and beliefs.

[15] See J. Bader's excellent exploration of the various hagiographic accounts of Śaṅkara's life: Bader 2000.

as pontiffs. This same person, it is said, also composed hundreds of philosophical works, developing abstruse topics in epistemology and metaphysics, as well as laying down the fundamental precepts guiding the social and religious thought of the Daśanāmī order.[16]

Potter thinks that Śaṅkara's philosophical views preclude the possibility of his being the founder of the centers of learning ascribed to him. "Śaṅkara the philosopher offers one consistently repeated thesis, viz., that the only way of getting liberated is by abandoning actions altogether...".[17] Śaṅkara's thesis, Potter thinks, has "social implications...which sit uncomfortably, to put it mildly, with the assumptions underlying the establishment and maintenance of a group founded on the principles set forth by Daśanāmīs as fundamental to their order."[18] Focusing on the identification of the two Śaṅkaras, he says: "We have no evidence, save the hagiographical literature...to substantiate the short life and the identification of the philosopher as the founder of the monastic order."[19] Thus, Potter concludes:

> Perhaps there was a man, possibly named Śaṃkara (it's a common Indian name), who was a social entrepreneur, an organizer. Advaita tradition also celebrates an outstanding philosopher, Śaṃkarācārya, whose works, especially the commentary on the Brahmasūtras, have earned him the serious respect of responsible Advaitins, from his pupils on downward. The followers of the entrepreneur find it advantageous to take advantage of the accidental identity of names. Since the general public doesn't understand philosophy very well, and since there is a deep-seated tendency within the Indian tradition itself to counter philosophical views of Śaṃkara's type with appeals to myth, devotionalism, or social necessity so as to bring the man-beyond-the-world back into it, this conflation of the two Śaṃkaras is not difficult. Notice that the authors of the hagiographies are all separated from the philosopher's time by at least 600–700 years. The result is a mythological creation, the philosopher-entrepreneur.[20]

Thus, the identification of author and *siddhāntin* becomes Potter's major (though implicit) presupposition and methodological tool. By identifying *siddhāntin* and author (merged as "the philosopher"), he is capable of denying the alleged historical reality of the active philosopher, the founding father of the *maṭhas*. Since the *siddhāntin* asserts the

---

16 Potter 1982: 111.
17 Ibid., p. 113.
18 Ibid., ibid.
19 Ibid., p. 111.
20 Ibid., 122–123.

necessity of action-renunciation, the author must be other than the founder of the *maṭhas*[21] (for they are the same person). But in truth, of course, if Potter is right on the issue of the *siddhāntin*'s doctrine of "non-action," the one who recommends non-action is the *siddhāntin*; the author of the BSBh could be someone else.[22]

Let us explore more closely the universe of connections and correspondence between *siddhāntin* and *pūrva-pakṣins*, a universe created (imagined) by the author who is, as suggested above, free of the mutual conditioning of winner/loser. I assume that quixotic aspects in the positions and arguments of the *siddhāntin* and *pūrva-pakṣin* point to the author's underlying presence, a presence palpably removed from both intellectual combatants: winner and loser.

By references to episodes of everyday life, Śaṅkara the author of the BSBh expresses his wit and talent, concomitantly suggesting his distinction from both *pūrva-pakṣin* and *siddhāntin*. The abysmal gap between the world as conventionally conceptualized (and "perceived") and the presupposed reality of *nirguṇa-brahman* makes room for the ironical expression of delicate, scholarly doubts. The author, in my view, finds it difficult to accommodate normal, *saṃsāric* perception and ontological commitment to the Upaniṣadic vision. Some scholars find Śaṅkara's references to worldly episodes an integral part of his argumentative structure. Others may think such analogies or illustrations do not constitute real arguments in favor of *ātman*'s or Brahman's existence.[23] Both attitudes to Śaṅkara's references to worldly episodes ignore the overt aesthetic dimension of his writing and its implications (in terms of the author's identity). Inasmuch as one focuses on Śaṅkara's art of writing, the character of the author as distinct from *siddhāntin* and *pūrva-pakṣins* alike stands out.

Grass, milk, and cow—what can one learn of the structure and evolution of the world from the relation of grass, milk, and cow? In his commentary on BS 2.2.1–10 Śaṅkara discusses instances of daily life as supposedly supporting the dualistic metaphysics of Sāṅkhya.

---

[21] Potter does not heed the (not unlikely) possibility that philosophers may not live up to their ideas or ideals.

[22] Though Potter writes of Śaṅkara's establishing of the *maṭhas*, his argument may include other activities of Śaṅkara's (such as roaming all over India, writing, speaking). Thus, according to this logic Śaṅkara might not have written the *Brahma-sūtra-bhāṣya* as well.

[23] See Halbfass 1991: 131–204.

The grounds for Śaṅkara's display of talent and wit is the essential tension between sublime experience of the innermost self where everything, so to speak, is unified and integrated, and ordinary, fragmentary perception or, in other words, the contradictory nature of Brahman and the "world." The underlying theme of the discussion of BSBh 2.2.1–10 is the logical force of observation with respect to metaphysics. What is the value of all sorts of daily episodes in the determination of the—most abstract—nature of reality? Śaṅkara is very close to his *siddhāntin*, and yet, a careful reading reveals a playful attitude towards his *siddhāntin* whose conception of Brahman and the world turns out to be similar to the improbable Sāṅkhya conception of *puruṣa* and *prakṛti* (or *pradhāna*).

In BSBh 2.2.2 the *siddhāntin* shares his acceptance of the strict correlation between perceptible phenomena and the nature of abstract reality with his opponent. "From what is seen one knows of the unseen" (*dṛṣṭāc câdṛṣṭa-siddhiḥ*). The Sāṅkhya *pūrva-pakṣin* says that the primordial potential of objectivity (*pradhāna*) evolves spontaneously, by its own nature, for the sake of the *puruṣa*, without any conscious intention of its own, as milk is generated by the action of grass and water.[24] The following *bhāṣya*s bring in other worldly episodes. Thus, discussions of grass and milk, magnet and iron, a lame person mounted on the back of the blind, all delve deeply into details supposedly relevant to the resolution of the greatest intellectual challenge conceivable—the feasibility of a world emerging from its abstract ground. As an illustration of this issue of emergence, here is a reconstruction of BSBh 2.2.5.

Opponent: *Pradhāna*, the primordial ground of objective existence transforms itself into the visible world as grass transforms itself into milk.
Siddhāntin: How do you know that grass transforms itself into milk without any other cause (*kathaṃ ca nimittântara-nirapekṣaṃ tṛṇâdîti gamyate*)?
Opponent: There is obviously no other cause in sight.... (*nimittântarâ nupalambhāt*).
Siddhāntin: But how is this possible? Can grass become milk of itself?
Opponent: Sure it can. For if we knew of any other cause in the production of milk we, by fetching more grass, could produce it as we like! But

[24] *yathā ksīram acetanaṃ sva-bhāvenâiva vatsa-vivṛddhy-arthaṃ pravartate yathā ca jalam acetanaṃ sva-bhāvenâiva syandata evaṃ pradhānam acetanaṃ sva-bhāvenâiva puruṣârtha-siddhaye pravartiṣyata iti.*

of course, we do not do it (*yadi hi kiṃcin nimittam upalabhemahi tato yathā-kāmaṃ tena tṛṇâdy upādāya kṣīraṃ sampādayemahi na tu sampādayāmahe*). Therefore, the transformation of grass is due to its inherent nature merely; and by the same token, the transformation of *pradhāna* is due to its own nature.

Siddhāntin: I could accept your point if grass were indeed transformed into milk spontaneously.

Implied Opponent: Indeed, so it does.

Siddhāntin: No. There is another cause (other than grass) (*nimittân-tarôpalabdheḥ*).

Implied Opponent: How is this possible? What is it?

Siddhāntin: Grass becomes milk only if eaten by a cow[25] or by some other female animal. It does not become milk if eaten by a bull or not eaten at all!

Implied Opponent: But what does it mean?

Siddhāntin: If there were no connection with a cow's body, grass and so forth would not become milk (*yadi hi nir-nimittam etat syād dhenu-śarīra-sambandhād anyatrâpi tṛṇâdi kṣīrī-bhavet*).

Opponent: But people cannot produce milk as they like (using all sorts of causes).

Implied *Siddhāntin*: True, people cannot produce milk by their own will.

Implied Opponent: Thus grass becomes milk spontaneously…

Siddhāntin: No. That does not mean that milk is produced spontaneously from grass.

Implied Opponent: How is milk produced then?

Implied *Siddhāntin*: Sometimes people do produce something. But sometimes there might be other causes involved.

Implied Opponent: Such as?

Siddhāntin: Sometimes there are divine causes (*daivata*) involved in producing certain effects.

Opponent: How is this connected with the production of milk?

Siddhāntin: Milk is not produced by spontaneous transformation of grass. Sometimes people can affect the production of milk.

Implied Opponent: How is this possible?

Siddhāntin: If people give a cow more grass and herbs, it can produce more milk.

Implied Opponent: And what is the meaning of this?

Siddhāntin: The meaning is, that (since grass does not become milk by itself) spontaneous transformation of pure objectivity (*pradhāna*) cannot be based upon observations of grass and the like (*tasmān na tṛṇâdivat svābhāvikaḥ pradhānasya pariṇāmaḥ*).

---

[25] The *siddhāntin*'s assumption is that a cow is an intelligent being. Such an assumption is expressed in BSBh 2.2.3: cows which are conscious beings are seen to produce milk through their will and love (for their calves) (*cetanāyāś ca dhenvāḥ snehêcchayā payasaḥ pravartakatvôpapatteḥ*).

Professional philosophers would argue that BSBh 2.2.5 illustrates the basic rule of Indian philosophical dialogue. The Advaita-*siddhāntin*, they would say, adjusts his arguments to the *pūrva-pakṣin*'s assumptions. This is true. However, the role of the author-narrator may not be equal to mere presentation of a dialogue between a Sāṅkhya loser-opponent and an Advaita winner-exponent. Re-labeling the underlying theme of the discourse, the author places the two participants in the debate on the same level. The presupposition shared by *siddhāntin* and *pūrva-pakṣin* alike is the legitimate use of worldly instances to determine the origin of the world and its nature. It seems to me that the author, conscious of himself as neither *siddhāntin* nor *pūrva-pakṣin*, ridicules the very presupposition of the debate. Probing into processes of grass-transformation and milk-production may not shed any light on the big issues of metaphysics. The presentation of the Sāṅkhya-opponent as one who does not know that a cow *is* required for the process as well as the dead-serious *siddhāntin*'s assertion that a cow *is* indeed necessary are both made into objects of fun. The author, though probably in doubt with respect to the reality of *ātman*, is unambiguous in his understanding of himself as different from *pūrva-pakṣin* and *siddhāntin* alike.

In making fun of a Sāṅkhya opponent, Śaṅkara also seems to ridicule the *siddhāntin*. In the course of reading a *bhāṣya* such as BSBh 2.2.5, the gap between the elaborate discussion of cow, milk and grass and the abstract issue of cosmic origin and essence becomes conspicuously absurd. The very presupposition of the debate—the strict correlation between "that which is seen" (*dṛṣṭa*) and the validity of one's metaphysics—becomes a joke, as it were, implicating the *siddhāntin* as much as the *pūrva-pakṣin*. Reading which resists the paradigm of author/*siddhāntin* identification can do so confidently in this case. In general, the dialogical situation itself invites differentiation between the author and his official delegate to the debate. As the *siddhāntin* shares the respective assumptions that rule the debate, his presuppositions are as unwarranted or as absurd as his opponent's and his Advaita-proposition may turn out to be as unlikely. According to the approach offered here, this must indeed be the case.

However, it is extremely difficult to read the BSBh while keeping in mind the distinction between author and literary hero. The first-person speech of both author and *siddhāntin*, the enchanting quality of the *siddhāntin*'s speech, the coherent, clear-cut commitment to the Advaita perspective, and the reader's inner urge for identification and merger—all these make the conflation of the voices of author and *siddhāntin* seem natural. Schechet's distinction between "the two readers, one resisting and one complicit, as a text's ideal or implied readers…" comes to mind:

> The reader I am calling a 'resisting reader' is one who is cued by a text to resist the text's narrator. The reader I am calling a 'complicit reader' is one who is cued to follow a text's narrator without questioning his/her reliability.[26]

While, I think, one should always look for cues conducive to resistance, the encounter of an Advaitin with certain types of opponents makes the distinction more discernible or natural. In general, the opponent's nature and presuppositions condition much of the *siddhāntin*'s corresponding attributes. Sometimes, the opponent's faults are shared by the *siddhāntin* as well. In such cases, the voice of Śaṅkara the narrator is more conspicuously distinct from that of his *siddhāntin* and *pūrva-pakṣin* alike. Training in resistance could start with the narrator's playful presentations of encounters between his Advaita-hero and the Sāṅkhya-opponent.

The *siddhāntin*'s assertion (BSBh 2.2.7) that the relationship of *puruṣa* and *prakṛti* is inherently obscure or impossible while the (obviously corresponding) relation of Brahman and the world (through Īśvara's agency by the force of illusion) is not, illustrates the *siddhāntin*'s unhappy situation. He is locked in debate with an unlikely opponent. The quixotic statement of the *siddhāntin*—that the emanation of the world from *nirguṇa-brahman* by virtue of Īśvara's power of illusion (*māyā*) is different from the *pūrva-pakṣin*'s statement of the (inherently impossible) connection between *puruṣa* and *prakṛti* (and the world's emanation therefrom)—is patently unconvincing, even grotesque. Following Śaṅkara's scathing criticism of the Sāṅkhya position based on the (truly) impossible relationship of pure subjectivity (*puruṣa*) with pure objectivity (*prakṛti*), the description of the Godhead as endowed with the power of *māyā* must be read as in a tone deliberately witty and ironical, audibly different from the words of exponent and opponent alike. In my reading, the narrator is consciously skeptical of the positions of the two opponents; with winner and loser similarly

---

[26] Schechet 2005: 30.

implicated in a discussion beyond their conceptual capabilities, the author remains identified with neither.

The correspondence of *siddhāntin* and *pūrva-pakṣin* is implied by the inherently dialogical quality of Śaṅkara's work. When the *pūrva-pakṣin* is ridiculous or quixotic, so is the *siddhāntin*. Here is a reconstruction of the *bhāṣya* mentioned above (2.2.7), in which the correspondence-in-nature of winner and loser is conspicuous even with respect to the validity of their metaphysical positions.

Implied Sāṅkhya opponent: Imagine to yourself a person who can see but cannot walk mounted on the back of a man who cannot see but can walk....

Implied *Siddhāntin*: Another bizarre episode of everyday life....

Opponent: Yes. And suppose the one who cannot walk makes the blind move (*pravartayati*)....

Implied *Siddhāntin*: Do such imaginary episodes mean anything?

Implied Opponent: Such episodes are pregnant with philosophical meaning.

Implied *Siddhāntin*: And what is the philosophical meaning of the lame man mounted on the blind's back?

Opponent: The *puruṣa*, of course, although passive and indifferent, could move the *pradhāna*.

Siddhāntin: The lame could indeed move the blind by speaking to him, and so forth. But the *puruṣa*, devoid of action and empty of any quality, cannot move anything.

Opponent: But suppose mere proximity between the two (*puruṣa* and *pradhāna*) would do the job.

Siddhāntin: If you mean proximity (*saṃnidhi*) such as making a magnet attract iron, this is also not an appropriate illustration of *puruṣa*'s moving power.

Implied Opponent: Why not?

Siddhāntin: For by virtue of the permanent proximity of *puruṣa* and *pradhāna* there would follow permanence of motion. This is unlike the case of the magnet and iron. In this latter case, the proximity is not permanent, and the action of the magnet depends upon the precise position of the iron, etc.

Implied Opponent: Is this such a grave problem?

Siddhāntin: Of course! If the proximity of *puruṣa* and *pradhāna* is permanent, *mokṣa* would be impossible.

Opponent: And yet, even if the instances of the lame and blind, the iron and magnet are not perfectly parallel to *puruṣa* and *pradhāna*, they are still valuable...

Siddhāntin: No. Let us be straightforward: since *pradhāna* is unconscious and the *puruṣa* absolutely indifferent (*udāsin*) or passive, in the absence of any third party any relation between the two is impossible!

(*tathā pradhānasyâcaitanyāt puruṣasya câudāsinyāt tṛtīyasya ca tayoḥ sambandhayitur abhāvāt sambandhânupapatteḥ*).

Implied Opponent: But what is the difference between our *puruṣa* and *pradhāna* and your *ātman* and the world?

Siddhāntin: The highest self is indeed absolutely indifferent by its inherent nature. And yet, it is endowed with the power to activate by virtue of illusion (*māyā*). It is therefore superior (*paramâtmanas tu sva-rūpa-vyapāśrayam audasinyaṃ māyāvyapāśrayaṃ ca pravartakatvam ity asty atiśayaḥ*).

It is noteworthy that Bādarāyaṇa's *sūtra* does not mention a lame or a blind person (it refers to stone [*aśma*] only).[27] Thus, the addition of the blind and lame is of Śaṅkara's own making. However humorous, some philosophical points of great interest and importance are also to be found here. The *siddhāntin* levels a devastating blow at his Sāṅkhya opponent, a blow consisting of a perceptive, penetrating statement aimed at the core of Sāṅkhya metaphysics of strict duality. If *puruṣa* is mere consciousness and inherently dissimilar and dissociated from objectivity (*prakṛti, pradhāna*), how could it make them move? And yet, at the end of his *bhāṣya* the author-narrator compares the relation of *nirguṇa-brahman* to the world to that of *prakṛti* and *puruṣa*. This is an interesting comparison. Yet any perceptive reader would sense that the suggested similarity between the *puruṣa* and *nirguṇa-brahman is* telling; both are inherently indifferent yet mysteriously active. The *siddhāntin*'s assertion of the difference between *puruṣa* and *ātman* is paradoxically juxtaposed with the author's notion of their similarity, thus implying the invalidity of a major Advaita principle. In this case, the author raises a doubt concerning Advaita through his criticism of an opponent. In my reading, the author's consciousness of the (perhaps disturbing) similarity of *ātman* and *puruṣa* is translated as the *siddhāntin*'s proposition of their difference.

By the power of his imagination, the author of BSBh brings the *siddhāntin* to life along with his rivals. Neither the literary figure of the Advaita-*siddhāntin* and his rivals, nor the flesh-and-blood master roaming the country are the same as the creative agent behind it all, the most real entity in the dialogic domain.

We can now re-approach the combinatory spirit in the various expressions of the autobiographical paradigm. As seen above, in the

[27] BS 2.2.7: *puruṣâśmavad iti cet tathâpi.*

course of traditional and scholarly research of the author's life and thought, denominations such as "Śaṅkara", or "Śaṅkarācārya," or "Ādi-Śaṅkarācārya" have invariably referred to the combined personality of narrator/Advaita-exponent (and sometimes also of the master/guru). See for example G.Ch. Pande, who promises "to reconstruct the life and thought of Śaṅkara on historical principles, i.e., to determine the age and biography of Śaṅkara and also his original ideas and writings within this framework" (p. x). Pande asks many questions such as the following:

> When did Śaṅkara live? What do we know of his history? Which works did he actually compose? Unless these questions are properly answered we cannot decide the relationship of Śaṅkara to his 'contemporaries' and would not be able to place his life, work and thought in a meaningful historical and cultural perspective. Nor would we be able to decide whether he was simply a dry philosophical commentator or also a saint-poet of no mean order who composed enchanting, popular as well as profound, hymns.[28]

Pande, like others, does provide some of the answers to the questions he asks. It is somewhat helpful to know that "Śaṅkara" lived in times of instability and upheaval.[29] Perhaps he was poignantly aware of *saṃsāra* and its troubles and hazards; perhaps he knew first-hand how inevitable death is. However, it seems to me that the respective answers provided by scholars about the age of Śaṅkara and the presumed, general circumstances of his life are insufficient for a determination of an effective context for a good-enough reading of Śaṅkara. For the combined personality of author/literary figure/master could hardly have existed. The presence of the autobiographical paradigm is most palpable in Pande's case; the possibility of a Śaṅkara different from his *siddhāntin* does not even occur to him. Whether "simply a dry philosophical commentator or also a saint-poet," the author is not distinguished from his hero, not even analytically. Among the three personalities set up by the dialogical domain of the text, the author is—paradoxically—less accessible than the master and *siddhāntin*.

---

[28] Pande 1998: ix. Pande surrenders to a curious dichotomy, namely, that Śaṅkara was either a "dry philosophical commentator" or a "saint-poet." Pande seems to suggest that if Śaṅkara is merely the author of the *Brahma-sūtra-bhāṣya* and the like (authorized compositions), he is a dry philosopher, whereas if he is also the author of two hundred or so compositions of poetry and bhakti, he is a saint-poet.

[29] See Pande 1998: ix.

Some scholars contextualize Śaṅkara's voice and writing by means of external sources such as historical evidence or the *dig-vijaya* tradition, while others resist such contextualization and stick to meanings strictly available in Śaṅkara's works. T.S. Rukmani is an eminent scholar of the first type, combining extensive and reliable analysis of Śaṅkara's philosophical writing with alleged evidence derived from history books and the *dig-vijaya* hagiographies (to which she refers as "biographies"). See for example Rukmani's combination of history and philosophy:

> But Śaṅkara, by his genius, was able to reinstate the Upaniṣadic heritage which was almost threatened with extinction due to the efforts of such stalwarts as Aśvaghoṣa, Nāgārjuna, Asaṅga and Vasubandhu, and put it in a strong logical framework. He was also responsible for taking the message of *advaita* throughout the length and breadth of the country. This is also amazing if one recalls the historical and political conditions of the country round about the eighth century A.D. At this period in India's history the north was reeling under a feeling of deep insecurity. The last of the emperors, Harṣavardhana was himself a Buddhist and the country had as yet not recovered from the onslaught of the Huns. Though politically this was not true of South India, the decline of *dharma-rājya* with the advent of reform movements like Buddhism and Jainism was as much true in the South as in other parts of the country. It was perhaps the strength and vigour of South India between A.D. 550 and 750 which threw up a leader of Śaṅkara's dynamism who with his clear insight was able to weave the various strands of philosophico-religious thought available into a single strand, and fit it into the traditional heritage without appearing to harm its fundamental tenets.[30]

Using the hagiographical *dig-vijaya* tradition as a reliable source, Rukmani makes efforts to integrate even minute episodes of the *dig-vijaya* with Śaṅkara's philosophical ideas. Thus, for example, she refers to the famous encounter of Śaṅkara with the Cāṇḍāla butcher as incompatible with his philosophy:

> Śaṅkara in his own life, on one or two occasions, behaved in a manner which appears incompatible to the philosophy he preached. In the famous Cāṇḍāla episode immortalized in the *Manīṣā-pañcakam*, Śaṅkara behaves like any orthodox Brahmin of that time. He had to be reminded of his own philosophy by the Cāṇḍāla. Thus the Cāṇḍāla asks Śaṅkara—O Brahmin, whom are you asking to get away? Your body is the product of food, so is mine. Are you asking one product of food to clear the way

[30] Rukmani 1991: 6.

> for another? Or, are you asking pure consciousness to get away from pure consciousness? In brief, we are both the same. Then whom are you asking to clear the way for another?[31]

Immersed in history, philosophy, hagiographies and varieties of *bhakti* and poetic texts thought to have been composed by Śaṅkara, Rukmani summarizes Śaṅkara's life and thought as an epitome of integration and combination:

> Thus Śaṅkara's life has many facets. If, on the one hand, he appears to negate life, and urges one to look for the underlying truth, on the other hand, his own life is an example of the values that one is asked to practise in this world in order to make living here and now fruitful. Qualities of compassion, filial duty,[32] and simplicity were the hallmarks of this intellectual giant who strode the Indian scene like a colossus in the time he lived.[33]

Whatever differences may exist among scholars of Śaṅkara's thought and life, the presupposition or paradigm underlying the prevalent vision of his work are rooted in the eager identification of Śaṅkara the author of the *Brahma-sūtra* with the literary figure of the *siddhāntin*. This presupposition is of course not necessarily untrue; the entire tradition of Advaita commentaries (such as Padmapāda, Sureśvara, Vacaspati Miśra) is grounded on this prima facie, yet unconscious identification.

But who then is the "invisible author"? Being consistently removed from *siddhāntin* and *pūrva-pakṣin* alike, the author's activity signifies

---

[31] Ibid., p. 20.

[32] With respect to Śaṅkara's filial duty towards his mother, Rukmani identifies the following tension and contradiction: "Again Śaṅkara's coming back to perform the last rites of his mother does not fit in with the *sannyāsa dharma* and is also against the *advaita* philosophy. He justifies it by the promise he had given her to be near her during her last days. Perhaps he felt that he had not looked after her when she needed him." (p. 21). On the ground of one of Śaṅkara's alleged compositions, Rukmani becomes specific about Śaṅkara's feelings of 1300 years ago: "Is there an echo of sadness in the verses addressed to *Devi* where he asks for her forgiveness in the *Devy-aparādha-kṣamâpana-stotram*?

Here in this world, O mother,
Many are thy guileless children,
But restless am I among them all,
And so it is nothing very strange
That I should turn myself from thee
Yet surely it were impossible that thou
Would ever turn away from me
A wicked son is sometimes born but an
Unkind mother there (never can) be." (p. 21).

[33] Ibid., p. 21.

the miraculous emergence of mind, thought and speech from an inarticulate abyss of pre-mind, pre-thought, and pre-speech. Although very real in the hierarchy of cause-and-effect, the author's presence is inherently inaudible, invisible, and mistakenly taken to be unreal as well.[34] Classical Indian tradition has often focused on the reversal of ontological order and priority; the more invisible is the more real. Thus, by separating the speaker from his speech, we may follow a recommendation of Kauśītakī Upaniṣad 3.8: Let a person know the speaker rather than speech (*na vācaṃ vijijñāsitā vaktāraṃ vidyāt*).[35] Speaking, indeed, is the "miraculous emergence" of something from nothing, as it were. In this sense, Śaṅkara's authorship of the BSBh is not different from any other episode of emergence of thought and speech (an emergence always mysterious). However, culture, tradition, learning, and talent constitute an intermediary context within which speech occurs. While the primordial emergence from the absolute *nirguṇa*-speaker into the BSBh speech-act is beyond comprehension, the transition from the partly objectified (*saguṇa*) author into the act of book writing is more accessible and tangible. The author's voice in the opening sections of the Veda-oriented *bhāṣyas* as well as in the composition of dialogues between *ātman* and mind (*manas*) in the Upad[36] expresses a condition of Advaita-doubt that consists of being aware of the gap between full-fledged self-identification with *ātman* and "mere familiarity" (however thorough and committed) with the Advaita ideal and goal.

---

[34] Śaṅkara speaks of the mysterious gap between the invisible agent (*viṣayin*) and the corresponding sphere (*gocara*) of his perception or referential emergence in the introduction to his BSBh: Though the agent (*viṣayin*) and his objectified field are necessarily disconnected, even mutually contradictory like dark and light, it is an invariable phenomenon in life that people conflate the two (*viṣayin* and *viṣaya*) (*yuṣmad-asmat-pratyaya-gocarayor viṣaya-viṣayiṇos tamaḥ-prakāśavad viruddha-svabhāvayor itarêtara-bhāvânupapattau siddhāyāṃ tad-dharmāṇām api sutarām itarêtara-bhāvânupapattir ity ato 'smat-pratyaya-gocare viṣayiṇi cid-ātmake yuṣmat-pratyaya-gocarasya viṣayasya tad-dharmāṇāṃ câdhyāsaḥ, tad-viparyayeṇa viṣayiṇas tad-dharmāṇāṃ câdhyāsaḥ, tad-viparyayeṇa viṣayiṇas tad-dharmāṇāṃ ca viṣaye 'dhyāso mithyêti bhavituṃ yuktam*).

[35] The Upaniṣad continues: Rather than smell one should seek to know the subject who does the smelling (*na gandhaṃ vijijñāsitā ghrātāraṃ vidyāt*); a person should seek to know the seer rather than the sight (*na rūpaṃ vijijñāsitā draṣṭāraṃ vidyāt*); One should not seek to know the sound, but rather the agent who hears; rather than the taste of food one should understand the subject who tastes; one should not seek to comprehend the deed but rather the doer (*na karma vijijñāsitā kartāraṃ vidyāt*); and so on.

[36] See below, Ch. 3.

And yet, the vision of the *Brahma-sūtra* of an author/Advaita exegete/guru-master as an intellectual autobiography holds its spell over the entire scholarly community. For another example of the autobiographical approach, see Ingalls' visualization of a Śaṅkara identical with Śaṅkarācārya and Ādi-Śaṅkarācāya:

> He wandered about India with nothing more than a cloth, a begging-bowl and a staff. What he wrote is in a language that only a handful of men still speak and very few men still read. And what he wrote of was not love or politics or war or any of the other things with which intelligent people are supposed to concern themselves. What is there here to excite one's curiosity? What first excited my own curiosity was the boldness of Śaṅkara's thought.[37]

Ingalls' references to Śaṅkara's thought and wanderings encapsulate the autobiographical paradigm. For Ingalls Śaṅkara's thought is that of author/*siddhāntin*/master (Śaṅkara/Śaṅkarācārya/Ādi-Śaṅkarācārya). Thus, Ingalls' Śaṅkara is a combination of the three speakers; the identity of author (Śaṅkara) and *siddhāntin* (Śaṅkarācārya) is taken for granted. The key words in Ingalls' passage are 'thought,' 'language' and 'wrote'. Śaṅkara is an original thinker and scholar as well as a master and wanderer. Though wandering under the hot Indian sun, the guru/writer keeps some palm leaves, ink, and feathers to write, probably early in the morning. During the day the master teaches and in the course of his short life he composes hundreds of pages (palm leaves) of eloquent philosophy. Thus, the *siddhāntin*'s philosophical positions turn into an author's autobiographical accounts of his thought and experience.

The autobiographical presupposition (as we see in Ingalls) excludes reflection on the possible distance between author and hero. Such exclusion may be costly, as issues of doubt and its handling hardly emerge into consciousness. When the autobiographical approach allows for doubt in Śaṅkara/Śaṅkarācārya's world, it is inherently trivial and technical, a mode of presentation rather than true doubt concerning the psychological reality of the Advaita vision.

According to Ingalls' view, Śaṅkara is a combination of a brilliant, thoughtful writer and an Indian sadhu. However, unlike other writing on Śaṅkara, Ingalls does recognize and acknowledge one of the most telling features of the author, namely, Śaṅkara's art of writing:

---

[37] Ingalls 1952: 2.

> Śaṃkara, I think, was not unaware of his literary gifts, but he makes no needless display of them and purple passages are rare in his works. When they come, however, their effect is overwhelming. Such are the full-dress arguments put in dialogue form in the Bṛhadāraṇyaka and Brahmasūtra commentaries. Quite aside from the question of philosophy, these dialogues simply as dramatic literature are magnificent.[38]

Ingalls does well to emphasize Śaṅkara's literary gifts with respect to his major commentaries. Such recognition makes room for fresh observations and a renewed overall evaluation of Śaṅkara's work and status as an author. The lifestyle of a virtuous author does not, I think, suit that of a public wanderer. At the very least, a preliminary, prudent act of scholarship would be to resist the conflation of the author and the literary figures who speak in his text. And yet Ingalls chooses to combine the three personalities of the "Śaṅkara world." Such a combination is not necessarily untrue or impossible. Wanderers and mystics are not lacking in the history of the Indian subcontinent, and Śaṅkara (author of the BSBh) could be one of them. However, the nature of Śaṅkara's scholarly output—eloquent, well written, structured, and aesthetic—may well point to directions different from the autobiographical approach.

Most probably there was a great master, Ādi-Śaṅkarācārya, who wandered through the sub-continent living by his begging-bowl, defeating rivals on the way, and so on. Indeed, the author of the BSBh could have created his *siddhāntin* in the image of the wandering master Ādi-Śaṅkarācārya. However, the sophisticated, scholarly, often ironical expression of Śaṅkara the writer suggests an invisible other in the shape of the author, probably stationary and often alone (like other great artists).

Who is Śaṅkara, the author of the BSBh? What is the relation between the two, author and *siddhāntin*, Śaṅkara and Śaṅkarācārya? Indeed, tradition and scholarly thinking are not totally at fault; the *siddhāntin* embodies aspects of the author's active conscience and innermost calling and articulates the philosophical challenges the author faced. But, however intimate the relationship between author and *siddhāntin*, they are not the same. Above all, the doubting author imagines a hero free of doubt. Indeed, the gap between Śaṅkara and Śaṅkarācārya suggests what we may call "creative doubt in Advaita".

---

[38] Ibid., pp. 2–3.

Like Uṣasta Cākrāyaṇa and Kahola Kauśītakeya (BU 3.4–5), Śaṅkara wishes to be *ātman*, to know him as one shows a cow by holding its horns.[39] The great scholarly author re-enacts an Uddālaka-like Ādi-Śaṅkarācārya, the master who sits in the shade of the tree. Although deeply familiar with the Upaniṣadic vision and intensely intimate with and committed to the existence of the one and only self (*ātman*), the author shares the lamentation of the disciple in Upad: I am one of *saṃsāra*-life (*samsārī*), I am one, and he is another.[40]

[39] These are Śaṅkara's own words in his commentary on Uṣasta's and Kahola's request to know the *ātman* in its actual presence and clarity (*sākṣād aparokṣāt*).

[40] Upad 2.25. The full quotation is the following: *anya evâham ajñaḥ sukhī duḥka-baddhaḥ saṃsāry, anyo 'sau mad-vilakṣaṇo 'saṃsārī devas, tam ahaṃ baly-upahāra-namaskārâdibhir varṇâśrama-karmabhiś cârādhya saṃsāra-sāgarād uttitīrṣur asmi, katham ahaṃ sa evêti.*

CHAPTER SEVEN

ON RICE AND MOKṢA: A NOTE ON ŚAṄKARA'S VOICES AND AESTHETICS

Who was Śaṅkara, the author of the BSBh, BUBh, BGBh and Upad? If we suppose that Śaṅkara possesses a particular quality of voice that is present in every piece of speech or writing and yet is significantly distinct from that of his sub-heroes (*siddhāntins* and *pūrva-pakṣins*), let us go further and ask what is the distinguishing quality of this voice? Let us suppose Śaṅkara was the single author of the compositions mentioned above. Is there a recognizable resonance that emerges in all of his writings? Just as voices in everyday life gesture to their sources, the voices heard in literary compositions can be telling with respect to their authors. Similarly, Śaṅkara's writings invite us to listen to the voices and echoes in his text. They require practice and competence if one is to hear the particular resonance of their author's voice. Śaṅkara is a gifted author who can speak in the name of others and can instill, as we shall see, Advaita propositions (of the great Brahman, pure consciousness, the self of all) in the mouth of an opponent, creating thereby a subtle and complex effect of irony, doubt, and—above all—self-confidence. Who else but the most self-confident of Advaitins could imagine Brahman speaking? Who else could tell a joke about Yājñavalkya's famous *nêti nêti*, or playfully compare the road to *mokṣa* with the cooking of rice? Thus, Śaṅkara's approach as an artist and author sheds light on the nature of Advaita philosophy as a way of life and experience. The author-Advaitin is a person possessing imagination, creativity, and freedom of spirit.

A close reading of Śaṅkara requires, among other things, the separation and identification of various voices. At least three voices of Śaṅkara's *bhāṣyas* are immediately noticeable: the author's, the *siddhāntin*'s, and the *pūrva-pakṣin*'s. These voices are interrelated, unified and embedded or contained within the author's. Though distinguished from one another—one is apparently winning, another is losing, a third (the author's) transcends them both—they all belong together.

In my view, the closer one reads the *bhāṣya*s, the more apparent the distinction between author and his sub-voices (notably the *siddhāntin*'s) becomes. Sometimes the author is closer to his chosen *siddhāntin*; sometimes he seems to be closer to his chosen *pūrva-pakṣin*. But who, then, is the author? Is he an Advaitin? Could a learned, intelligent city-dweller (*nāgarika*) scholar uncommitted to Advaita metaphysics and way of life compose the BSBh? According to the principle of "resisting confluent reading as much as possible," this option is not completely absurd. Once the separation between the voices of author and *siddhāntin* is established, one can apply this voice-sensitive approach indefinitely. However, to assume that the *bhāṣya-kāra* does not commit himself to the truth of his chosen *siddhāntin*'s teachings is an unwarranted generalization, in my view. The author is deeply knowledgable of the *ātman*; he loves the *ātman* and professes to hear its echo everywhere in the Vedānta-texts (*sarveṣu hi vedānteṣu*).

Our opponent would argue that knowledge of the Vedānta-texts and professed love for the *ātman* emerge out of the *siddhāntin*'s mind! If you separate author and *siddhāntin*, he might say, you are bound to deny everything, and this can result in an overwhelming lack of confidence (*sarvatrânāśāsvāsa-prasaṅgāt*). But in fact, we argue that a close reading of the *bhāṣyas* succeeds in shedding light on the forcefulness and quality of the differentiated chorus articulated by the master-Advaitin whose depth and complexity of vision exceed those of his *siddhāntin*'s in gravity and conviction.

In our search for symptoms (or expressions) of the particular quality of the author's voice, let us attempt a close reading of a few *bhāṣyas*, such as BSBh 1.1.22, 2.3.45–6, 1.1.4, and 3.2.22. Like other *bhāṣyas*, these sections invite engagement by virtue of their rich texture and philosophical content.

The underlying topic of BSBh 3.3.32 is the relation of body and self. The *bhāṣya-kāra* presents questions about the fate of persons who know Brahman or the self yet continue to live and act, even taking upon themselves new bodies till their work in the world is done. How is this possible? In the course of his composition the author imagines the *siddhāntin* dealing an allegedly critical blow to his rival. Mockingly, the exponent takes into consideration the most sacred of Advaita statements, "You are that" (*tat tvam asi*). He says: This *maha-vākya* cannot be assumed to be a reference to the future, namely, to mean: "Once dead, you will become that (Brahman)" (*tat tvaṃ mṛto bhaviṣyasi*). The *siddhāntin*'s allegation is the essence of the *pūrva-pakṣin*'s position. The apparently absurd paraphrase of *tat tvam asi* as *tat tvaṃ mṛto bhaviṣyasi* is a true summary of the *siddhāntin*'s relegation of *mokṣa* to a future. Thus, the master author presents the *siddhāntin* (in this case) as an innocent Advaitin unaware of the true import of his speech. The apparent winner is here a true loser.

I do not know, of course, whether in the course of composing the BSBh, Śaṅkara was playfully aware of himself as a master-writer inherently different from his heroes. One can never be sure whether he identified with the exponent or the opponent or with neither, or both. However, my hypothesis in the following discussion is that the structure and course of the argumentation as well as the content articulated therein point to a subtle yet tangible presence behind the composition of the text. Thus, in my view, close reading of the *bhāṣya* corroborates the proposition that the author must have been intensely aware of the difference between the Advaita-*siddhāntin* and himself.

BS 3.3.32 says: For those holding particular entitlements (roles, or assignments), there is maintenance (of the body) as long as the assignment persists (*yāvad adhikāram avasthitir adhikārikānām*). Śaṅkara the *bhāṣya-kāra* glosses the *sūtra*, identifies the topic and rephrases the question: may a liberated "person"—knower of *ātman*—be born in a new body, or is he necessarily released of his last body (in a state of embodiment) (*viduṣo vartamāna-deha-pātanânantaraṃ dehântam utpadyate*?) It is a question related to the very nature of *mokṣa* and the significance of the *jīvan-mukta* in Advaita. Some Advaitins could argue that the term *jīvan-mukti* (embodied liberation) is self-contradictory. For the reality of "a liberated person in the body" means that *mokṣa* is not necessarily (strictly speaking) a body-free condition, and that knowledge of self does not terminate a measure of self-identification with the body. In this matter we assume that such a measure of self-identification is necessary for activating the body (voluntary acting in the body).[1]

Questions about knowledge of self and embodiment are naturally present in Advaita-Vedānta thought. Following Bādarāyaṇa's *sūtra*, Śaṅkara's BSBh 3.3.32 reflects on such questions. Can liberated *saṃnyāsins* be re-born? Can currently true cognitions of the self and the absolute be translated into *future* transformation? What precisely does *mokṣa* mean for one's relationship with the body? On the one hand,

---

[1] I wonder whether scientific data (e.g. neurology) are relevant in this matter. My present intuition, namely, that voluntary action is impossible without a minimal sense of "I" and self-identification with one's body, could, perhaps, be corroborated by neuro-science.

mokṣa-transformation implies—by definition—non-identification of self with the body—*aśarīratvaṃ mokṣaḥ*.[2] On the other hand, questions such as Arjuna's in the *Bhagavad Gītā*—regarding the relationship of a *jīvan-mukta* with "his" body—necessarily come to mind: How does a *jīvan-mukta* move? How does he talk?[3]

The question of liberation and the possibility of a new body originates on the *sūtra*-level and then surfaces in the *bhāṣya-kāra*'s mind, articulated by the author's voice. The question presupposes the entire Advaita universe of discourse; assumptions of *ātman*'s existence, knowledge of Brahman, and its power of subverting *saṃsāra*, re-birth and embodiment are taken for granted.

The author's preliminary *pūrva-pakṣin* seems to undermine the presupposition of the entire discourse. He says: there is no room at all for doubt. Since knowledge (of *ātman*) is brought about (necessarily) by certain means, one does not say that the separation of the I from the body is either accomplished or not (*nanu vidyāyāḥ sādhana-bhūtāyāḥ saṃpattau kaivalya-nirvṛttiḥ syān na vêti*). There is no room for doubt in this respect (*nêyaṃ cintôpapadyate*). As cooked rice does not require one to question whether the rice is made or not, and as there is no question as to whether a person who has eaten is satiated, likewise there is no room to doubt whether knowledge results in complete disembodiment and cessation of re-birth (*na hi pāka-sādhana-saṃpattav odano bhaven na vêti cintā sambhavati. nâpi bhuñjānas tṛpyeta na vêti cintyate*).

The preliminary opponent paraphrases the well-known Advaita thesis: knowledge of *ātman* irreversibly terminates one's self-identification with the body. The relation of the self to the body is due to a wrong perception. The individual self (connected with a body) is projected upon *nirguṇa* Brahman as a snake is projected onto a rope. We would expect that the *bhāṣya-kāra* would endorse such a view from the very beginning. But no; the author introduces a *siddhāntin* who asserts that there *is* room for doubt. Thus, if the author holds the foundational position with respect to liberation as the necessary termination of embodiment (self-identification with a body) one suspects that the author shares the *pūrva-pakṣin*'s rather than the *siddhāntin*'s position. However, we

---

[2] BSBh 1.1.4.

[3] See BhG 2.54. *sthita-prajñasya kā bhāṣā samādhi-sthasya keśava/sthita-dhīḥ kiṃ prabhāṣeta kim āsīta vrajeta kim//*

should notice the author's caution. The preliminary *pūrva-pakṣin* does not assert tautology of *mokṣa* and disembodiment but rather a causal, empirical relation (like cooking of rice which makes the rice cooked, or eating and satiety). Thus, Śaṅkara the author of BSBh 3.3.32—presenting throughout the BSBh exponents insisting on the deeply rooted Advaita truth of liberation as disembodiment—creates an opening for the debate between *siddhānta*-Advaita and *pūrva-pakṣa*-Advaita, while removing himself from both parties to the debate. In fact, the distinction between *siddhāntin* and *pūrva-pakṣin* is not so clear-cut. The preliminary *pūrva-pakṣin* who denies room for doubt is closer, one would assume, to the author's position in terms of contents. But on the other hand, the author's affirmation of the legitimacy of doubt nourishes the entire discussion, and is thus of the author's making.

The author, as we have seen, is in favor of doubt; thus he controls the discourse. He introduces examples of persons who—though knowing Brahman—continue to live in their old bodies or acquire some new embodiment. Such persons—Apāntaratama, Kṛṣṇa Dvaipāyana, Vasiṣṭha, Sanatkumāra, Nārada, etc., known from the Purāṇas and the Mahābhārata—are like the sun (*savitṛ*), who watches over the worlds for thousands of eons (*yuga*) by virtue of its entitlement, or role (*adhikāra*). Having finally fulfilled its role, the sun enjoys *mokṣa* (*kaivalyam anubhavati*),[4] and neither rises nor sets. Likewise, says the *siddhāntin*, all those sublime persons appointed by Īśvara to carry out certain tasks in the world continue to live in the body, although they know Brahman.

The *pūrva-pakṣin* responds to the insightful doubt raised by the preliminary *siddhāntin* (who insisted on the legitimacy of doubt) by making a somewhat surprising and brilliant move; if what you say is so, he says, let doubt exist with respect to the power of knowledge to generate liberation (disembodiment). Then knowledge of Brahman may or may not produce *mokṣa* (*tad eteṣāṃ dehântarôtpatti-darśanāt prāptaṃ brahma-vidyāyāḥ pakṣikaṃ mokṣa-hetutvam ahetutvaṃ vêti*).

Now, the *pūrva-pakṣin*'s assertion goes deep; he exposes *jīvan-mukti*, namely, *mokṣa* embodied, as not *necessarily related* to knowledge of self. His argument is simple: if indeed there are individuals embodied and knowing themselves as Brahman, and if *mokṣa* is necessarily a

---

[4] The *siddhāntin* suggests that someone who knows himself to be Brahman may not "experience *mokṣa*" (*anubhava*). Thus, the experience of *mokṣa* (*kaivalya*) is not, according to this view, an integral dimension of knowledge of self.

disembodied state, then knowledge may not be considered a sufficient cause of liberation, for if it were a sufficient cause, it would invariably lead to disembodiment (which, according to the *siddhāntin*, is not the case). Sometimes, argues the *pūrva-pakṣin, mokṣa* follows knowledge of self, sometimes it does not. Thus, the opponent makes use of the illustrations brought forth by the *siddhāntin* (of Vasiṣṭha, Nārada, Sanatkumāra, etc.) in order to jeopardize one of Advaita's central propositions—the inherent connection between self-knowledge and liberation. Śaṅkara the *bhāṣya-kāra*—if he shares such a central proposition of Advaita—creates the *pūrva-pakṣin* in his (the author's) image.

The illustrations offered by the *siddhāntin* highlight another aspect of his inherent weakness and (consequently) the distance between the author and his apparent exponent. The distinction between the authority of *śruti* (revealed knowledge) and *smṛti* (transmitted knowledge) is intensely present in Śaṅkara's mind.[5] Man-made *smṛti*-illustrations from *itihāsa* (Mahābhārata) and the Purāṇas are notably of lesser significance. For his *siddhāntin*'s sake, Śaṅkara the *bhāṣya-kāra* could have selected other examples of higher authority (the Upaniṣads). The author is explicit with respect to the inferior quality of his *siddhāntin*'s position. The exponent says: Stories such as those of Dakṣa, Nārada, etc. are known from mantras and *arthavāda* portions of *śruti (śrutāv api mantrârthavādayoḥ prāyeṇôpalabhyate*). The relegation of the main datum in the *siddhāntin*'s argument to the domain of *arthavāda* and *mantra*[6] bespeaks a somewhat skeptical or ambivalent attitude toward his chosen *siddhāntin*.

As if in need of further explanation with respect to the possibility of *mokṣa*-life in the body, the *siddhāntin* offers at this point a theory of karma and causality. There is a condition of unexhausted karma, he says, like an arrow suspended in mid-air. The tense, apologetic tone is evident:

> And as the present knowers of Brahman reach the state of isolation after the enjoyment of those results of action, which have begun to operate, has come to an end, according to ChU 4.14.2—"For him there is only delay so long as he is not delivered from the body"; so Apāntaratamas

[5] Thus, reasoning as man-made *smṛti* is explicitly inferior and without foundation, according to Śaṅkara. See for example BSBh 1.3.28, BSBh 2.16, 2.1.11. W. Halbfass 1991: 131–204.

[6] One recalls Nārada's confession according to ChU 7.1: I am a knower of mantra (*mantra-vid*), not a knower of the self (*ātma-vid*).

> and other Lords to whom the highest Lord has entrusted certain offices, last—although they possess complete knowledge, the cause of release—as long as their office lasts, their works not yet being exhausted, and obtain release only when their office comes to an end.[7]

The tension embedded in the *siddhāntin*'s stance is obvious. He recognizes true knowledge of self as the cause of *mokṣa* or separation of self and body (*saty api saṃyag-darśane kaivalya-hetau*) and yet concomitantly endorses the connection of self and body in the lives of those special persons (Īśvaras) who are destined to fulfill certain assignments. A question naturally arises: how can knowledge produce dissociation of self and body and at the same time preserve such an association?

The *siddhāntin* proceeds in his selection of illustrations from secondary sources (*smṛti*). "*Smṛti* tells us, e.g. that Sulabhā, a woman conversant with Brahman (*brahma-vādinī*), wishing to dispute with Janaka, left her own body, entered into that of Janaka, carried on a discussion with him, and again returned into her own body."[8] (The author of BSBh 3.3.32 is indeed acquainted with yoga traditions of transference to other's bodies, and so forth.)[9]

The opponent's forceful argument survives while his opponent's (the *siddhāntin*'s) appears insufficient, even weak. The author again makes the *pūrva-pakṣin* raise a proposition about the possibility of fresh karma generated in the lives of those knowers of self and liberated personalities mentioned above. If such karma were indeed generated there would be sufficient reason to cut off the inherent relationship between knowledge of self and *mokṣa*; knowledge of self would in that case not be a sufficient cause for the attainment of *mokṣa*.

> If in addition to the works the consequences of which are already in operation, other works manifested themselves, constituting the cause of further embodiments, the result would be that in the same way further works also, whose potentiality would in that case not be destroyed, would take place, and then it might be suspected that the knowledge of Brahman may, indifferently, either be or not be the cause of final release.[10]

---

[7] Thibaut 1890: v. 2, p. 236.

[8] Thibaut 1890: v. 2, p. 237.

[9] The BSBh touches here upon a well-known theme of Pātañjala-yoga (see YS 3.38) as well as the famous tale of the *dig-vijaya* tradition.

[10] Thibaut 1890: v. 2, p. 237.

At this point of the debate, towards the end of the *bhāṣya* the *siddhāntin* brings forth a totally different argument, mentioned above, based on the foremost of Vedāntic statements, *tat tvam asi*. One does not say *tat tvam asi* and mean thereby: you will be that when you are dead (*na hi tat tvam asi ity asya vākyasyârthas tat tvaṃ mṛto bhaviṣyasîty evaṃ pariṇetuṃ śakyaḥ*). The *siddhāntin* seems to say that liberation comes about simultaneously with true knowledge or understanding of *tat tvam asi*. And this, of course, is the opponent's major proposition. The obvious implication is that illustrious figures such as Dakṣa, Nārada, Vasiṣṭha, and so forth had indeed absorbed the sublime truth of *tat tvam asi*, but their final disengagement from the body had been mysteriously relegated (by the exponent) to the future. The *siddhāntin*'s rephrasing of the opponent's alleged position as *ta ttvaṃ mṛto bhaviṣyasi* seems unfair; after all, the *pūrva-pakṣin* insists that disembodiment or liberation follow simultaneously upon knowledge of the self (or understanding *tat tvam asi*). Relegation of the impact of Advaita truth to the future is of the exponent's, not the opponent's making.

Thus, the curious statement voiced by the *siddhāntin* seems to invite further reflection on losing and winning, and the nature of the *siddhāntin*'s voice. For indeed, the quotation of *tat tvam asi* in the context of BSBh 3.3.32 bespeaks a remarkable failure on the *siddhāntin*'s part. At issue is the self-contradictory nature of *mokṣa* in the body; if *mokṣa* is a necessary and complete separation of self and body/mind, correct understanding of *tat tvam asi* stands in opposition to any future-life in the body. The continuation of life in the body following knowledge of *ātman* is a true problem for Advaita theory. The author, I suggest, shares the *pūrva-pakṣin*'s position and doubt (with respect to the possibility of *jīvan-mukti*). Keeping in mind the fundamental position of Advaita that the self *appears* (by virtue of *adhyāsa* or *avidyā*) associated with a body but is in reality absolutely different from the body,[11] the author of BSBh 3.3.32 favors the *pūrva-pakṣin* rather than the *siddhāntin*.

Close reading is critical to making the distinction between author and *siddhāntin* alive and tangible. If the apparent winner is unresponsive to the true philosophical challenge put forth by his rival; if he loses

[11] See for example BSBh 1.4.20–22, where Śaṅkara reviews three possibilities with respect to the relation of the individual self to the one *ātman*.

the debate; if his argument is patently inconclusive, and rests on secondary, inferior sources (*smṛti*)—then the distinction between Śaṅkara the master Advaitin and his sub-voices is compounded.

Currently, readers and scholars regard the difference between the voices of author and the *siddhāntin* as insignificant; the author seems, according to their view, truly identical with his chosen *siddhāntin*. The different registers in the voices, though undeniable—the author introduces both exponent's and opponent's positions—is no more than a literary device. Yet we have seen that the author's voice *is* different from his Advaita sub-voices; Śaṅkara's art of writing seems to require a corresponding art of listening.

The presupposition underlying listening of this kind is as follows: voices are different from abstract (unvoiced) overt contents. Under certain circumstances, the effective philosophical unit is explicitly voiced. In other words, in this context, truth-value belongs to vocal speech-acts. Vocalization is philosophically significant. Thus, as we shall show below, an Advaita message put in the mouth of a Mīmāṃsaka exponent may be false, and—by the same token—an Advaita message generated by an Advaitin who is a *pūrva-pakṣin*'s *pūrva-pakṣin* may also be significantly false. The voice is an integral dimension of the message.

Let us assume then that Śaṅkara's writing is inherently philosophy-in-context, namely, voiced and origin-dependent, etc. What does this mean? An assumption like this initiates a quest after Śaṅkara, the somewhat distant, obscure, inherently free and highly imaginative author of the BSBh, who has remained largely unknown. And yet, in a sense he is, and remains, the true Advaitin, the channel through which Advaita-Vedānta has been conceived in history.

CHAPTER EIGHT

ON MUD, NEGATION AND THE HUNGRY SPACE

The greatest Upaniṣadic sage, Yājñavalkya, points to the one self as "not this, not this" (*nêti nêti*) (BU 2.3.6). Yājñavalkya seems to point to a frustration inherently pertinent to knowledge of the so-called absolute, *nirguṇa-brahman* (or *ātman*). What does it mean to know something which is by definition beyond word and mind? For Śaṅkara, author of the BSBh, this is an occasion to introduce Advaita-discourse focused on negation, its scope and philosophical meaning. He creates a dialogue in which a *siddhāntin* and opponent have important things to say. Thus, the exponent says that any act of denial implies recognition of (an existing) something else; the opponent asserts that an entity allegedly existent but by definition inaccessible to speech and thought might be denied existence altogether.

The Advaita-discourse of negation concerns a foundational idea underlying the Advaita perspective on experience and life: the force and quality of empty space opened up by negation (or resistance). Translation of *ātman*-knowledge into referential subject/predicate language is inappropriate; thus says Yājñavalkya in his *nêti nêti*, according to Śaṅkara's two debaters (*siddhāntin* and opponent) displayed in BSBh 3.2.22. The quality of empty space thus focuses the attention of author, exponent, and opponent. A hungry space opens up (it is assumed by the three voices), in which unfamiliar phenomena of consciousness might happen. How empty are spaces generated by all sorts of negation? How hungry is the empty space of which Yājñavalkya speaks in his *nêti nêti* proposition? The opponent says that—possibly—the empty space suggested in Yājñavalkya's vision is of infinite depth; Brahman itself, the allegedly ultimate reality is negated, subverted, as it were. However, like his creator the opponent is apparently openminded, heeding various possibilities; if one has to accept something real, namely, if complete, total negation "of everything" is impossible, let objects of sense and reasoning exist. The author's consciousness has room for the ideas of both opponent and exponent. He is, as repeatedly suggested above, in doubt. However, the *siddhāntin*'s choice should not be ignored; Śaṅkara the philosopher, author of the BSBh finds immeasurable attraction in negation of the familiar and visible in favor of touching the unfamiliar, unseen Brahman (the self).

Freedom from the familiar won by the force of negation (applied to duality, multiplicity and congealed boundaries "of the world") seems to be the essence of the Upaniṣadic experience. Freedom, however, is of many kinds; for the Upaniṣadic sage, says Śaṅkara in his introduction to the BSBh, it is freedom from the mysterious and false fusion of subject (*viṣayin*) and object (*viṣaya*), of misconception (*avidyā*) in the form of *adhyāsa* (projection of subject on object and object on subject). For our author of the BSBh, we suggest, it is also freedom from complete self-identification with his hero (the *siddhāntin*). In both cases a modulation of fusion or conflation conditions the flavor of freedom or of auspicious empty space.

Since Śaṅkara's text is the only source by which we can derive our notion of the author's identity, the meaning of the text cannot be informed by the identity of its author. In other words, if the author's nature is conceived after the text, then any notion of the identity of the author would be patently derivative and of no value insofar as the meaning of the text is concerned. In these circumstances, a reading that conflates author and exponent is natural and legitimate. And yet, as we have seen, the author is a palpable presence in the text; his point of view, his talent and imaginative power, his freedom of spirit, his scholarship—all are worthy of attention. Here is a scholarly sage capable of imagining the *ātman* more vividly and animatedly than anyone has ever done before him: both as terribly real and yet as significantly distinct from himself. The author of the BSBh is a sage who boldly utilises the existential or philosophical doubts gnawing at him to create a dynamic and unexpected dialogic exploration of Advaita—Vedānta thinking. Thus, a new personality emerges; a great philosopher, Śaṅkara the author of the BSBh, is an arch-adversary (or rival) of the familiar in favor of the unfamiliar and real.

Indeed, the more familiar a phenomenon is, the more it needs to be resisted. I take resistance to mean energetic negation, saying "No" (in our case, to the familiar). Handelman and Shulman articulate in the following the particular force of creative resistance (negation):

> A violent negation effectively nourishes and affirms. Creation itself seems to proceed, in such a cosmos, in the sudden twists and involutions of generative rejection, or of an emphatic 'no' that gives life. The very energy that moves this cosmos through its constant turns is somehow produced out of the act that denies its wholeness, or that, negating, emp-

> ties out its partial or superficial forms. More precisely, 'no' takes away, opening space that can now become full (of god).[1]

Indeed, Advaita-Vedānta is about negation. An underlying question of this tradition would be, using Handelman's and Shulman's phrase: how violent can negation be? And what precisely is negated? In Advaita, acceptance of plurality or duality is negated. The title of this tradition, *advaita*, posits negation as the apex of liberating knowledge. This is, according to Śaṅkara,[2] the Upaniṣadic function. An opponent in BSBh 1.1.4 proclaims that since Brahman is not an object, the Veda may not be the source of the desired knowledge (namely, the Veda cannot teach but of Brahman devoid of any trace of objectivity) (*aviṣayatve brahmaṇaḥ śāstra-yonitvânupapattir*). The intention of the Upaniṣads is to remove the notion of "difference" (*bheda*), namely, plurality, which is considered wrong metaphysics, the essence of *avidyā* (*avidyā-kalpita-bheda-nivṛtti-paratvāc chāstrasya*). In other words, the Veda teaches about the one self (Brahman, *ātman*) by stimulating resistance and instigating negation. Vedic power is the power of negation.

The author of BSBh 3.2.22 treats Upaniṣadic negation in its most explicit occasion, namely, Yājñavalkya's "not this, not this" (*nêti nêti*) proposition. In response to the opponent's claim that this saying negates Brahman (but not the world!) the *siddhāntin* cites a mundane, everyday cliché:

> For, as the common saying goes, better than washing it is not to touch dirt at all (*prakṣālanād dhi paṅkasya dūrād asparṣanaṃ varam*).[3]

This witty truism is voiced twice, first by the exponent and then by the opponent. In both cases, we sense the presence of an author different than his two sub-voices.

Sensing the presence of an author gifted with humor, irony, freedom of mind and literary talent, readers feel pleasure; the juxtaposition of sublime teaching with a mundane illustration is hilarious. Our partial reconstruction of the *bhāṣya* points to the quality of the

---

1 Handelman and Shulman 2005: 35. And elsewhere: ('no') is thus the creative word par excellence (p. 104).

2 Note that I, too, do not always distinguish between Śaṅkara the author of the BSBh and the *siddhānta*-exponent. I assume a measure of intimacy between the two: both author and *siddhāntin* are exponents of Advaita.

3 The cliché is also found in the *Hitôpadeśa* 1.181. *dharmârthaṃ yasya vittêhā varaṃ tasya nirīhatā/prakṣālanād dhi paṅkasya dūrād asparṣanaṃ varam//*

Advaita discourse; in some respects, the exponent and opponent share their being; dialogue is real, and so is Śaṅkara's presence as the gifted author of the BSBh.

Opponent: Yājñavalkya's statement (*nêti nêti*) negates the two modes of Brahman (*mūrta* and *amūrta*) as well as Brahman itself.
Implied *Siddhāntin*: How do you reach such a far-fetched interpretation?
Oppponent: By a method you yourself often make use of.
Implied *Siddhāntin*: And what is this method?
Opponent: By force of context (*prakaraṇa-sāmarthyāt*).
Implied *Siddhāntin*: What is the context you have in mind?
Opponent: Look. The word "no" is uttered twice. This means that there are two negations involved (*dvau câitau pratiṣedhau dvir nêti-śabda-prayogāt*).
Implied *Siddhāntin*: What could these two negations be?
Opponent: As I suggested above, one negation of the two is of the cosmic material nature (form) (*saprapañca*) of Brahman; the other negates that which has this form, namely, Brahman itself.
Implied *Siddhāntin*: But the second "no" is for emphasis only.
Opponent: Very well; Yājñavalkya's *nêti nêti* negates Brahman itself only (*athavā brahmâiva rūpavat pratiṣidhyate*).
Implied *Siddhāntin*: Are you serious?
Opponent: Yes, I am.
Implied *Siddhāntin*: Your proposition is audacious and unwarranted. After all, all the Vedānta texts assert the existence of Brahman which is the self, one without a second!
Opponent: Since the Upaniṣads assert that Brahman is beyond speech and mind, its very existence might be negated (*vāṅ-manasâtītatvād asambhāvyamāna-sad-bhāvaṃ pratiṣedhârtham*).
Implied *Siddhāntin*: If the existence of Brahman is negated, what is left?
Opponent: The entire universe accessible to sense-perception and the other means of knowledge (such as reasoning) may not be negated (*na tu rūpa-prapañcaḥ pratyakṣâdi-gocaratvāt pratiṣedhârham*).
Implied *Siddhāntin*: You accept sense-perception and deny the authority of the Veda!
Implied Opponent: I did not say that. I said that Brahman is beyond speech and mind; this is a major tenet of the Veda.
Implied *Siddhāntin*: Ah! Does Brahman exist or it does not? Dare you say that Yājñavalkya denies the existence and reality of Brahman, which is *ātman*, the self of everything?
Implied Opponent: I followed your suggestion that Yājñavalkya's second "no" is for emphasis only. That's why I said that Brahman alone should be negated. For the world accessible to sense-perception may not be denied reality.
Implied *Siddhāntin*: So what about the second "no"?
Opponent: As you yourself have suggested, it might be taken as mere emphasis. Brahman alone is negated in Yājñavalkya's *nêti nêti* proposition.

Siddhāntin: I have had enough. Following your talk, I shall give you a decisive response (*evaṃ prāpte brūmaḥ*).

Implied Opponent: What can you say?

Siddhāntin: It is impossible to deny Brahman and the world. If you deny the existence of both (Brahman and the world), a false theory of emptiness is implied (*na tāvad ubhaya-pratiṣedha upapadyate śūnya-vāda-prasaṅgāt*).

Implied Opponent: Are you suggesting that I am a Buddhist?

Implied *Siddhāntin*: Yes, I am.

Implied Opponent: I only interpreted Yājñavalkya's *nêti nêti* the best I could. After all, he did say "not this, not this," which means that he denies existence of everything!

Siddhāntin: If we deny something as unreal, we accept something else as real (*kiṃcid dhi paramârtham ālambyâparamârthaḥ pratiṣidhyate*).

Implied Opponent: Give me an example.

Siddhāntin: The existence of a (real) rope is concomitant with the denial of a snake (*yathā rajjv-ādiṣu sarpâdayaḥ*).

Implied Opponent: What is the meaning of this particular illustration?

Siddhāntin: As I said, whenever you deny the existence of something you approve of the reality of something else. In the denial of a snake's existence, one approves of that of a rope.

Implied Opponent: And so?

Implied *Siddhāntin*: You cannot deny everything.

Implied Opponent: I have not denied everything.

Siddhāntin: Yes, you did. In your denial of Brahman and its forms, what other thing is left? (*ubhaya-pratiṣedhe tu ko 'nyo bhāvaḥ pariśiṣyet*).

Implied Opponent: I have not denied everything.

Siddhāntin: And if you deny everything, and nothing is left, then you cannot deny anything else since there is nothing left to approve of! (*apariśiṣyamāṇe cânyasmin ya itaraḥ pratiṣeddhum ārabhate pratiṣeddhum aśakyatvāt tasyâiva paramârthatvâpatteḥ pratiṣedhânupapattiḥ*).

Implied Opponent: But I have not denied everything. I have my doubts about the existence of Brahman.

Siddhāntin: You cannot deny the existence of Brahman (*nâpi brahma-pratiṣedha upapadyate*).

Implied Opponent: As I said, it is reasonable to deny the reality of Brahman after Yājñavalkya's emphatic negation ("not this, not this").

Implied *Siddhāntin*: Your statement is absurd.

Implied Opponent: Why?

Siddhāntin: It blatantly contradicts the opening statement of the passage (BU 2.1.1); "I am going to tell you about Brahman" (*brahma te bravāṇi*).

Implied Opponent: A single statement is not enough.

Implied *Siddhāntin*: All the Vedānta texts speak of Brahman which is *ātman*, the self of everything.

Implied Opponent: Do you really mean that the one and only object of the Upaniṣads is Brahman and *ātman*?

Siddhāntin: Yes, I do. See Taittirīya 2.6.1:—"Whoever conceives of Brahman as non-existent becomes non-existent himself" (*asann eva sa bhavati asad brahmêti veda cet*).

Implied Opponent: This is frightening indeed.

Implied *Siddhāntin*: You'd better take care of yourself.

Implied Opponent: Please tell me more.

Siddhāntin: Kaṭhôpaniṣad 2.6.13 asserts: "Brahman should be conceived as 'He exists'" (*astîty evôpalabdhavyaḥ*).

Implied Opponent: Sometimes, indeed, the Upaniṣads speak of Brahman. Sometimes they deny the existence of Brahman (as in Yājñavalkya's *nêti nêti*).

Siddhāntin: No, no. If you ever deny the existence of Brahman, you contradict all the Vedānta! (*sarva-vedānta-vyākopa-prasaṅgāt*).

Implied Opponent: But Brahman is beyond speech and mind!

Siddhāntin: Brahman is indeed beyond speech and thought but that does not imply its non-existence! (*vāṅ-manasâtītvam api brahmaṇo nâbhāvâbhiprāyeṇâbhidhīyate*).

Implied Opponent: If something cannot be touched by the senses or thought, it is as if it does not exist.

Siddhāntin: No. If the Vedānta texts assert so many times that Brahman exists; see for example the following statements of Taittirīya 2.1.1—"The one who knows Brahman obtains the highest" (*brahma-vid āpnoti param*); "Brahman is truth, infinite knowledge" (*satyaṃ jñānam anantaṃ brahma*).

Implied Opponent: And yet, I have my doubts.

Siddhāntin: Considering the sublime Upaniṣadic propositions concerning the reality of Brahman as the pure, eternal, infinite ground and the self of everything, which is one, made of consciousness (knowledge), one cannot all of a sudden negate its existence. Indeed, it is better not to touch mud than to wash your hands of the dirt.

Implied Opponent: Please explain.

Implied *Siddhāntin*: The Veda asserts the existence of Brahman; it does not contradict itself by negating the same.

Implied Opponent: Do you deny the force of Upaniṣadic negation?

Implied *Siddhāntin*: No. I am only saying that Yājñavalkya denies certain attributes of Brahman, but not Brahman itself.

Implied Opponent: Who is Brahman?

Implied *Siddhāntin*: Brahman is pure consciousness, eternal, omniscient, the origin of the world, the cause of its subsistence as well as of its imminent destruction…

Implied Opponent: But Brahman itself is said to be beyond speech and mind.

Implied *Siddhāntin*: I am doing my best.

Implied Opponent: Why do you speak of Brahman's attributes and then deny that any attribute belongs to Brahman? It seems better to stay clean rather than touch mud and then wash your hands.

Implied *Siddhāntin*: True.

Implied Opponent: Is not Yājñavalkya's statement *nêti nêti* like washing one's hands (after having touched dirt)? It is apparently better not to describe Brahman than to touch dirt afterwards.

Along with an abstract, liberating metaphysics of the one reality which is the self, the author of the BSBh inserts the worldly mud-cliché. Combining the utterly familiar with the unfathomable, incredible truth of the one self is a characteristic feature in Śaṅkara's art of writing.

The opposite of the familiar is the incredible. In some circumstances, especially where the familiar is untrue in significant ways, truth is a hallmark of the incredible. See, for example, Freud's association of truth and incredibility:

> There is a very convenient method by which we can sometimes obtain a piece of information we want about unconscious repressed material. 'What,' we ask, 'would you consider the most unlikely imaginable thing in that situation? What do you think was furthest from your mind at that time?' If the patient falls into the trap and says what he thinks is most incredible, he almost always makes the right admission.[4]

But the universe of negation is immense and varied. Notwithstanding Freud's fascinating discovery of a transformational negation, the Upaniṣadic negation discussed below is inherently different from the neurotic negation discussed by Freud. We can accept Freud's proposition that "negation is a way of taking cognizance of what is repressed' (p. 438), but the challenge to be met is the nature of that which is affirmed by transformational negation in different contexts of negation.[5] We must also concede that Śaṅkara, the author of the BSBh, uses a different type of negation (let us name it the Upaniṣadic 'no'), which offers a significant clue to the nature of Vedic power conceived by Śaṅkara (above) as the negation or removal (*nivṛtti*) of plurality.

There are, for Freud, significant negations whereby hidden (repressed) contents are suggested. But could *ātman*, the one and only self, be the

---

[4] Freud 1984: 437.

[5] In some places Freud suggests that negation is not only a hallmark of repression but a precondition of thought and thinking: "affirmation—as a substitute for uniting—belongs to Eros; negation—the successor to expulsion—belongs to the instinct of destruction. The general wish to negate, the negativism which is displayed by some psychotics, is probably to be regarded as a sign of a diffusion of instincts that has taken place through a withdrawal of the libidinal components. But the performance of the function of judgment is not made possible until the creation of the symbol of negation has endowed thinking with a first measure of freedom from the consequences of repression and, with it, from the compulsion of the pleasure principle..." (p. 441).

repressed emerging from the Vedic negation of plurality? Is *ātman* the incredible-yet-true Advaita? The Advaita idea of the one true self is grounded, as suggested above (BSBh 1.1.4), in resisting familiar plurality; and it is incredible indeed. And, in a sense, as a vehicle conducive to the emergence of truth, negation or resistance seems to be recommended by Śaṅkara and Freud alike.

Indeed, Śaṅkara the author of the BSBh was, according to our view, a resisting agent (he resists the necessity of committing to the reality of everyday life—*saṃsāra*, autonomy of reasoning, etc., as well as self-identification with his chosen *siddhāntin*). Could he have composed the BSBh without such resistance? Could he take into consideration his *siddhāntin*'s weaknesses without being detached, separate from his hero?

As we see in the passage just cited, sometimes the *siddhāntin* fails. Sometimes the winner's argument is inherently the loser's. Sometimes apparent messages change voice. Sometimes an author's voice is dissociated from the dialogue between exponent and opponent. The closer and more resistant our reading, the more palpable becomes our perception of the autonomous, independent author's point of view.

Let us explore the subject-matter of our author's negation and resistance (to his hero) in more detail, looking further into Śaṅkara's *bhāṣya* on BS 3.2.22. The opening paragraphs are set out in the author's voice, the author who presides over the *siddhāntin* and his opponent, who imagines the winning exponent as well as his rivals. The author presents the Upaniṣadic teaching of the two modes of Brahman—with form (*mūrta*) and without form (*amūrta*), and introduces the scope of negation as the issue:

> Now we know that the word "so" (*iti*) is used with reference to approximate things, in the same way as the particle *evam* is used; compare, e.g. the sentence "so (*iti*) indeed the teacher said" (where the "so" refers to his immediately preceding speech). And, in our passage, the context points out what has to be considered as proximate, viz. the two cosmic forms of Brahman, and that Brahman itself to which the two forms belong. Hence there arises a doubt whether the phrase 'Not so, Not so!' negates both Brahman and its two forms, or only either; and if the latter whether it negates Brahman and leaves its two forms, or if it negates the two forms and leaves Brahman.[6]

[6] Thibaut 1890: v. 2, 167.

BSBh 3.2.22 recapitulates the general pattern of Veda-oriented *bhāṣyas*. It opens with the uncertainty generated by three possible (apparently legitimate) interpretations of a Vedic statement. Thus, the author of BSBh 3.2.22 considers three objects of negation intended in Yājñavalkya's *nêti nêti*; the two forms of Brahman, and Brahman itself.

The opponent suggests that Brahman itself—with form and without form—is negated by Yājñavalkya's *nêti nêti*. We notice the breadth and freedom of his mind and his ability to express more than one legitimate interpretation of the *nêti nêti* assertion. In this respect, he is significantly closer to the author than the *siddhāntin* (who never expresses doubt or more than one interpretation). Considering the various options, the opponent goes for the most violent negation:

> As the word 'no' is repeated twice, there are really two negative statements, of which the one negates the cosmic form of Brahman, the other that which has form, i.e. Brahman itself.

Thus, the author lets the opponent resist the apparently most familiar presupposition among Vedānta sages: the very existence of the absolute. Indeed, the *pūrva-pakṣin* puts forth a most straightforward statement: since Brahman is beyond speech and mind, it cannot be said to exist as all!

This is a moment to diagnose and assess the nature and significance of the opponent's stance as articulated by the author. His assertion that Yājñavalkya's *nêti nêti* negates the existence of Brahman is of two parts; in the first he says that Brahman is beyond speech and thought (*vāṅ-manasâtīta*) and (therefore) its true existence should be negated; in the second he concludes that in contradistinction to the objects of perception, Brahman does not exist (*vāṅ-manasâtītatvād asaṃbhāvyamāna-sad-bhāvaṃ pratiṣedhârham/ na tu rūpa-prapañcaḥ pratyakṣâdi-gocaratvāt pratiṣedhârhaḥ*). On the surface, the opponent's two-part statement is well taken; anything unperceived cannot be said to exist. And yet the opponent's statement is seemingly self-contradictory, for if Brahman is beyond thought and speech, it must exist. However, the opponent might say that the reference to Brahman's inaccessibility is suggestive of a deeper-level idea with respect to the proper means of knowledge (*pramāṇa*); sense-perception (*pratyakṣa*) is the only true means of knowledge. However, the opponent does not say anything like this; he is committed to the validity of the Veda as a means of knowledge and he denies—concomitantly—the existence of Brahman (the main principle of the Upaniṣads). Indeed, readers experience a strangely double sensation from the self-contradiction embedded in the *pūrva-pakṣin*'s statement. The first part is an exemplary Upaniṣadic definition of the essence of Brahman (inaccessible to speech and ordinary mind) (see TU 2.4); the second is a blatant denial of Vedic authority. Thus, the opponent's statement contains a contradiction of central importance within the universe of Indian discourse of knowledge and adequate means of knowledge (*pramāṇa*); if one accepts the Upaniṣads as an authoritative means of knowledge (acceptance implied by the proposition about Brahman which is beyond speech and thought) one cannot deny the existence of Brahman. The reader knows, as the author must have been aware, that underlying the Upaniṣadic statement of Brahman's inaccessibility is the recognition of its very existence. For Indian thinkers and even for the "educated public" of the eighth century A.D. the opponent's presupposition of the validity of "sense perception" as the only means of right knowledge is naïve or unwarranted. The inaccessibility of Brahman or *ātman* to speech and thought is not evidence of non-existence but, on the contrary, a major sign of reality; the apparent plethora of worldly phenomena contacted by the senses and mind—subject to incessant change—occupies a much lower position in the hierarchy of being and existence than inaccessible *ātman* or Brahman.

Then who is the *pūrva-pakṣin* here? He is a joker, conspicuously unrealistic and even grotesque. He may not be a Buddhist (for he accepts the Veda); he may not be an Advaitin (for he denies Brahman). He is not a serious logician (*tārkika*, for he contradicts himself so blatantly), nor a materialist (*lokāyata*, for he implicitly accepts the authority of the Veda). As a "self-contradictory opponent" he is patently unidentified or unreal. Heeding the opponent's non-identification and unreality, a question arises with respect to the *siddhāntin*.

Who is the *siddhāntin*? And how does the *pūrva-pakṣin*'s unreality affect the *siddhāntin*'s nature? And what does it all mean in regard to the relationship of the author with the "creatures of his mind"? I suggest that the split between exponent and opponent is not as radical as it appears and that the *pūrva-pakṣin*'s nature in fact corresponds with that of his rival, the Advaita-*siddhāntin*. The particularly quixotic quality of our *siddhāntin*, 'crippled by certainty,' becomes evident. He supports the teaching of the principal Upaniṣads, of the oneness of everything, of the underlying ground and essence of existence which is the self (*ātman*—a great discovery indeed) by the truism of the mud-cliché; better not to touch mud in the first place than to touch it and then wash your hands.

The *siddhāntin* commits himself to the authority of the Veda (as means of true knowledge) and concomitantly brings forth an illustration from a conspicuously mundane occurrence. Thus the most essential, central, elemental of the Upaniṣadic teachings (that *ātman* exists) is exemplified—supported—by a *dṛṣṭānta* of a particularly low order, as it were. Tension and beauty are obvious. As seen above, the quotations from the *Bṛhadāraṇyakôpaniṣad*, *Taittirīyôpaniṣad*, and *Kaṭhôpaniṣad* are well known, inherently familiar and authoritative for any audience receptive to Advaita sources. The addition of the low-order illustration is strictly unnecessary, almost inappropriate, vulgarizing, one could say, the knowledge of Brahman. The authorship of the BSBh is behind the strictly unnecessary addition; opponent and *siddhāntin* are somewhat unlikely figures of the author's sophisticated, playful mind.

The gap between the sophisticated author and the two creatures of his mind is made evident by further consideration of the mud-illustration in the context of commenting on the Upaniṣadic *nêti nêti*. The mud-*dṛṣṭānta* joke seems to hit at Yājñavalkya's own *nêti nêti*; for why negate the world and *saguṇa-brahman* (by *nêti nêti*) rather than directly affirm the existence of *nirguṇa* Brahman? Why, indeed, wash one's hands rather than avoid dirt altogether? In this context, I think, the mud-*dṛṣṭānta* is subtly suggestive of Vedic insufficiency as an effective means of knowledge. Thus, the *siddhāntin* becomes somewhat self-contradictory (like the *pūrva-pakṣin*).

Changes of voice are succinct expressions of the content-free dimension of the author's voice. Thus, the author feels free to embed the mud-cliché in the opponent's mouth. The opponent—wisely and deliberately—makes use of the cliché for his own purpose; if the Veda endorses the two modes of Brahman—with and without form—why should it negate the same? The *siddhāntin* asserts that Brahman is not an effect but rather the real ground and cause of everything. As such it cannot be negated.

Effects we know to have no real existence, and they can therefore be negated; not so, however, Brahman, which constitutes the necessary basis for all fictitious superimposition. The *siddhāntin*'s assertion of the scope of negation sounds throughout the BSBh. For example, heeding the inherently subjective nature of Brahman (made of self), the author introduces a statement such as "I do not exist" (*nâham asmi*)[7] as an impossibility (*na nâham asmîti*). Thus, the *siddhāntin*'s opening statement is truly profound, and echoes some of the prevailing themes in Śaṅkara's work. Resistance to multiplicity breeds affirmation of oneness; negation of the seen or familiar brings about knowledge of the unseen, etc. But why indeed wash one's hands rather than remain unsoiled? The opponent has his own sense of humor. Embedded in the *siddhāntin*'s voice, namely, within the winner's position, the opponent asserts that the Veda contradicts itself; and he makes ironical use of the cliché:

> Nor must the question be asked here, how the sacred text, after having itself set forth the two forms of Brahman, can subsequently negate them, contrary to the principle that not to touch dirt is better than bathing after having done so.[8]

The voice uttering the mud cliché the second time is thus patently different from the first voicing of the utterance. In the first occurrence it is the exponent's voice (saying that it is inconceivable that the Upaniṣads negate the existence of Brahman after having established its existence throughout). In the second occurrence it is the *pūrva-pakṣin* who makes use of the cliché, apparently much loved by the author. He says that the Upaniṣad cannot negate the two forms of Brahman after having established their existence. Thus, the proposition of both exponent and opponent is apparently the same; it is unlikely that the Veda contradicts itself. If the Veda asserts the existence of Brahman (says the *siddhāntin*), it cannot negate this existence by Yājñavalkya's *nêti nêti*.

The mud-cliché is ultimately a blatant denial of the value of negation. Better to affirm initially rather than to lose oneself in the complexities of negation-affirmation. The logical force of the cliché implied by exponent and opponent alike seems to be grounded in the notion of coherence; to negate something assumed elsewhere to have a measure of existence implies a contradiction (rather than transformation). Thus, the mud-cliché voiced by the exponent as well as by the oppo-

---

[7] See BSBh 1.1.1. This is "Śaṅkara's cogito" argument.

[8] Ibid., p. 168 (*na câtrêyam āśaṅkā kartavyā—kathaṃ hi śāstraṃ svayam eva brahmaṇo rūpa-dvayaṃ darśayitvā svayam eva punaḥ pratiṣedhati—prakṣālanād dhi paṅkasya dūrād asparśanaṃ varam iti*).

nent is incompatible with Yājñavalkya's *nêti nêti* and with Śaṅkara's (the author's) view of transformational negation.

As seen above, the author of the BSBh (1.1.4) suggests that Vedic power as a reliable means of knowledge (*pramāṇa*) consists in negating (removing) plurality (rather than straight affirmation of Brahman). Śaṅkara, as we have seen, recommends positive, transformational negation, which generates truth, or affirmation of Brahman or *ātman*. Keeping in mind Freud's evaluation of negation as a move toward discovering deeply buried truths, we observe that the author's relationship with his exponent is infused with ambivalence. The exponent, to be sure, holds a position which is very close to that of the author, asserting that Yājñavalkya's *nêti nêti* negates everything but (*nirguṇa*) Brahman. However, his doubt-free expression and the apparently inappropriate use he makes of the mud-cliché suggest the author's dissociation from his chosen *siddhāntin*. Embedding the cliché into the arguments of the *siddhāntin* as well as the *pūrva-pakṣin* suggests a palpable gap between the author and his characters.

Thus, if the author's voice is to be distinguished from those of his various sub-heroes', who is the author? Was he an energetic scholarly sādhu of the eighth century, a hectically active personality, who came to dominate the intellectual life of the Indian subcontinent, unifying India under the flag of Advaita-Vedānta? In that case, we could assume that the text would include notes of urgent communication and would reveal an awareness of his audience. Was the author a lonely mystic intoxicated with the discovery of the Self? Was he a scholar immersed in texts and polemics and tormented by far-reaching doubts? In my view, these questions are pertinent and need to be raised. However, the circumstances of Śaṅkara's childhood, adolescence, education, even the date and place of his birth are shrouded in uncertainty. Information about such circumstances is unavailable, or flimsy.

And yet, we have at our disposal a solid start: The author of the *Brahma-sūtra-bhāṣya*, *Upadeśa-sāhasrī*, etc. was the author of the *Brahma-sūtra-bhāṣya*, *Upadeśa-sāhasrī*, etc. The process of composing such works presupposes an author who imagines a variety of characters, winners and losers, more or less clever. The author's imagination of his exponents and opponents is, in fact, our only clue to the otherwise invisible source of the BSBh and Śaṅkara's other works. Suppose for a moment that the Upad is Śaṅkara's work; the following first-person statement (Upad 2.7.2), verbalized by the absolute self himself, becomes an example of a telling statement in regard to the author:

> As I am the witness (*sākṣin*) of everything whatsoever, I see others' objects of thought as I see my own. I may neither be rejected nor approved of. Therefore I am supreme (*yathâtma-buddhi-cārāṇāṃ sākṣī tadvat pareṣv api/ nâivâpoḍhuṃ na vâdātuṃ śakyas tasmāt paro hy aham//*).

The *siddhāntin*'s mind, we suggest, could by no means produce such a statement. As we read the BSBh, BUBh, and Śaṅkara's other works, we become attuned to the differing registers and resonances of the multiple voices. The voice of *ātman* speaking in the first-person has a very different tone from that of the *siddhāntin*'s staunchly Advaitin, doubt-free and seemingly uni-dimensional exclamations.

But even if we resist including the Upad among our author's works, we see that the definitive *bhāṣya-kāra* of the BS provides us with clues to his rich, complex, somewhat liberated identity, significantly free from the dichotomy between winner and loser. The mud-cliché, as we have seen, used by both exponent and opponent, is a "negation of negation" (namely, denying the value of negation). Contrary to both his exponent and opponent, the author seems to say that it is better to get dirty and then wash one's hands than to stay out of the mud and thereby make no use of the transformational power of negation.

CHAPTER NINE

ADVAITA MESSAGES AND FOREIGN VOICES: SOME PHILOSOPHICAL MEANINGS OF ŚAṄKARA'S ART OF WRITING

The distinction between author and *siddhāntin* raises questions about the author; who exactly was he? The author, some would argue, is inherently unknown; Śaṅkara the writer of the eighth century is beyond our reach. So why raise questions about an unknowable author? Thus, under the circumstances of the "inherent unknowability of the author," the mechanical identification of author and *siddhāntin* underlies any speech-act about Śaṅkara the author of the BSBh. And yet, the composition itself reveals aspects of the author lurking behind the interplay of voices. The masterly creation of the voices of exponent and opponents, the wit and nature of the text's scholarship, the role of reasoning and its relation to Upaniṣadic origins, the relationship of message to source—all these are signposts to the author's presence, his point of view, his metaphysics. Thus, "the author of the BSBh is the author of the BSBh" is far from being an empty tautology.

Śaṅkara's creation is evidently scholarly and based on written texts. Like Bādarāyaṇa, Śaṅkara studies the Upaniṣads (and Bādarāyaṇa's *Brahma-sūtra* as well). Śaṅkara's written composition is a quest after coherence and inter-textuality and leaves no doubt with respect to the scholarly, literary nature of Śaṅkara's work. Thus, Śaṅkara the author of the BSBh is grounded in study as "extended sequential analysis."[1] If Śaṅkara was ever a sage speaking to an audience, the BSBh does not show any evidence of that; the BSBh is essentially a study of the BS and the Upaniṣads. There is no trace of orality in the BSBh. "Human beings in primary oral cultures, those untouched by writing in any form, learn a great deal and possess and practice great wisdom, but they do not 'study.'"[2] However, the distinction between the orally transmitted and the written text does, I think, present itself in Śaṅkara's writing. Quotations from the Veda, particularly from the Upaniṣads and also

---

[1] Ong 1982: 9.
[2] Ibid. ibid. Close reading means enhanced attention to multi-vocality.

from *smṛti* compositions such as the Bhagavadgītā, seem to be deeply ingrained, memorized, internalized and ready for use.

The complexity of the composition is striking; quotations from the Upaniṣads as well as illustrations from everyday life are brought together by the author's rigorous reasoning and the inherent multivocality of the text, suggesting an intense imagination controlled by a synthesizing aesthetic drive. Bakhtin sums up the difference between an author's truly dialogical mood and a philosophical monologue:

> In an environment of philosophical monologism the genuine interaction of consciousnesses is impossible, and thus genuine dialogue is impossible as well. In essence idealism knows only a single mode of cognitive interaction among consciousnesses; someone who knows and possesses the truth instructs someone who is ignorant of it and in error; that is, it is the interaction of a teacher and a pupil, which, it follows, can be only a pedagogical dialogue.[3]

Consider, for example, the multi-vocality in the piece of literature to be discussed below (BSBh 1.1.4). The exponent's opponent introduces the exponent's position in a subdued voice; a Mīmāṃsaka asserts that statements of fact are subordinate to imperative ones. Indicative statements which do not serve some imperative—statements such as "This king marches on" or "There are seven continents in the world"—are, he claims, insignificant and ineffective. But, says the exponent in his *pūrva-pakṣin*'s role, sometimes statements of mere facts do have some use; thus, for example, "This (apparent) snake is (really) a rope" is a statement effective in the removal of fear (of the snake). Very nice, says the victorious *siddhānta-pūrva-pakṣin*, I concede such a possibility. But statements of Brahman's being are not like this. A Brahmin who listens to such statements (such as *tat tvam asi*) remains the same, untransformed, as he had been before (*yathā-pūrvam*), affected by pleasures and pains.

Embedding the winner's voice in the loser's one reveals a simple truth: here is a writer who lets his chosen *siddhāntin* lose the battle, at least for the length of a long paragraph. Witty, enjoying himself, the author allows philosophical foreplay to unfold. Stitching voices together, the author of the BSBh stands apart from the sounds and voices he plays with.

---

[3] Bakhtin 1993: 81.

Śaṅkarācārya is known to have been a good writer. Even scholars who conflate the voice of author and *siddhāntin* recognize his greatness. In Ingalls words:

> Śaṅkara, I think, was not unaware of his literary gifts, but he makes no needless display of them, and purple passages are rare in his works. When they come, however, their effect is overwhelming. Such are the full-dress arguments put in dialogue form in the Bṛhadāraṇyaka and Brahmasūtra commentaries. Quite aside from the question of philosophy, these dialogues simply as dramatic literature are magnificent.[4]

What, then, is the philosophical meaning of Śaṅkara's art of writing? Is the author's metaphysic different from that of his chosen *siddhāntin*'s? Is there, as we have asked previously, a particular quality of voice present in the various compositions ascribed to Śaṅkara?

But then one could argue that the author of the BSBh is not the one who composed the Upad or the BUBh. In response, I would say that we trust the work of great scholars and authorities such as Ingalls, S. Mayeda, H. Nakamura, and others, who like other serious scholars, identify the author of the BSBh with the author of the BUBh, BGBh, and Upad.

Yet there are controversies with respect to many issues in Śaṅkara's authorship. Take, for example an eerie statement such as Upad 2.7.1: "I am the supreme Brahman, omniscient, omnipresent" (*paraṃ brahma sarva-jñaś câsmi sarva-gaḥ*) or "Since I am free of any particular quality, I have no benefit whatsoever from your doings."[5] The statements are unlikely to have been composed by a sober theologian and logician of Śaṅkara's nature; the author of the BSBh never speaks in the first-person from the *ātman*'s point of view. But, an opponent's opponent would say, is it really so unlikely? Though Brahman is inherently, necessarily silent, a great and gifted writer, confident of his vision and art, could have been creative enough to imagine the one self speaking. This first-person speech is a radical and effective technique. *Ātman*, the motionless, self-sufficient innermost self rebukes the congealed, egocentric, unceasingly active individual self as a nuisance! This is new, revealing an Advaitin's inner thinking (or psychology); his *ātman* is disturbed, as it were (see above, Ch. 3). However, if we require consistency with the strict philosopher/theologian Advaitin figure, Śaṅkara

---

[4] Ingalls 1952: 1–14.
[5] Upad 8.2.

the author of the BSBh may not be the author of the Upad (or of some portions thereof).

Let us, then, renounce the identification of the author of the BSBh with the author of the Upad. Let us suppose only that the author of the BSBh is the author of the BSBh. Who was he? But, an opponent could say, why identify the author of the first *adhyāya* with that of the second *adhyāya*? Why, in other words, consider the author of the BSBh as one agent? Let it be so (we say). Let us address only one paragraph as Śaṅkara's. Well done and said, says the opponent. What portion would you choose? I would go for BSBh 1.1.4, opening with statements of the omniscient and omnipotent Brahman, which is the cause of the emergence, existence and disappearance of the universe, to be known by means of the Upaniṣads only. It then proceeds to reflect on the difference between "acting" and "knowing", and various expressions of the abysmal split of *dharma* and *mokṣa*, of natural existence and liberation, disembodiment as a definitive aspect of *mokṣa*, and so on.

Thus, our initial question is rephrased as follows: who was Śaṅkara the author of BSBh 1.1.4?

BSBh 1.1.4 is Śaṅkara's longest commentary on Bādarāyaṇa's *Brahma-sūtra*. It is rich in metaphysical content, offering Śaṅkara's entire metaphysics of the unity of self; there is no principle of philosophy absent in this large *bhāṣya*. It is also one of the most successful artistic expressions of Śaṅkara's *bhāṣya*. In its reflections on the relevance of voice to the location of Vedic truth (and the nature of "knowledge"), it is also philosophically significant.

In Śaṅkara's BSBh 1.1.4, centered on the efficacy of Upaniṣadic speech, an Advaitin and a Mīmāṃsaka express similar statements about Brahman or *ātman*. The *ātman* is eternal (*nitya*), pure, free. However, as Śaṅkara suggests, the force of the knowledge of Brahman manifested in the Mīmāṃsaka's verbalization is strikingly different from that (knowledge) verbalized by the Vedāntin. At the climax of the debate, the Mīmāṃsaka says that knowledge of *ātman* does not make one free of *saṃsāra*. Therefore, he concludes, it is and should be subordinate to the prescriptive mood of the Veda, a mood grounded in a vision of multiplicity. However, according to Śaṅkara's Advaitin, the Vedāntin's knowledge of Brahman and *ātman*, while apparently similar (in its verbalized references to Brahman), is totally different in force from the knowledge possessed by the Mīmāṃsaka. The Vedāntin's knowledge is powerful, liberating from *saṃsāra*. Manipulating rival speech through an aesthetically rewarding presentation of voices, Śaṅkara says something about the force of Vedic speech, its potency suggested in voice no less than in content.

What is the difference between an Advaita proposition articulated by an Advaitin and the "same" proposition uttered by someone else? Perhaps we should preface this question with another: Is there a difference between an Advaita idea expressed by a "primary Advaitin" and the "same" idea offered by a "secondary Advaitin" (created by a non-Advaitin as a *pūrva-pakṣin*)? Such questions are of philosophical significance; they raise issues of language, truth, meaning, and the adequate voice of liberation. Underlying such questions is the assumption of the possible distance between oneself and one's speech, and the relevance of voice as a dimension of authority and truth. Under some circumstances the linguistic unity pertinent to the discourse is voiced, and its truth-value is qualified and conditioned by its auditory dimension. Thus, Śaṅkara, I suggest, deals with auditory dimensions of speech and truth in his artful exposition of encounters with opponents who speak of the self and the absolute as if they shared knowledge of Advaita, and likewise with opponents who invoke their shadow-Advaitins who speak, as Advaitins should, Advaita messages of *ātman* and Brahman.

The potency of metaphysics is a major underlying theme of Śaṅkara's philosophical interests. Since Advaita metaphysics is—if truly understood—inexorably powerful, metaphysical discussion is fateful. Vedic speech, according to Śaṅkara, highlights and creates a new self, *ātman*. Sacred speech correctly understood (absorbed in its true voice) thus carries a benevolent, healing truth. If misunderstood, establishing a false or liable-to-sorrow self, the Veda may bring terrible pain. Thus, for example, says Śaṅkara, if by hermeneutical accident one concludes that scripture upholds a dualist (Sāṅkhya) vision of existence, along with a particular self-understanding commensurate with it, disaster awaits.[6] The power of Vedāntic speech, however, is associated with its being uniformly, inherently, and necessarily true.

Intellectual disputes, dialogues with opponents (*pūrva-pakṣins*), are foundational to Śaṅkara's exposition of Advaita discourse and Advaitic views. The opponents' presence is essential, inherent in Śaṅkara's presentation and production (performance) of the Vedāntic voice. None of the *Brahma-sūtra-bhāṣyas* is opponent-free. As Advaita messages

[6] See, for example, BSBh 1.1.7.

dubbed in conventional meanings of words may be materialized by foreign voices, the difference between an "authoritative Advaitin" and his opponent cannot be exhausted by reference to conventional meanings alone. Some sort of "Vedic intention" must be assumed to exist in Śaṅkara's horizon if he embeds Vedic meanings within his opponents' voices. Such meanings must be allowed to be untrue if dissociated from the "right voice."

Indeed, the structure of the *pūrva-pakṣin*'s assertions reveals the coherence of Śankara's argument. Evidently, the *pūrva-pakṣin*'s is by definition a loser's voice, and as such cannot carry truth (even if literally "correct"). Thus, the "primary *pūrva-pakṣin*" (the Mīmāṃsaka) is explicitly incapable of performing (expressing) Vedic truth (if only for the reason that such performance undermines his very existence as a Mīmāṃsaka). The Vedāntin as "secondary *pūrva-pakṣin*" (*pūrva-pakṣin's pūrva-pakṣin*) is also necessarily a loser, reacting to, adjusting himself to his opponent's vision (grounded in the perspective of multiplicity). The *pūrva-pakṣin's* subordination in the debate reflects the necessarily inferior quality of his voice. It is necessarily weak, subdued, untrue. Vedic truth thus—and this is one major philosophical significance of "Śaṅkara's art of writing"—abides in adequately voiced, register-bound propositions rather than in abstract, voiceless sentences.

In the course of BSBh 1.1.4, Śaṅkara creates two contexts of incongruity between voice and message. In one, a Mīmāṃsaka asserts Vedāntic messages; thus, for example, in section 53 of my translation (below): "As you know, the Veda teaches us all that Brahman is eternal, omniscient (*sarva-jña*), existing everywhere (*sarva-gata*), ever-content, inherently and always pure, conscious, free (*nitya-śuddha-buddha-mukta-svabhāva*); it is consciousness, joy, and so forth." Such statements are naturally understood as "Advaita messages." Śaṅkara embeds them in the Mīmāṃsaka 's voice, creating thereby an aesthetic effect (the reader's pleasure).

The second context of incongruity between voice and message is somewhat more difficult to notice. It is the incompatibility of an Advaita message which, while pronounced through an Advaitin's voice, is spoken in his loser's (*pūrva-pakṣin*'s) role. I will attempt to illustrate this incongruity through the creation of "implied" speakers alongside the actual textual voices, trying thus to tease out textual voices which are present, though not spoken. For example, according to statements 41–49 (below):

41) **Mīmāṃsaka**: If you accept—as you hopefully do—that Vedānta is necessarily connected with (underlying) prescriptions, then just as sacrifices like the *agnihotra* are means for people desiring conditions such as heaven (*svargâdi-kāma*), the knowledge of Brahman is prescribed for one who wishes for immortality (*amṛtatva*)!
42) **Advaitin**: Yes, but there is still a difference concerning the thing to be known. For in the Karma-kāṇda the thing to be known is *dharma*, which may come into being (*bhāvya)* (but is not necessarily existent), whereas here (in our Vedānta texts) what is to be known is Brahman, always existent (*nitya-nirvṛtta*), which is an established reality (*bhūta*).
43) **Implied Mīmāṃsaka**: [And yet, the Veda is one, and as such is necessarily instrumental in achieving results.]
44) **Advaitin**: But due to the difference in the nature of Brahman and *dharma*, there must be a difference in the fruits resulting from the knowledge of *dharma* (*dharma-jñāna-phala*) and those consequent upon the knowledge of Brahman (*brahma-jñāna-phala*). It is only appropriate (to respect the aforementioned difference in this way) (*tatra.....bhavitum arhati*).
45) **Mīmāṃsaka**: No; it is inappropriate (*nârhaty evaṃ bhavitum*).
46) **Implied Advaitin**: [Why?]
47) **Mīmāṃsaka**: For the Veda teaches of Brahman as connected with actions according to prescription.
48) **Implied Advaitin**: [But Vedic statements of fact are distinct from prescription! Especially with respect to Brahman—as I have already said—there is not even a touch of prescriptive attitude visible in the Veda! The Vedānta texts are in danger of being utterly useless.]
49) **Mīmāṃsaka**: Oh, no. Please notice the following assertions: "The *ātman*, lady, should be seen" (BU 2.4.5); "This *ātman*, free of any blemish, is what should be sought after, that which should be known" (*ya ātmā 'pahata-pāpma so 'nveṣṭavyaḥ sa vijijñāsitavyaḥ*) (ChU 8.7.1); "let a man meditate on the *ātman* only" (BU 1.4.7); "let a man meditate on the world as the *ātman* only" (*ātmānam eva lokam upāsīta*) (BU 1.4.15); "whoever knows Brahman becomes Brahman" (*brahma veda brahmâiva bhavati*) (MU 3.2.9). [You see, the knowledge of Brahman embedded within the prescriptive mood of the Upaniṣads, expressed in the gerundive (*anveṣṭavya*, *vijijñāsitavya*) and optative (*upāsīta*) endings, naturally and beautifully makes sense.]

This presentation has a significant shortcoming; it suppresses the distinction between the *siddhāntin* and the *pūrva-pakṣin*, a distinction foundational and evident in reading Śaṅkara. While the transitions of thought are made more apparent and clear-cut (aided by the insertion of "implied speakers"), the distinction between the *siddhāntin* and *pūrva-pakṣin* is somewhat blurred. Especially in cases—such as BSBh 1.1.4—when *pūrva-pakṣins* and *siddhāntins* speak similar "truths" (such as that of the immortal *ātman*), it is strictly necessary to listen to their respective voices. Consequently, a representation of the Advaitin/ Mīmāṃsaka exchange such as the above, mitigating the distinction between primary speaker and *pūrva-pakṣin* is significantly misleading. However, the clear-cut distinction is always there in Śaṅkara's *bhāṣyas*, as G. Thibaut's excellent translation of the same text (sections 41–49 in our presentation) clarifies:

> (The Mīmāṃsaka speaking): "Hence the Vedānta texts also as likewise belonging to the Veda can have a meaning in the same way only. And if their aim is injunction, then just as the agnihotra-oblation and other rites are enjoined as means for him who is desirous of immortality.—But—somebody might object—it has been declared that there is a difference in the character of the objects enquired into, the object of enquiry in the karma-kāṇḍa (that part of the Veda which treats of active religious duty) being something to be accomplished, viz. duty, while here the object is the already existent absolutely accomplished Brahman. From this it follows that the fruit of the knowledge of duty which depends on the performance of actions.—We reply that it must not be such because the Vedānta texts give information about Brahman only in so far as it is connected with injunctions of actions. We meet with injunctions of the following kind, 'Verily the Self is to be seen' (Bṛ Up ii.4.5); 'The Self which is free from sin that it is which we must search out, that it is which we must try to understand' (Kh. Up viii.7.1); 'Let a man worship him as Self' (Bṛ Up i.4.7); 'Let a man worship the Self only as his true state' (Bṛ Up i.4.15); 'He who knows Brahman becomes Brahman' (Mu Up iii.2.9)."

Thibaut beautifully presents the Advaitin in his role as *pūrva-pakṣin*; ("—But—somebody might object—"). The "somebody" is obviously the Advaitin in his *pūrva-pakṣin*'s weak, subdued, loser's voice. The Mīmāṃsaka controls the debate. Pleading for the unity of the Veda, he generously offers a big benefit for the knowledge of Brahman (immortality). Moreover, he cites well-known Upaniṣadic passages, all of them very close to Śaṅkara's heart. The Advaitin's response is inferior in voice. He suggests a difference between the *jñāna-kāṇḍa* and the *karma-kāṇḍa*, rejecting the Mīmāṃsaka's graceful offer of meaning and purpose for knowledge of Brahman. While insisting on his views, the Advaitin (as the Mīmāṃsaka's "somebody") is invoked by his rival and is defeated in due course. Closely listening to the relationship of the speaking selves to the contents of their speech, one realizes that Śaṅkara's art of writing reflects on the significance of voice in the adequate reception of Vedic truth.

For most philosophers, truth abides in voiceless, register-free propositions or texts.[7] The philosopher's voice is made to sound consciously abstract, scientific, clear: "Entification begins at arm's length; the points of condensation in the primordial conceptual scheme are things glimpsed, not glimpses."[8] Such a statement appears context-free, voiceless; it has a seemingly objective, autonomous meaning in the sense that it may in principle be read in silence in one's room, recited in the presence of a devoted student, uttered in a classroom or elsewhere. Its validity is explicitly independent of the context of its production or performance. Prevailing philosophical discourse rests upon reduction in the dimensions of speaking. It is thus grounded solely in the use of clear-cut language and on the power of argument. For example:

> The *I think* must be *capable* of accompanying all my presentations; otherwise something would be presented to me which could not be thought at all, which means no less than: the presentation could be either impossible, or at least nothing to me.... Consequently every manifold of perception has a necessary relation to the *I think*, in the same subject in which the manifold is found.[9]

But as suggested above, according to Śaṅkara's presentation, Vedic truth may abide in fuller, multi-dimensional speech, not necessarily in abstract propositions received solely by attending to conventional meanings. However, representations of "Indian philosophy" have often reflected premises of the voicelessness characteristic of philosophical expression. An aggressive orientation has often accompanied such decontextualization of Vedic speech, and the results have sometimes been of a somewhat denigrating nature. This is how A.B. Keith sums up the teaching of the Upaniṣads (along with his evaluation):

> But the identity of the self and the absolute is based merely on the abstraction of the self as subjectivity, and that of the absolute as subjectivity, and the identity is therefore meaningless and a mere matter of words.[10]

---

[7] L. Wittgenstein, in his *Philosophical Investigations*, challenges context-free philosophizing.
[8] W.V.O. Quine, 1973: 1.
[9] E. Kant, *Critique of Pure Reason*, 108, B 131, in S. Korner 1982: 61.
[10] Keith 1925: 593.

Thus, the momentous discovery of Upaniṣadic culture—the unity, identity of pure subjectivity with the—seemingly, mistakenly, allegedly objective—essence of the "world"—becomes void under the scorching eyes of the philosopher. But is not Keith's rendering of the Upaniṣadic essential statements of identity (such as *tat tvam asi*) too harsh? In Keith's mode of analysis, any statement of identity may be said to be "a mere matter of words". However, the tautology "The morning star is the morning star" and the meaningful "The morning star is the evening star" (a real discovery) are patently different.[11] Why reduce the *tat tvam asi* to tautology? Though the reference of *tat* and *tvam* may be the same (and this is the apex of the Upaniṣadic discovery), the meanings of these terms (as the vehicles to reach the moment of identifying their respective references) have attracted the attention and concentration of the best minds in the history of Indian reflection on such statements of identity.

> However, it is also important for Śaṅkara that before one can properly execute such an analysis of the sentence "That thou art" one must first of all, as with the analysis of any sentence, call to mind the correct meanings of the individual terms. This process of recollection involves the application of the method of retaining what is constant and abandoning what is not constant (*anvaya-vyatireka*) in order to determine the proper sense of the word *tvam*. Once accomplished, this automatically makes the proper sense of the word *tat* clear and, in turn, leads to the possibility of understanding the meaning of the sentence "That thou art" in the correct manner.[12]

Vedic statements such as *tat tvam asi* may be more fully contextualized.[13] The semantics of Advaita messages may not be enough—in Śaṅkara's view—to move the listener to a full understanding of the message.

Can the highest truths of Vedānta be significantly voice-free? Would Śaṅkara consider anybody's recitation of *tat tvam asi*—say in a

---

[11] This is a well known illustration dealing with the difference of meaning and reference, found in G. Frege's "On Sense and Reference." See Frege 1952.

[12] Kocmarek 1985: 23–4.

[13] See Paul Ricoeur: "...if a text can have several meanings, for example a historical meaning and a spiritual meaning, we must appeal to a notion of signification that is much more complex than the system of so-called univocal signs required by the logic of argumentation.... the very work of interpretation reveals a profound intention, that of overcoming distance and cultural differences and of matching the reader to a text which has become foreign, thereby incorporating its meaning into the present comprehension a man is able to have of himself." (Ricoeur 1974: 4).

classroom—as asserting *tat tvam asi*? As suggested above, in his BSBh 1.1.4, Śaṅkara points out the importance of voice (a type of context) by his art of writing centered in the presentation of the dialogue between the Advaitin and his (Mīmāṃsaka) opponent.

As noted above, Śaṅkara's *Brahma-sūtra-bhāṣya* is the norm of his authority and authorship; all other works ascribed to Śaṅkara are measured against the BSBh. However, the BSBh reaching our eyes is a skeleton, abstracted from rich, fulfilling exchanges of thought and emotion, and thus in need of clothing, re-enactment, embodiment, fulfillment, and interpretation.[14] Such re-embodiment is concomitantly an unearthing, as it were, since the flesh in this case is less accessible than the skeleton, consisting of fundamental yet less accessible differences in vision.

In this chapter I offer close reading of Śaṅkara's longest *bhāṣya*—1.1.4—in the spirit of embodiment and "fulfillment." One of its expressions is the identification of the "main concern" of the text (dialogue). Though the ideas and various contents discussed in BSBh 1.1.4 are numerous, it is possible to locate the true center of the verbal exchange between the two rivals, the real issue of the fight. The focus of the debate between the Advaitin and the Mīmāṃsaka is the commensurability of Vedānta (and the knowledge of Brahman) with the universe of multiplicity grounded in the distinction between agent, action, and result. According to both (Advaitin and Mīmāṃsaka), if truly potent, knowledge of Brahman is incompatible with Vedic prescriptions of *dharma* and *adharma*, prescriptions rooted in embodiment, pleasure and pain, and multiplicity (*saṃsāra*). The essential disagreement is whether knowledge of Brahman is indeed truly potent. Since it is not, says the Mīmāṃsaka, Vedānta is compatible with ("subordinate" to, part of) the prescriptive Veda. Since it is (truly potent), says the Advaitin, it is *incompatible* with Vedic prescriptions of *dharma* and *adharma*, with embodiment, pleasure and pain, multiplicity, and *saṃsāra*. The issue is thus an aspect of the nature of knowledge of Brahman, an aspect different from the merely conceptual contents of such knowledge, since the Advaitin and Mīmāṃsaka seem to share such contents while differing radically in other respects.

[14] These were David Shulman's instructive words, addressed to me some 15 years ago, in the course of a talk on the nature of Śaṅkara's texts and their availability to us. It is now obvious to me that close reading of Indian philosophical masterpieces (such as Śaṅkara's BSBh) implies recognition of their skeletal presence, and a spirit of clothing, "fulfillment," etc.

The dialogue opening BSBh 1.1.4 is rich in content; the nature of Brahman, Vedic authority, the relationship of "knowledge" to prescription, the relationship of revelation to reasoning (*anumāna*), the scope and essence of *mokṣa*—these are among the topics discussed. Most of these issues have been raised in the opening *bhāṣyas* (BSBh 1.1.1–3), especially in the *bhāṣya* preceding BSBh 1.1.4 (namely, 1.1.3). In particular, topics especially pertinent to the Advaitin/Mīmāṃsaka dialogue, such as the Veda's primary mood (prescriptive or indicative), are salient in BSBh 1.1.3. Such topics may be considered as background to the debate unfolded in of BSBh 1.1.4. Thus, even if reformulated in BSBh 1.1.4, they may still be regarded as an active context for the new and attractive underlying theme suggested in the long opening section of BSBh 1.1.4.

In Śaṅkara's presentation unfolded in BSBh 1.1.4, the core controversy between a Pūrva-Mīmāṃsaka and an Advaitin is the assessment of the efficacy and force of Vedānta assertions about the self. It is an occasion to express a typically dramatic aspect of metaphysical discourse in India; differences of outlook are often seen to involve differences of experience and vision inadequately mediated by reasoning. Specifically, the subject discussed in Śaṅkara's presentation of BSBh 1.1.4—the rivals' differing assessments of the force of Vedic speech (and therefore the nature of "knowledge")—nicely illustrates characteristic aspects of Indian philosophical discourse. The apparent similarity between the rivals' surface-meanings ("knowledge") concerning *ātman* and Brahman highlights, somewhat paradoxically, vast experiential differences. As seen above, the Mīmāṃsaka concedes that the Vedānta texts speak of *ātman* as eternal, pure, omniscient, bliss. However, he maintains that such Vedāntic references to Brahman are weak, unable to overrule the viable vision of reality of multiplicity based on distinctions such as those between agent, action, and results. In contrast, the Advaitin considers Vedāntic speech as inherently effective, sufficiently powerful to undermine the reality of the distinctions (necessary for the Mīmāṃsaka's universe of instrumental sacrifice to exist). Thus, the Advaitin negates the possibility of co-existence with the Mīmāṃsaka, since knowledge of the absolute makes the culture of *dharma*, sacrifice and its agents and fruits futile, or even impossible.[15]

[15] Such a possible interpretation of the tension between action and knowledge is succinctly expressed by K. Potter: "As he (Śaṅkara) sees it, an agent cannot have

The Mīmāṃsaka shares with the Advaitin the impossibility of their mutual co-existence (if knowledge of self is powerful as the Advaitin proposes). However, he argues about the force of knowledge provided by the Vedānta-texts. At the climax of the dispute articulated in BSBh 1.1.4, the Mīmāṃsaka asserts that Vedānta is incapable of delivering the end of *saṃsāra*. Though having heard about Brahman, one remains deeply mired in the sorrows and joys of transmigratory existence. Unlike statements such as "This is not a snake, but a rope"—assertions patently effective under certain circumstances—the propositions of Vedānta are not potent enough to change one's vision of reality. In Śaṅkara's *pūrva-pakṣin's* (Mīmāṃsaka's) language, if Vedāntic speech were indeed like the statement of the snake and the rope, it *would* undermine (*nivarteta*) *saṃsāra*. However, it does not (*na tu nivartate*)! This exchange of attitude over the efficacy of Vedāntic knowledge is the new, exciting theme developed throughout the opening section of BSBh 1.1.4. Indeed, this moment in the course of the Advaitin/Mīmāṃsaka encounter according to BSBh 1.1.4 is the apex of Śaṅkara's playful, artistic enterprise.

What is the nature of the Mīmāṃsaka's negative appraisal of the efficacy of Vedāntic knowledge of the self? Although hearing of Brahman, one stays as before (*yathā-pūrvam*), attached to pleasures and woes in *saṃsāra*, says the Mīmāṃsaka. Such a statement—the alleged climax of the Advaitin/Mīmāṃsaka encounter—is an occasion for "fulfillment" of the skeletal presentation of the debate. The first question to be raised concerns the identity of the unregenerated person presented by the Mīmāṃsaka as proof (or illustration) of the inefficacy of Vedāntic knowledge. Who is the poor Brahmin unable to extricate himself from *saṃsāra* (though hearing of Brahman so many times)? Is it anyone and everyone (including the Vedāntin)? Or is the poor Brahmin the Mīmāṃsaka himself, confessing his failure (assessing it as of universal significance with respect to the power of Vedāntic speech)?

---

knowledge, and a true knower cannot act. Thus, it is knowledge which leads to the abandonment of action, not the reverse. Nonattached action is always action, and actions breed karmic consequences inexorably. The only way finally to destroy all actions is by gaining the knowledge which makes acting impossible—the awareness of the lack of distinctions in reality. 'Nonattached action' is a contradiction in terms for Śaṅkara—action must involve intentionality, the purposive interest of an agent for a distinct outcome to be gained through a specific activity. Only the realization that all these distinctions are illusory can undermine karma-producing activity; as a result of knowledge one can get nonattachment, but only so." Potter 1982: 113.

I believe the latter interpretation more appropriate, and aesthetically more satisfactory; in his very person the Mīmāṃsaka illustrates the Advaitin's allegations that whoever does not understand Vedānta remains as he was. Taken as a confession, the Mīmāṃsaka attests to his own failure! However, the Mīmāṃsaka's assertion is of double meaning; he confesses to being a *saṃsārin* (though having often heard of Brahman), but he also blames the Vedānta texts for their impotence. It is a complex moment of apparent victory and actual defeat, terminating the Mīmāṃsaka's role as a *siddhāntin* (see below).

For his part, Śaṅkara's Advaitin asserts that a true understanding of Vedānta propositions transforms one's vision of reality. Such propositions do—irreversibly!—remove the vision of agents, actions, and consequences. The Advaitin's obvious suggestion is that if the Mīmāṃsaka understood Vedānta, he would not be a Mīmāṃsaka. Thus the true center of the Advaitin/Mīmāṃsaka dispute is the transformative power of Vedāntic speech. No compromise on this issue seems possible for either of the rivals; one of them must be a more adequate exponent of Upaniṣadic meanings.

In order to facilitate discussion of Śaṅkara's "art of writing" I have reconstructed the opening section of BSBh 1.1.4, emphasizing the theme I consider as underlying Śaṅkara's presentation of the Advaitin's encounter with his Mīmāṃsaka opponent (the force of Vedic voice). In order to embody the skeletal exchange between the two rivals and to elucidate its structure, I have written this opening section of BSBh 1.1.4 as a "philosophical play." To account as much as possible for every transition of thought in the course of this seemingly repetitive debate, I have inserted "implied" Mīmāṃsakas or Advaitins to amplify unspoken voices in the exchange. I think this insertion is in the spirit of Śaṅkara's own (however concise) invocations of *pūrva-pakṣin*s. It is, however, advisable to consult Thibaut's translation in order to experience more fully, if desired, the status (*siddhāntin*, *pūrva-pakṣin*, *pūrva-pakṣin*'s *pūrva-pakṣin*) of the speakers involved.

1) **Implied Mīmāṃsaka**: [The Veda prescribes actions to be undertaken or avoided. This is the fundamental sacred presence underlying all Vedic speech. If there were any assertion devoid of direct or indirect imperative mood, it would be useless. Under no circumstances is the universe, structured by distinctions among agents, actions, and results, undermined; for multiplicity is ultimately real, underlying and implied by the imperative mood of the Veda.]

2) **Implied Advaitin**: [But the Vedānta texts are non-prescriptive statements about Brahman. Dare you say that they are useless or impotent?]
3) **Implied Mīmāṃsaka**: [No. The Vedānta texts are meaningful. Yet, insofar as they refer to entities such as Brahman or any deity they imply prescription of actions such as meditation (*upāsana*). Other than that kind of exhortation to action, what could the Vedānta texts say in a purely non-prescriptive way?]
4) **Advaitin**: Brahman is omniscient and omnipotent, the cause of the creation, continuity, and dissolution of the world. This Brahman is known only by the Veda (and is indeed its only concern).
5) **Mīmāṃsaka**: But how do we know this? [The Vedāntic texts speak on many subjects other than Brahman. Why select Brahman as a particularly significant reference of Vedic speech?]
6) **Advaitin**: By virtue of the connection (commensurability—*anvaya*—of all Vedic propositions). The statements in all the Vedāntic texts follow this very meaning with the same intention of transmitting the teaching of Brahman. Numerous sayings in the Upaniṣads attest to this message; "One only, my dear, was in the beginning, one with no second," (ChU 6.2.1), "The one *ātman* only was here in the beginning," (AitBr. 2.1.1), "This Brahman is without anything prior to it, highest, eternal, with no interior and exterior, seeing everything" (BU 2.5.19), "This immortal Brahman is before" (MuU 2.2.11), and other phrases like these. [These statements are all purely matter-of- fact references to Brahman.]
7) **Implied Mīmāṃsaka**: [These may be some instances where the Veda speaks, indeed, on Brahman. But there are other assertions not connected with Brahman at all!]
8) **Advaitin**: As the reference of these Vedic sentences in their entirety has been ascertained to be Brahman, any idea of another reference is improper; for such an idea would entail the fault of forsaking a scriptural meaning in favor of an unscriptural one *(śruta-hāny-aśruta-kalpanā-prasaṅgāt)*
9) **Implied Mīmāṃsaka**: [Be it as you say. But even the assertions apparently pointing to Brahman express the vision of plurality, a multifarious reality in which there are agents, actions, results].
10) **Advaitin**: No, no! For by no means can the import of these statements of the Veda be thought to involve agents, actions, and results; for there are explicit Vedic statements such as in BU 2.4.13: "By what can it see whom?" and so forth which deny (any association of Brahman with) agency, action, and results. [The knowledge of Brahman is necessarily accompanied by the cessation of the vision of plurality. If only you understood this, you could not stay a Mīmāṃsaka!]
11) **Implied Mīmāṃsaka**: [But how is it that I do not grasp Brahman? If you, the Vedāntin, insist that Brahman is an extant entity, it must be perceived somehow!]

12) **Advaitin**: Though Brahman is a well-established entity (*pariniṣṭhita-vastu*), it cannot be grasped by the senses; (for only scripture can testify): *tat tvam asi* (ChU 6.8.7); there is no other means of knowledge but the Veda to teach of Brahman.
13) **Mīmāṃsaka**: But pending reference to (actions) prescribed or prohibited, scriptural teaching would become useless! [Given that the essential mood and presence of the entire Veda is the imperative, speech dissociated from this presence and mood would be nothing but digression].
14) **Advaitin**: No, this is not a real fault. For man's highest success—accompanied by forsaking any weakness or blemish—consists of the understanding of Brahman as not susceptible to being associated with anything to be done or to be avoided. [True knowledge of Brahman is not connected at all with the imperative mood; it is the end of the universe of means-and-ends (*sādhya-sādhana-bhāva*).
15) **Implied Mīmāṃsaka**: [But the Veda prescribes meditation on various deities.]
16) **Advaitin**: Even Vedic teachings of deities to be meditated upon do not involve any contradiction. [Knowledge of Brahman is essentially different from the relationship with any deity.]
17) **Implied Mīmāṃsaka**: [Why not? After all, even Brahman is a kind of deity, having a role in the context of prescription. For the Veda prescribes meditation on Brahman and other deities.]
18) **Advaitin**: No; by such meditations, Brahman does not become subordinate to the prescription of meditation (*na tu tathā brahmaṇa upāsanā-vidhi-śeṣatvaṃ sambhavati*).
19) **Implied Mīmāṃsaka**: [But whence the distinction between Brahman and other deities? Commitment to the dual nature of reality is assumed by knowledge of Brahman as well as by meditation on any other deity].
20) **Advaitin**: No; (knowledge of Brahman is inherently different from meditation on any deity). For in the arousal of the insight of unity, by the (understanding of) the complete non-association of Brahman with anything to be done or avoided, the (previous) vision of duality—accompanied by distinctions of agent, action and so forth—is destroyed (*ekatve heyôpādeya-śūnyatayā kriyā-kārakâdi-dvaita-vijñānôpamardôpapatteḥ*). [Knowledge of Brahman and the perception of multiplicity in reality cannot co-exist.]
21) **Implied Mīmāṃsaka**: [However, even if the vision of unity arises once—like in a trance—man may awake again to normal reality, which is essentially dual, in which agents, actions and fruits thereof are discernible].
22) **Advaitin**: No; by the established insight of unity, the destroyed vision of duality does not rise again. [Transformation into Brahman knowledge is irreversible.]
23) **Implied Mīmāṃsaka**: [Let it be so. Yet, knowledge of Brahman makes Vedic prescriptions more pervasive; the existence of *ātman*

provides confidence in future benefits of present performances of Vedic sacrifices.]

24) **Advaitin**: (No. Since knowledge of Brahman sublates duality, it cannot subserve any existence based upon such duality.) In this way, the Veda teaches the non-subordination of the knowledge of Brahman to any prescription.

25) **Mīmāṃsaka**: In some parts of scripture, Vedic authority does not exist apart from the connection with prescriptions.

26) **Advaitin**: This does not invalidate the authoritativeness of the Veda in the contexts where it refers to Brahman; for knowledge of *ātman* has its own end (and cannot be conceived as means to other ends).

27) **Implied Mīmāṃsaka**: [But even if Vedic testimony does not directly imply sensual perception, yet the use of reasoning (*anumāna*)—obviously a mode of speech underlying the scriptures—does depend upon observed instances (significant in the course of reasoning).]

28) **Advaitin**: Nor does Vedic authoritativeness consist in the power of arguments (*anumāna*), depending on instances observed elsewhere (beyond Vedic assertions). Therefore, it is established that the Veda is (the sole) authority with respect to Brahman (depending on nothing else).

29) **Mīmāṃsaka**: All this is true, and the Veda does teach us about Brahman. Yet, it teaches about Brahman as an object of certain commands or prescriptions (not as an entity valuable on its own). Thus, for example, the Veda informs us about the sacrificial post, the *āhavanīya* fire, and other things irrelevant in the course of everyday, profane transactions.

30) **Implied Advaitin**: [Indeed, the Veda gives us information about entities!]

31) **Mīmāṃsaka**: However, the Veda does give us such information only in correlation with certain prescriptions (not, of course, for information's sake) (*yathā yūpâhavanīyâdīni alaukikāny api vidhi-śeṣatayā śāstreṇa samarpyante tadvat*).

32) **Advaitin**: How do you know this? [Why do you judge the subordination of knowledge to prescription?]

33) **Mīmāṃsaka**: We do know this since the Veda (essentially and always) prescribes either action or restraint from action (*pravṛtti-nivṛtti-prayojanatvāc chāstrasya*).

34) **Implied Advaitin**: [On what grounds do you base such an overall, simplistic and uniform interpretation of Vedic speech?]

35) **Mīmāṃsaka**: We have our authorities knowledgeable about the Veda and its meaning. Thus the commentary on Jaimini's sūtra 1.1.1 says: "The goal of the Veda is known to be prescription of actions"; and the same commentary on sūtra 1.1.2: "Prescription means assertions driving to action." Jaimini's sūtra 1.1.5 asserts that "the knowledge of this (*dharma*) comes from prescription." Jaimini's sūtra 1.1.25: The assertions referring to those things should be connected (with

the appropriate verbal imperative) which has action (to be undertaken) as its goal. And finally, Jaimini's sūtra 1.1.2: The meaning of the Veda is action; whatever does not aim at action is meaningless." From all this it follows that the Veda has a single purpose: to drive man to certain actions and to restrain him from other actions.

36) **Implied Advaitin**: [But what is thus the fate of all the Vedānta texts which refer to matters of fact such as Brahman?]

37) **Mīmāṃsaka**: No need to worry; such Vedānta texts do—of course—have their meaning (and are never meaningless), since they are part of the Veda!

38) **Implied Advaitin**: [But what role can be assigned to our Vedānta texts?]

39) **Mīmāṃsaka**: Being parts of the Veda, they must be understood as complementary to commands of actions to be done or actions to be avoided.

40) **Implied Advaitin**: [Be it as you say. But sometimes Vedāntic assertions do not seem to have *any* purpose. How would we then construe them as meaningful?].

41) **Mīmāṃsaka**: If you accept—as you hopefully do—that Vedānta is necessarily connected with (underlying) prescriptions, then just as sacrifices like the *agnihotra* are means for one desiring conditions such as heaven (*svargâdi-kāma*), the knowledge of Brahman is prescribed for one who wishes for immortality (*amṛtatva*)!

42) **Advaitin**: Yes, but there is still a difference concerning the thing to be known. For in the *Karma-kāṇḍa* the thing to be known is *dharma*, which may come into being (*bhavya*) (but does not necessarily exist), whereas here (in our Vedānta texts) what is to be known is Brahman, always existent (*nitya-nirvṛtta*), which is an established reality (*bhūta*).

43) **Implied Mīmāṃsaka**: [And yet, the Veda is one, and as such is necessarily instrumental towards the achievement of results.]

44) **Advaitin**: But due to the difference in the nature of Brahman and *dharma*, there must be a difference in the fruits resulting from the knowledge of *dharma* (*dharma-jñāna-phala*) and those emerging from the knowledge of Brahman (*brahma-jñāna-phala*). It is only appropriate (to respect the aforementioned difference in this way) (*tatra…bhavitum arhati*).

45) **Mīmāṃsaka**: No; it is inappropriate (*nârhaty evaṃ bhavitum*).

46) **Implied Advaitin**: [Why?]

47) **Mīmāṃsaka**: Because the Veda teaches of Brahman as connected with actions to be done according to prescription.

48) **Implied Advaitin**: [But Vedic statements of fact are distinct from prescription! Especially with respect to Brahman—as I have already said—there is not even a touch of a prescriptive attitude visible in the Veda! The Vedānta texts are in danger of being utterly useless.]

49) **Mīmāṃsaka**: Oh, no. Please notice the following assertions: "The *ātman*, lady, should be seen" (BU 2.4.5); "This *ātman*, free of any

blemish, is what should be sought after, that which should be known" (*ya ātmā 'pahata-pāpma so 'nveṣṭavyaḥ sa vijijñāsitavyaḥ*). (ChU 8.7.1); "let a man meditate on the *ātman* only" (BU 1.4.7); "let a man meditate on the world as the *ātman* only" (*ātmānam eva lokam upāsīta*) (BU 1.4.15); "whoever knows Brahman becomes Brahman" (*brahma veda brahmâiva bhavati*) (MU 3.2.9). [You see, the knowledge of Brahman embedded within the prescriptive mood of the Upaniṣads, expressed in the gerundive (*anveṣṭavya, vijijñāsitavya*) and optative (*upāsīta*) endings, naturally and beautifully makes sense.]

50) **Implied Vedāntin**: [But knowledge has nothing to do with prescription and effort! What possible use could there be for prescriptive pressure in arousing knowledge! Suppose you look at a post. Knowledge of the existence or nature of the post cannot be prescribed or affected by will or effort; it depends solely on the object (post). It thus either comes into being or not, independent of any action whether prescribed or not!]

51) **Mīmāṃsaka**: (Vedic prescriptions, as always, do have their uses.) As the prescriptions offered above (from major Vedāntic sources) become noticed, questions pop up in one's mind: Who is this *ātman* (*ko 'sāv ātmā*); what is this Brahman (*kiṃ tad brahma*)? With respect to this desire (to know Brahman/*ātman*), all the Vedānta texts are committed to teaching of Brahman by references to its essential nature.

52) **Implied Advaitin**: [But what, in your opinion, is this nature of Brahman taught by the Veda?]

53) **Mīmāṃsaka**: As you know, the Veda teaches us all that Brahman is eternal, omniscient, omnipresent (*sarva-gata*), ever-content, inherently and always pure, conscious, free; it is consciousness, joy, and so forth.

54) **Implied Advaitin**: [This is, indeed, precisely what we Vedāntins consider the nature of Brahman to be! But the effortless openness to the nature of Brahman—followed by mere recognition of matter-of-fact Vedic speech—is evidently enough for obtaining *mokṣa*. Nay, it is *mokṣa* itself!]

55) **Mīmāṃsaka**: (No; an effort—following the prescription of the Veda—is needed.) By the force of meditation on this (Brahman) the unseen liberation made known by scripture—(similarly to the unseen (*adṛṣṭa*) outcome of sacrifice)—will follow as the fruit (of meditation) (*tad-upāsanāc ca śāstra-drṣṭo 'dṛṣṭo mokṣaḥ phalaṃ bhaviṣyati*).

56) **Implied Advaitin**: [But mere openness to and understanding of Vedic statements of fact is evidently the means of knowing *ātman* and thus the means to liberation!]

57) **Mīmāṃsaka**: No. If there is no prescription of actions to be done or avoided, in the absence of any command to mandatory action, in the mere indifferent mood of statements of fact....

58) **Implied Advaitin**: [But statements of fact are exciting, bursting with their own meanings!]
59) **Mīmāṃsaka**:...indeed, like the following statements of fact: "The earth consists of seven continents" (*sapta-dvīpa-vasumatī*), "this king is walking (*rājâsau gacchati*)..." (These, indeed, are your statements of fact, "exciting, bursting with meaning...").
60) **Implied Advaitin**: [But pray, do you suggest that our Upaniṣads consist of such useless statements of fact?]
61) **Mīmāṃsaka**: Oh, no. However, if you do insist that the Vedānta statements are like the mere statements of fact cited above, then your Vedānta texts would be useless all the same! (... *ityādi-vākyavad vedānta-vākyānām ānarthakyam eva syāt*).
62) **Advaitin**: (But there are statements of fact which are evidently not useless). Even though a statement such as "This is a rope, not a snake" is a mere statement of fact, it obviously has value and impact through removal of the fear generated by the mistaken perception (of the rope being a snake).
63) **Implied Mīmāṃsaka**: [But what does it have to do with the power of Vedānta—statements? These—unlike statements about snakes and ropes—do not of course address any matters of fact in the world.]
64) **Advaitin**: The case of our Vedānta statements of fact is exactly similar to the case of statements concerning the snake and the rope. Although mere statements of fact, the Vedānta texts, by mere telling of the facts concerning the nature of *ātman* as inherently different from *saṃsāra*, remove the wrong notion concerning the reality of *saṃsāra*, and thus (our Vedānta statements) obtain their use and value (*tathêhâpy asaṃsāry-ātma-vastu-kathanena samsāritva-bhrānti-nivartanenârthavattvaṃ syāt*).
65) **Mīmāṃsaka**: This indeed could be as you say if the wrong notion about *saṃsāra* were removed (*nivarteta*) by merely hearing (of Brahman), as the wrong perception of the snake is removed by merely hearing about the rope.
66) **Implied Advaitin**: [So, if *saṃsāra* were removed (*nivarteta*) upon hearing of *tat tvam asi*...]
67) **Mīmāṃsaka**: But it (*saṃsāra* cognition) is *not* actually removed (*na tu nivartate*) (by the statements of Vedānta).
68) **Implied Advaitin**: [Pray, how do you know this?]
69) **Mīmāṃsaka**: Well, it is well-known that even though someone listens to the matter-of-fact statements of Brahman, he is found to be in *saṃsāra*, along with its sorrows and pleasures, and remains the same, as before! (*śruta-brahmaṇo 'pi yathā-pūrvaṃ sukha-duḥkhâdi saṃsāri-dharma-darśanāt*).
70) **Implied Advaitin**: [Do you suggest that Vedic speech of matters of fact invariably fails to abolish *saṃsāra*?]
71) **Implied Mīmāṃsaka**: [Of course. Reality consists of agents, actions, and results. Vedic teaching is necessarily founded on such a reality. You do not expect the Veda to undermine its own basis!].

72) **Implied Advaitin**: [But then there would be no sense in one's mere openness to Brahman through hearing Vedic matter-of-fact propositions...]
73) **Implied Mīmāṃsaka:** [That is true.]
74) **Implied Advaitin:** [How will the Veda address us then in matters concerning our self?]
75) **Mīmāṃsaka**: You know, it is explicitly prescribed in the *Bṛhadāraṇyakôpaniṣad* 2.4.5: "This self should be heard about, should be thought over, should be contemplated." Thus, you see, it is established that thinking and contemplation must follow the hearing about Brahman. [Thus, the invariably prescriptive mood of the Veda—including Vedānta—is always primary and present. It is inconceivable that a subordinate portion of Vedic speech—indicative references to Brahman—would be detrimental to the overall, primary prescriptive presence of the Veda]
76) **Implied Advaitin**: [But what would in this case be the power of scripture to teach about Brahman?]
77) **Mīmāṃsaka**: Brahman is thus taught by the authoritative Veda only as it is referred to by Vedic prescription. Vedic voice is necessarily prescriptive [and thus upholds the true reality of agents, actions, and fruits.]
78) **Advaitin (Summary of the main body of BSBh 1.1.4):** Your Mīmāṃsaka's arguments are not valid, on account of the difference between the results of *dharma* and those of the knowledge of Brahman. *Dharma* is conducive to pleasure, *adharma* to pain. The embodied condition is the ground of both pain and pleasure, and thus of *dharma*. *Mokṣa*, on the other hand, is a disembodied state, and thus beyond pleasure and pain, and has nothing to do with the knowledge of *dharma*.

With respect to the Mīmāṃsaka's assertion that though one has heard about Brahman he yet remains as before in *saṃsāra*: this is impossible, since Vedic speech, correctly understood, is effective. Insisting on the inefficacy of Vedic speech implies contradicting the authoritative Veda, which asserts that the nature of being in *saṃsāra* cannot be applied to one who has understood his self to be Brahman (*nâvagata-brahmâtma-bhavasya yathā-pūrvaṃ samsāritvaṃ śakyaṃ darśayituṃ, veda-pramāṇa-janita-brahmâtma-bhava-virodhāt*). There are observations of worldly phenomena that illustrate the power inherent in changes of mind akin to the conversion from being immersed in *saṃsāra* to obtaining knowledge of Brahman. A rich and conceited householder is greatly disturbed over losses of his property. But if he renounces his conceit (*abhimāna*), he is no longer as troubled over such losses. Similarly, one may find great pleasure in having beautiful earrings. However, such pleasure vanishes when one loses the earrings or renounces conceit. Thus, the Upaniṣads tell us that one free of the body is free of both pleasure and pain (*priyâpriya*).[16] One is wrong to think that disembodiment is obtained by death; for the condition of being embodied is grounded solely in wrong knowledge (*śarīratvasya mithyā-jñāna-nimittatvāt*). As soon as the insight of the unity of Brahman and the self arises, expressed in the sentence "I am Brahman" (*ahaṃ brahmâsmi*), all the agents, actions, conceptions of body, relatives, etc., come to end. Even ordinary means of knowledge production cease to function. Since knowledge of Brahman, which is *mokṣa*, implies a disembodied state inaccessible to considerations of *dharma* and *adharma*, pain and pleasure, a state in which action is impossible (at least in so far as action constitutes a universe of distinctions), such knowledge of self is utterly incompatible with the prescriptive presence of the Veda. Indeed, knowledge of *ātman* is inherently different from so-called knowledge generated by ordinary means of knowledge; knowledge of self is a condition in which elephants, pride, action, *dharma*, texts and Mīmāṃsakas lose their foundation.

Śaṅkara's playful orchestration of the voices of Advaitin and Mīmāṃsaka underlies the obvious similarities between the "philosophical contents" of the two rivals in the section from BSBh 1.1.4 studied above. Looked at closely, differences in content between the two positions seem rather inconspicuous. The Mīmāṃsaka and the Advaitin accept the authority of the Veda, of course. The Vedāntin does not deny that the Veda includes prescriptive components (say in the *Karma-kāṇḍa*); moreover, he does not contest the allegedly prescriptive assertions of Vedānta (such as: the *ātman* should be searched for; *anveṣṭavya*). Such prescriptive statements divert one's attention from worldly phenomena. Thus, the Vedāntin accepts that human curiosity with respect to the *ātman* may arise in the context of prescription; "The *ātman* should be heard about," says BU 2.4.5. The apparent prescriptive tone may well serve the Vedāntin's case, for implied by such prescriptive language is the utmost importance of knowledge of self. The Mīmāṃsaka concedes that knowledge of the *ātman* is very important and duly prescribed by the Vedānta texts. The Mīmāṃsaka recognizes the nature of Vedānta as consisting of numerous matter-of-fact assertions concerning Brahman/*ātman*. He agrees with the Vedāntin

---

[16] Śaṅkara quotes here ChU 8.12.1: *aśarīraṃ vāva santaṃ na priyâpriye spṛśataḥ*.

about the major attributes of Brahman, referring to it as eternal, omniscient, joyous, ever-existent, and so forth.

As seen above, Śaṅkara inserts the dearest, most beloved words of Advaita in a foreign, opponent's voice. The opponent praises the *ātman*/Brahman just as an Advaitin would. The reader, however, recognizing inter-textuality and an "original voice" (an Advaitin's, resonant as primary and victorious in many other texts), remains aware that the "Advaitin himself" has planted these cherished code-sentences in a rather hostile context. He feels a touch of pleasure; consciousness of inter-textuality has aesthetic value in this context. The reader experiences the difference between the message and its somewhat incongruous context, and he shares with the author the efficacy of this technique of foreign-voice contextualization.

To be sure, the author is helpful on the level of the verbalized message, inserting somewhat unusual characterizations of Brahman among some other, more familiar ones. In BSBh 1.1.4, Śaṅkara's opponent depicts Brahman as omniscient, eternal, ever-content (*nitya-tṛpta*), inherently ever pure, conscious, free (*nitya-śuddha-buddha-mukta-svabhāva*), etc. Most of these epithets of *ātman* do appear elsewhere in Śaṅkara's *bhāṣya*.[17] However, the characterization of Brahman as ever-content (*nitya-tṛpta*) is somewhat unusual. It is found in *Bhagavadgītā* 4.20, but is of use neither in the Upaniṣadic literature nor in Śaṅkara's BSBh (apart from the context of the Mīmāṃsaka's attributes of Brahman in BSbh 1.1.4). There is thus a slight touch of otherness in the false Advaitin's voice.

The Advaitin is necessarily invisible to the Mīmāṃsaka. Not only is a subject inherently unheard; the Advaitin's "visibility," in Śaṅkara's view, his being fully understood, implies the Mīmāṃsaka's destruction. This is the underlying theme and issue behind the repetitive talk of the subordination (*śeṣatva*) of the teaching of Brahman to the prescriptive mood of the Veda, its being or not being a part of the teaching of *dharma* and sacrifice. Indeed, the Advaitin is dangerous for any resistant *saṃsārin* eager to remain in *saṃsāra*, who uses his brain to "subordinate" the Vedic voice of liberation to contexts and voices where it becomes weaker and ineffective. Channeling

---

[17] See, for example, BSBh 1.1.1; BSBh 1.3.19; BSBh 2.1.22; BSBh 3.2.22; BSBh 4.1.2. Slight variations of this expression are found in BSBh 2.1.14, BSBh 1.1.2, BSBh 2.3.40, and more.

Advaita messages into foreign voices—be it the opponent's or that of the Vedāntin as *pūrva-pakṣin*—is the main purpose of Śaṅkara's Mīmāṃsaka, struggling for his existence, according to BSBh 1.1.4.

Śaṅkara's insistence on the uniform reference of the Vedānta (to Brahman) suggests resistance to the ambiguity that normally contaminates human speech. The voice of the other-than-human (*apauruṣeya*) Veda is necessarily unambiguous, leaving no distance between self and speech. This voice only, according to Śaṅkara, can highlight and create the new self (*ātman*).

CHAPTER TEN

COMMENTATOR'S ADVAITA, EXPONENT'S ADVAITA

In the course of my studies in Śaṅkara's Advaita (or Viveka-Vedānta), it dawned on me that the author of the *Brahma-sūtra-bhaṣya* (BSBh) and his dialogical hero, the winner-exponent (*siddhāntin*), could be viewed as separate entities on a number of different levels. To distinguish a gifted writer from the creations of his mind (including an ever-winning exponent) is in a sense trivially true; an author cannot help being other than his hero. This is especially true of an author who, by his very act of imagination and his dialogue-bound discourse, is aware of an ice-cold vision of the utterly lonely one self, a seer dissociated from any trace of relationship with objective reality. As repeatedly suggested above, this is the core of the author's voice in the introduction to the BSBh.

Having distinguished the author and the "creatures of his mind," we made room for questions regarding to the author and his voice. The author's confessions of doubt, we argued, should be accepted in earnest, and his *viveka*-metaphysics present most palpably in the introduction to the BSBh is the essence of his innermost voice. As a staunch *vivekin*, Śaṅkara differs from his exponent in some important respects. Following his focus and emphasis on the difference between seer and seen he rejects Upaniṣadic theories of creation (and consequently the absolute authority of the Veda), he lives by a (poetic) figurative state of mind, sharing in earnest his exponent's assertions of doubt rather than his alleged victories, and so on. Thus, everything depends upon the separation of Śaṅkara the author of the BSBh from his verbalized hero.

However, our suggested separation of voices in the case of Śaṅkara (author) and his chosen winner has at least two apparent shortcomings. First, to distinguish author and *siddhāntin* seems opposed to the entire volume of traditional and scholarly study. The apparent negation of the fruitful paradigmatic conflation of author and exponent implies the attempt to resist or renounce the rich findings accumulated within this paradigm. Thus, complete resistance to the allegedly inappropriate author/*siddhāntin* combination would be very costly. Second, in the light of our recommended distinction, Śaṅkara's work would seem less coherent, and would consist of varying incompatible visions of reality. Cogently integrated ideas and a coherent world-view are obviously of great value; they allow for complexity and depth. However, the combination of substantially different voices sometimes results in a blurred vision. By splitting the voices of a mixed vision of unified Advaita, we can generate a clearer, more focused vision of Advaita philosophy. In theory, we conclude that the distinction between author and hero is a worthy presupposition. The hero may represent his creator's ideal, his dream, his mask. Indeed, he shares with his *siddhāntin* the vision of the one self (*ātman*) expounded in the Upaniṣads. However, in his wonder over the reality of objectivity, living the paradoxical, poignant condition of living in a body he stands for himself. In our case as in others, the author is not necessarily identical with his exponent; though seemingly invisible, the composer of the BSBh exists somewhere as a separate entity.

Śaṅkara the commentator on the Upaniṣads and Bādarāyaṇa's *Brahma-sūtra* is crucial to the Hindu tradition. Deeply familiar with Hindu scriptures and schools of thought, Śaṅkara is a great scholar; but he is seemingly a commentator on the work of others. Even an apparently independent work such as the Upad is not truly independent. It seems a commentary on a specific, though implicit, body of knowledge, which is present before the commentator's eyes. Being explicitly aware of his dependence on other people and other texts, the commentator openly declares his dependence or inter-dependence; his is an inherently humane discipline. But through his commentary he also imbues these texts with an implicit yet real difference. Śaṅkara's method of employing rhetorical tools such as dialogue, questioning, doubt, and imaginative projections significantly distinguishes the author of the BSBh from his exponent, who is bound by incessant certainty. If we allow for the commentator's distinct identity, a more intelligent, alive, probing persona emerges. At the very least we become aware of a commentator who offers a metaphysics of wonder and a recalcitrant sense of plurality concomitant with a comprehensive familiarity with Upaniṣadic knowledge of the one and only self (*ātman*), etc. Should we ignore such a complex metaphysics of *viveka*, wonder and doubt? The authority of the text might perhaps be enhanced if fusion of author and exponent were assumed. However, such a fusion detracts, as Bakhtin says, from the aesthetic value of a work of art:

> If, in a monologic world, an idea retains its power to signify as an idea, then it is inevitably separated from the fixed image of the hero and is no longer artistically combined with this image; the idea is merely placed in his mouth, but it could with equal success be placed in the mouth of any other character. For the author it is important only that a given true idea be uttered somewhere in the context of a given work; who utters it, and when, is determined by considerations of composition, by what is convenient or appropriate or by purely negative criteria: it must not jeopardize the verisimilitude of the image of him who utters it. Such an idea, in itself, belongs to *no one*. The hero is merely the carrier of an independently valid idea; as a true signifying idea it gravitates toward some impersonal, systematically monologic context; in other words, it gravitates toward the systematically monologic worldview of the author himself.[1]

Still, a sensitive reading of the *bhāṣya* also means recognizing the close relationship between the voices of the author and his arch-exponent. Sometimes, of course, the author explicitly merges his voice with that of his exponent's. This uniformity of voice is most visible in the opening paragraphs of major sections of the BSBh, wherein the author/*siddhāntin* seems to sum up his achievements in the previous section. See for example a characteristic passage (BSBh 2.1.1):

> It has been shown in the first *adhyāya* that the omniscient Lord of all (*sarvêśvara*) is the cause of the origin of this world in the same way as clay is the material cause of jars and gold of golden ornaments; that by his rulership he is the cause of the subsistence of this world once originate, just as the magician (*māyāvin*) is the cause of the subsistence of the magical illusion; and that he, lastly, is the cause of the emitted world finally reabsorbed into its essence, just as the four classes of creatures are reabsorbed into the earth. It has further been proved, by a demonstration of the connected meaning of all the Vedānta texts, that the Lord is the Self of all of us.[2]

However, we know that the author of the BSBh rejects the Upaniṣadic theory of creation, and in the light of his "secret teaching" would not accept that "the omniscient Lord of all (*sarvêśvara*) is the cause of the origin of this world in the same way as clay is the material cause of jars and gold of golden ornaments". And yet, the voices of the author and the *siddhāntin* sound inseparable and unified in this excerpt (BSBh

[1] Bakhtin 1993: 79.
[2] Thibaut's translation, v. 1, p. 290.

2.1.1), as they do in other introductory statements to major sections. In such passages, the author reinforces his choice of *siddhāntin*. Thus, throughout the BSBh (and Śaṅkara's other works) the author chooses his Advaita exponent. That is why, we say, both (author and *siddhāntin*) are Advaitins. And yet, the author's Advaita is moderated by his bold version of Viveka-Vedānta, along with continual allusions to doubt (or wonder) expressed in dozens of references to uncertainty (*saṃśaya, saṃdeha, cintā*) in the opening paragraphs of so many *bhāṣyas*. Seen in conjunction, they point to the presence of an author whose underlying metaphysics (or perception of the real) is somewhat different from his exponent's.

It is often a matter of choice whether to separate author and *siddhāntin* or to conflate them. This essay is devoted to the exploration of the first option, namely, the viability of reading works such as the BSBh and Śaṅkara's other works in the light of the distinction between author and exponent.

The author of the BSBh is occupied with commentary, namely, the articulation and interpretation of the thoughts and writings of others. Listening to the thoughts of others—whether of opponent or exponent—he gives voice to the dialogues resounding in his mind. There is a dialogical quality to the commentator's thought or process of thinking. As a thinker, philosopher and writer, Śaṅkara cares about the textures of dialogue, eloquence, coherence and beauty. He uses humor, sarcasm and witty illustrations from everyday life (often strictly unnecessary, even patently redundant within a given structure of argument) in order to make his point. His main business is the description of a hero who knows a profoundly important Advaita truth of the self (*ātman*). We assume that the commentator shares the notion of the revolutionary force of Advaita with his *siddhāntin*; like the author himself, the exponent thinks that knowledge of self is the only thing of true value. Moreover, knowledge of this one self generates knowledge of everything, says the exponent,[3] following in the steps of Uddālaka (ChU 6). The exponent's foundational recommendation or challenge to mankind is thus the following: the self (*ātman*) is the only subject worthy of attention. The opponents, however, whoever they are, do not share the same opinion. Some of them (Buddhists, Jainas) oppose the exponent altogether. Others (Sāṅkhyas, Mīmāṃsakas, Yogins, etc.) are

---

[3] See for example BSBh 1.4.21, BSBh 3.3.17, etc.

not as harsh in their opposition; they share with our exponent some principles or attitude (such as, e.g. the authoritativeness of the Veda). None of the opponents concedes to the *siddhāntin*'s insistence on consciousness associated with the connectedness of everything (Brahman or *ātman*) as the only issue dealt with in the Veda; none of them consider the one primordial self the only subject worthy of attention. Thus, opponents who accept the authority of the Veda propose that scriptures such as the Upaniṣads speak of many entities (breath, light, ether, pots, the individual self, etc.) other than *ātman* the one self. In this sense, by his vision of *viveka*, the unabridgeable gap between self and non-self the commentator shares the views of his *siddhāntin*'s opponents in acknowledging an objective presence, thinking that many things other than Brahman or *ātman* are significant, worthy of attention. He considers other voices and positions, and as commentator he is bound to contain the dialogical structure (or essence) of thought and, in this respect, is his exponent's opponent. But, our own opponent might interpose, the exponent responds to his opponents' charges and propositions and thus, too, attends to things other than *ātman*! In this respect, indeed, we say, the commentator creates his hero in his own image. The *siddhāntin*, if left to his own devices (or by remaining true to his basic commitment regarding the one thing worthy of attention) would never attend to his *pūrva-pakṣins*' assertions. But he does, and thus makes the BSBh possible.

The scope of one's resistance to the conflation of author and exponent is thus an object of attention or research, and a matter of choice. Choices are made in every act of reading. Primary among them is how we read the relationship between the author and the creation of his mind, his alleged spiritual hero, the *siddhāntin*. One may reasonably choose to envision the author as a veiled and inherently invisible commentator, of no standing whatsoever as an independent point of view. It is, however, more intriguing from a scholarly perspective, to distinguish the two voices. This is, of course, the case if we accept the suggestion made above concerning the exponent's foundational axiom (that the *ātman* is the only worthwhile object of attention). Upon such a reading of the exponent's vision or encounter with the Upaniṣads, the *viveka*-commentator who considers so many things other than the *ātman* is necessarily his exponent's other. Commenting on texts such as the BS, the Upaniṣads and the *Bhagavad-gītā*, he also comments on the veracity and coherence of the various participants in the debates. The commentator on Bādarāyaṇa's *Brahma-sūtra* is also a commentator on Sāṅkhya, Yoga, the Buddha, and so forth. And he (also) comments on his *siddhāntin*, the exponent of Advaita-Vedānta. There is, of course, a judgment in favor of Advaita, but, in our view, the *siddhāntin*'s proposition that *ātman* is the only entity worthy of attention becomes subordinated to the recurring doubts that arise regarding this very subject. Thus the author's measure of freedom is expressed in the dissociation of the commentator from his favorite exponent.

The author imagines a doubt-free, coherent, ever-winning exponent, a victorious *siddhāntin* who is often extremely forceful and penetrating but, sometimes, less than convincing. The author who imagines his exponent comparing someone's remaining, unexhausted karma to a king's servant left after many years of service with only an umbrella and a pair of shoes may be seen as subverting his exponent's ideology or cogency of argument (see discussion of BSBh 3.1.8, below). Similarly, as we have seen, when the commentator announces that a sentence such as 'bring the pot,' *āhara pātram* and *pātram āhara*, 'the pot, bring it' has the same meaning, he leaves the reader wondering about his intentions.

A major motive for investigating the author's invisibility (or presence) is indicated by his own confessions of doubt or wonder. As discussed above, such confessions are numerous and particularly significant. The author of the BSBh discusses doubt (*saṃśaya, saṃdeha, cintā*) and the resolution of doubt in contexts that I consider to be the core of Śaṅkara's writings; these are his playful presentations of inner-circle debates with opponents committed to the Upaniṣads as means of knowledge (*pramāṇa*) with respect to Brahman or *ātman*. Such opponents allow for alternative meanings of words in reference to Brahman or *ātman*. The significance of the opponents' view in such inner-circle contexts of interpreting *śruti* passages of the sacred Upaniṣads is the recognition of their relevance to worldly phenomena. While the *siddhāntin*, crippled by certainty, accords reality to Brahman alone, inner-circle opponents (and, in my view, also the author voicing his uncertainty) ascribe presence and a measure of truth and reality to plurality. Thus, the opponents who consider ether, light or breath as references to Upaniṣadic speech articulate an aspect of the commentator's being.

The verbal confrontation between the *siddhāntin* and the inner-circle opponents recapitulates the primary theme of mysticism on the textual level—perception of the beyond; the inter-connectedness of meanings (*anvayatva*) parallels the interconnected-ness of the world. As the words become meaningful in accordance with their connectedness (context, *prakaraṇa*,[4] underlying subject of the passage—*prakṛta*, relationship to other occurrences in different contexts—*vākya-śeṣa*) so too is the universe unified in the one *ātman*. But doubt persists; for the words have conventional meanings which are difficult to transcend in favor of the one *ātman*.

The word 'doubt' (*saṃśaya*, etc.) provokes some thought; what does it mean in the context of the BSBh? To be sure, it means full recognition of Vedic authority regarding the oneness of *ātman* followed by a composite flavor of intense expectation, attraction, and an impulse towards understanding. Secondly, it implies a flaw, a vacuum made of the inexplicable gap between seer and seen, which desires to be filled through articulation, imagination, thought. Let us suppose that our author's self-understanding finds expression in words such as *saṃśaya* occurring at the initial paragraphs of inner-circle debates. Since interpretation of Upaniṣadic words is the means of knowing Brahman or the self, we must assume that correct interpretation allegedly generates correct vision, or is in fact such vision. The *pūrva-pakṣin* can hardly resist interpreting Upaniṣadic words by their conventional meanings. The *siddhāntin* adheres to Brahman and *ātman* as his sole reference for establishing the meanings of numerous nouns such as *prāṇa*, *jyotis*, *ākāśa*, and so on. The commentator, I think, stands in the middle, aware of the other-than-*ātman* presence, open to the ideas of plurality and 'conventional perception' articulated by the various opponents. Thus, wonder articulated as doubt keeps coming to the fore; how can the one become many? How is the one present in the many? Or, in a more personal vein: Am I inflicted by *adhyāsa*? The author's credo or cry of wonder is thus: How is the world possible? Committed to his secret teaching of *viveka*, namely, of the unabridgeable gap of seer and seen, the author of the BSBh keeps wondering over the viability of his own living experience "in the body": what is this connection of worldly plurality to the one Brahman? How is everything felt to be unified in the one truly existing self? Is this world connected with Brahman,

[4] Since rejection of ordinary meanings (in favor of Brahman or *ātman*) is a major move in Śaṅkara's writings, the semantic field associated with 'context' (as a means to replace conventional denotation) is very rich. See for example *prakaraṇa-sāmarthya* (BSBh 3.2.22, BSBh 3.3.49, BSBh 3.4.14, and more. Also *prakaraṇa-vaśa* (BSBh 2.4.6), *prakaraṇântara-kāraṇa* (BSBh 1.3.39), and more.

or with something else? What then is the connection between Brahman and allegedly objective reality? It seems impossible to know, says Śaṅkara the author of the BSBh. (*kiṃ brahmaṇā sambaddhaṃ, kim anyena kenacit sambaddham iti na śakyaṃ niścetum*).[5] The *siddhāntin*, however, provides answers of many kinds. Brahman is the cause of the world; Brahman is a juggler (*māyāvin*). Brahman is real but the world is unreal. The sense of questioning and wonder behind the BSBh is the commentator's, not the *siddhāntin*'s.

In his imaginative evocation of the *siddhāntin*'s rivals, of worldly phenomena vaguely or otherwise connected with Brahman as the pure abstract subject completely dissociated from any trace of objectivity yet the forceful origin of the world (according to the Upaniṣads), in his portrayal of the exponent's weaknesses and so on the commentator reveals a theoretical boundary between himself and his hero. While for the *siddhāntin* conventional perception (implying committed acceptance of plurality) is an utter illusion, a dream, entirely untrue, for his creator, it seems, it contains a trace of disturbing truth or reality. That is how "*ātman* himself" (if we are allowed to use the term) appears, disturbed at the sight or presence of the mind (*manas*), in the Upad (see chapter 3). Thus, though he apparently shares almost every principle of Advaita ideology and knowledge (and the fundamental belief in the Upaniṣads as the only source of such knowledge) with the *siddhāntin*, the author's wonder and doubt imply metaphysics different from his confident *siddhāntin*'s. The metaphysics of the latter (the exponent) are explicit, while the metaphysics of the author are implicit in the act of imagination and composition.

The only methodology available for assessing the intensity of the author's presence is a close reading of the *bhāṣyas*. For in terms of voice-free philosophical contents we perceive the two allies (author and exponent) as highly similar. However, a close reading of the comparison made between the Sāṅkhya-made relation of *puruṣa* and *prakṛti* and the relation of Brahman and the world (see chapter 5) reveals doubt in relation to the positions of both the *siddhāntin* and *pūrvapakṣin*. Though apparently in agreement with the winner's position, the author remains aloof, playfully expressing his reservation about the explication of any relationship between an invisible Brahman and a perceptible world (also, of course, about any possible relationship of

[5] BSBh 1.1.2.

subject [*puruṣa*] and objectivity [*prakṛti*]). A close reading of Śaṅkara's reflection (BSBh 3.2.22) on Yājñavalkya's *nêti nêti* reveals a playful use of the mud-cliché ("better to stay clean of mud rather than wash it") (see chapter 8). The author identifies himself with neither the winner nor the loser. Likewise, in discussing his view on the possibility of life in the body after attainment of knowledge of self (BSBh 3.3.32), the commentator remains skeptical, expressing doubts about the cogency of his exponent's integration of liberation with a continuous sense of active agency (see chapter 7). By embedding Advaita messages in an opponent's mouth (see chapter 9) the author reveals a measure of inner freedom unavailable to his (content-bound) exponent.

And yet: is there really sufficient reason to divide the author from the *siddhāntin*? Paradigmatic reading, conflating author and *siddhāntin*, has been useful and, as previously mentioned, the author's voice is often seen to merge with the *siddhāntin*'s. After all, the *siddhāntin* is the winner who champions Advaita. By definition, the denomination 'Advaita' is Śaṅkara's exponent's Advaita. Why, then, violate the convention of author/*siddhāntin* identification?

As stated at the outset (see Chapter 1), we accept in earnest Śaṅkara's confessions of doubt in the opening paragraphs of what we consider his core-*bhāṣya*s. (The "secret teaching" forcefully embedded in the introduction conditions the sense of doubt but is not, strictly speaking identical with it). The paradigmatic conflation of the voices of author and exponent is grounded in the didactic nature of articulating doubts (*saṃśaya, saṃdeha, cintā*) and questions. The author, it is assumed, does not really ask questions or use the *vā* operator with respect to the meaning of certain Upaniṣadic terms. Rather than reflecting on existential issues, questions and disjunctions (*vā*-uses) are common modes of presenting intellectual situations or debates. The author is moved to action (for composition is action) by conviction and probably compassion, not by doubt or wonder. Fully secure in his reading of the Veda and perception of ultimate reality, he knows himself to be the *ātman*, speaking solely for the benefits of others. Though reading Śaṅkara like this is not necessarily unwarranted or wrong, the alternative, namely, taking the author's questions and doubts seriously should also be considered. After all, the Advaita theory of the illusionary boundary between the individual self (*jīva*) and the one *ātman* is in a sense incredible. Every "I" speech-act in everyday life bespeaks an experiential incredibility. In his author's imagination, even the one and only self (*ātman*) speaks in the first-person in the presence of another, thus acknowledging a measure of ignorance about his allegedly one true self.[6] The familiar notion of the separate existence of the lively individual self (*jīva*) forcefully resists rejection; it is perhaps the most recalcitrant root of *saṃsāra*. In BSBh 1.3.19 Śaṅkara jokes about the doubts which spring to mind incessantly in regard to the individual self (an entity resisting disappearance or merger in the one *ātman*); the author compares a *pūrva-pakṣin*'s recurring doubt in this respect to ambrosia (*amṛta*) sprinkled on a dead person (*athêdānīṃ mṛtasyêvâmṛta-sekāt punaḥ samutthānaṃ jīvâśaṅkāyāḥ kriyate*). In our view, the author of the BSBh is familiar with doubts about the true non-reality of worldly plurality, and especially of the individual soul (*jīva*).

The author's doubt and wonder-informed creativity differs from his exponent's unwavering certainty, invariably articulated as a response to an opponent's challenge. To be sure, the author and his creation are both Advaitins. They share a deep commitment to the Upaniṣads. And yet the *siddhāntin* never uses the 'or' (*vā*) component in his speech, while the *vā* attitude is inherent to the author's stance or being. In a sense, the *siddhāntin* is the true successor of the great Upaniṣadic sages. For indeed, Uddālaka and Yājñavalkya never use the *vā* operator.

The question of identifying or distinguishing the voices of author and exponent is sometimes context-dependent and sometimes a matter of choice. Let us take the example of Śaṅkara's commentary on the famous dialogue between Yājñavalkya and two sages who challenge his knowledge of the Veda (BU 3.4–5). The two sages, Uṣasta and Kahola are familiar with the Upaniṣadic teaching of Brahman and *ātman*, but they avoid identifying themselves with the *ātman*. According to our exposition of the commentator's self as charged by doubt or wonder, we choose to identify the author with the two sages who challenge Yājñavalkya (rather than with Yājñavalkya himself). A conflated author/*siddhāntin*, on the other hand, would read the dialogue between Yājñavalkya and Uṣasta and Kahola (BU 3.4–5) as the complaints of weak-minded disciples or rivals who miss the main point of Yājñavalkya's teaching (namely, that the one *ātman* is their own). But if Śaṅkara the composer of the BSBh shares these doubt and is reluctant to know that he knows the *ātman*, he would expose his frus-

[6] See the metrical part of the Upad discussed above, chapter 3.

tration at Yājñavalkya's teaching. Consider the vividness of Śaṅkara's articulation of Uṣasta's complaint to Yājñavalkya:

> Why all this excessive talk? Man, stop your tricks generated by your desire for cows, and show us this Brahman—which is the self (*ātman*) within everything—clearly, in a tangible and lucid way (*kiṃ bahunā? tyaktvā go-tṛṣṇā-nimittaṃ vyājaṃ, yad eva sākṣād aparokṣād brahma ya ātmā sarvântaras tam me vyācakṣvêti*).

It is, as suggested above, a matter of choice. The commentator (Śaṅkara) can be seen to present Uṣasta's challenging phrase as illegitimate. But we choose to see Śaṅkara's articulation of Uṣasta's complaint as reenacting his own mode of existence. It is, according to our speculation, revealing of a complex life-style consisting of a committed reading of the Upaniṣads and full-fledged acceptance of Upaniṣadic contents or principles (such as the oneness of Brahman which is the *ātman*), while also admitting to a certain lacuna or emptiness which generates the impulse towards wonder or doubt.

But what, our audience would like to know, is the exact nature of this lacuna or empty space, which contains or *is* the author's wonder or doubt? What is its origin? Whence does it arise? As one can say that Uṣasta is familiar with the teaching of the *ātman* (the self within all) but does not know that he knows, so one can say the same of Śaṅkara, the author of the BSBh.[7] Thus, the recognition of one's individual self as the one *ātman* is the core of the Upaniṣadic norm as well as the origin of Śaṅkara's wonder. Though you know, as the master says to his disciple in the Upad, you think you do not. Like Uṣasta's and Kahola's complaint, the disciple's statement is also lively and true; I am one, he says, and *he* is another. This vivid articulation of doubt in Uṣasta's voice is strangely resonant. It seems to be a personal matter shared by numerous Advaitins. The difficulty in recognizing the individual self within the great oneness of *ātman* points to the origin of an Advaita sense of wonder.

Like the 'or' (*vā*) stance, the question is the author's distinctive speech-act. Indeed, in a sense, the author of the BSBh is his exponent's disciple; the *siddhāntin* answers the author's questions as the master

[7] Yājñavalkya's response to Uṣasta's challenge is noteworthy. The only addition to Uṣasta's succinct summary of the Upaniṣadic norm (of the one *ātman* within all) is the enclitic '*te*' (your). This Brahman which is *ātman* is your self, he says.

does in Śaṅkara's Upad. The disciple asks: how can I, who am different from this Brahman (*tad-vilakṣana*), I who live in *saṃsāra*, I who am attached to numerous aspects of *saṃsāra*, consider myself as the ultimate self? It is as if I see fire devoid of heat![8]

Unacknowledged assumptions in reading may sometimes be challenged. We are tentatively resisting the assumption that the author of the BSBh, as distinct from his exponent, is inherently invisible. Yet the question arises: How may an author be as invisible as Śaṅkara has been made to be?

This slim volume consists of a few studies inspired by the author's visibility or presence in the BSBh. The very distinction of author and *siddhāntin* points to the reality of the human being who produced the BSBh; he must have lived somewhere at some point in time. However, the texts he composed are the only evidence at our disposal.[9]

Of course, valuable observations can be offered without references to the distinction made here. The 'Śaṅkara' denomination may often be used indiscriminately, and there are many contexts in which the distinction between author and *siddhāntin* is not worth applying. See, for example, the following passage (BSBh 2.1.6), in which a Śaṅkara/Śaṅkarācārya integrates intense reasoning with openness to axiomatic authority of the Veda:

> And if it has been maintained above that the scriptural passage enjoining thought (on Brahman) in addition to mere hearing (of the sacred texts treating of brahman) shows that reasoning also is to be allowed its place, we reply that the passage must not deceitfully be taken as enjoining bare independent ratiocination, but must be understood to represent reasoning as a subordinate auxiliary of intuitional knowledge. By reasoning of the latter type we may, for instance, arrive at the following conclusions; that because the state of dream and the waking state exclude each other the Self is not connected with those states; that, as the soul in the state of deep sleep leaves the phenomenal world behind and becomes one with that whose Self is pure Being, it has for its self pure being apart from the phenomenal world; that as the world springs from Brahman it cannot be separate from Brahman, according to the principle of the non-difference of cause and effect, etc.[10]

---

[8] *kathaṃ tad-vilakṣaṇo 'aneka-saṃsāra-dharma-saṃyuktaḥ paramâtmānam ātmatvena ca māṃ saṃsāriṇaṃ paramâtmatvenâgnim ivâśītatvena pratipadyeyam?*

[9] As J. Bader says: "This text (the *Upadeśa-sāhasrī*) and the commentaries comprise a substantial and coherent body of work from which we can derive a clear picture of the nature of Śaṅkara's thought, but not of his life." Bader 2000: 18.

[10] Thibaut's translation. P. 307–8.

On the other hand, the author's presence often requires attention. The interpretation of specific words in Upaniṣadic passages are particularly significant in this respect; in our view, such examples are the stuff of Śaṅkara's core-*bhāṣyas*[11] and invariably begin with questions and doubts. BSBh 1.1.22 is one of these *bhāṣyas*; we read it as a work of art that ends on a note of ambivalence. The winner announces that the word *ākāśa* in Chāndogya Upaniṣad 1.9 means Brahman, not ether, as the opponent asserts. It is, he says, like a sentence such as "Agni studies a passage" (*agnir adhīte 'nuvākyam*). Although the conventional meaning of *agni* is fire, within the verbal environment of "Agni studies a passage" the word *agni* must be taken as a personal name. An immediate association is rejected in favor of a meaning implied by context. Indeed, the interpretation of Agni (as a personal name) arises immediately (*śīghram*) and naturally (*prasiddham*) in the reader's mind. But ether—rather than Brahman—arises in the mind (in Chāndogya Upaniṣad 1.9) naturally and immediately (in the opponent's view). And moreover, unlike the Agni-illustration, the conventional meaning of *ākāśa* (ether) remains legitimate and viable even after the possibility of reading Brahman for *ākāśa* has been presented and defended. There is thus a significant difference between the *agni*-illustration and what is illustrated. But there is no doubt with respect to "Agni studies a passage;" fire cannot read and therefore cannot be the subject of the sentence. In the case of the Upaniṣadic text, doubt lingers on with respect to the reference to *ākāśa*. Moreover, *ākāśa* as ether remains the more natural and immediate reading of ChU 1.9. One could ask: if the Upaniṣad points to Brahman, why the use of *ākāśa*? Why not simply use the word Brahman? In terms of worldly existence and plurality, it seems that recognition of the individual soul (*jīva*) never vanishes.

In the paradigmatic conflation of commentator and *siddhāntin*, the weakness inherent in the *siddhāntin's* comparison of *ākāśa* and *agni* is shared by the commentator. According to such a reading, every weakness of the *siddhāntin's* is necessarily the commentator's as well. In our view, this major presupposition does not do justice to our author. Preserving a boundary between himself and the exponent, he is capable of commenting on the latter. Think about the author of this argument. The exponent is not wholly ridiculous (for fire cannot read a passage

[11] See above, chapter 1.

and context often defeats a word's primary meaning). The commentator, we argue, is aware of his *siddhāntin*'s weaknesses.

What then, is the timbre of the voice heard in the concluding statement of BSBh 1.1.22? Is it the voice of a truly victorious exponent? Or is it the voice of an author expressing his wonder at the connectedness of meanings, or the connection of Brahman and apparent plurality in existence? In our view, the author's awareness of his exponent's weakness and his ability to distance himself from his subject constitute the most individual expressions of the commentator's creativity.

As a *bhāṣya* presenting a *siddhāntin* who is bound to reject an ordinary meaning or denotation in order to apply another (*ātman* or Brahman), BSBh 1.1.22 is characteristic of the core-*bhāṣya*s of the BSBh. Moreover, I consider such a *bhāṣya* a reenactment of the fundamental challenge faced by Advaitins of many kinds (and humanity at large as well); namely, the challenge of coping with the immediacy and ease of taking in the world in its plurality. Pūrva-Mīmāṃsakas insist upon the force of the conventional perception of plurality, a perception impossible to reject or overcome (which is also true perception). Indeed, Śaṅkara himself insists that the Veda does not deny the validity of sense-perception (*pratyakṣa*); the Veda does not assert that fire is cold.

Still, however lively and visible the author of the BSBh may become in such a reading, the exponent should not be disregarded. He is truly remarkable as an ideal guide to the forceful theory of Advaita-Vedānta. Almost everything achieved in the study of Śaṅkara's output applies to the *siddhāntin*'s Vedānta. Though we sometimes speak of him as 'crippled by certainty', somewhat invalidated by his incapacity to question and express doubt, he is still superb in the effects he exerts on so many minds and hearts. After all, he is the one who envisions horizons of liberation, the renunciation of self-identification with the body, salvation of the non-instrumental mode of being, the freedom of nature, and so on. Scholarship, traditional and otherwise (including that of our commentator), has invariably been attracted to the exponent's teaching of one *ātman* as the only reality. Thus, for example, J. Bader's articulation of the *siddhāntin*'s attraction:

> Perhaps Śaṅkara's presence makes itself most strongly felt when old age approaches, and people find it difficult to avoid the fact of their own mortality. At this time the atavistic call of the forest *ṛṣis* is more easily

> heard, and there is impetus for reflection on the ancient ascetic values, which Śaṅkara represents.[12]

True, the author of the BSBh and his exponent are Advaitins whose visions—however different—appeal to an older generation. A call for recognition of a life-giving, exceedingly subtle omnipresent self (*ātman*), a sense of intense reality associated with this self made of freedom and consciousness, and acceptance of the Upaniṣads as the exclusive means of knowledge, are some of the preeminent attitudes shared by the *bhāṣya-kāra* and his *siddhāntin*. Such attitudes and principles make for a palpable intimacy between the two speakers. For all sorts of practical reasons, the difference between an author's voice charged by wonder ('doubt') and that of a winner—*siddhāntin* voice 'crippled by certainty' is not complete or final. However, for scientists of the true self, or for those curious about Advaita forces in action, or simply in the variety of Advaita visions and experiences, the difference between the Advaita of the author and that of his exponent is not trivial. The author's Advaita is presented here as consisting of wonder—which means the recognition of worldly phenomena as inherently significant (as well as the variable presence of Brahman), and the acceptance of a multiplicity of truth-values.

The author's presence is felt throughout the BSBh; his is a playful imagination, which allows for the emergence of uncertainty and yet yearns for true knowledge of the self, or self-identification with the one *ātman* (the nature of such oneness is perhaps the greatest mystery in life). The author is not as invisible as one may at first assume. Analytically, at least, he differs from his hero. Perhaps, an opponent would say, the author imagines his hero in perfect resemblance to himself (and thus is as visible as his exponent is, or invisible if conceived as different). But we return to our argument; whatever the perfect resemblance between author and *siddhāntin* may signify, the very act of creating and imagining the *siddhāntin* means that the author maintains a type of existence or level of being beyond his creation.

The outlook of Viveka-Vedānta generates doubt and wonder; the cognition of the void existing between seer and seen is hard to maintain as life goes on. Thus, one can say that the choice is between certainty

---

[12] Bader 2005: 5.

and coherence, on the one hand, and levels of doubt and ambivalence, on the other. The crux of the Advaita vision is the connection of Brahman or *ātman* with the world of plurality. In terms of Advaita metapsychology, it is the power of Vedic speech to 'sublate' or transform one's committed acceptance of a world of plurality. Conflation of the voice of the author and *siddhāntin* finds its tangible expression in scholarly literature in the subconscious assumption of omnipresent coherence. Coherence in this sense means a one-voice speech-act. With his usual philosophical acumen, W. Halbfass senses a possible tension between the autonomy of the worldly means of knowledge (such as *pratyakṣa* and *anumāna*) and the power of the Veda to transform 'worldly plurality.' Committed to the purpose of the uniform, coherent, doubt-free voice of the author/*siddhāntin*, Halbfass integrates the two principles (autonomy of the diverse means of knowledge and the power of the Veda) into one synthetic whole. On the one hand, Halbfass asserts that Śaṅkara accepts that the Veda does not contradict sense perception, but on the other hand, of course, Halbfass's Śaṅkara asserts that the Upaniṣads have the power to affect a radical change in one's vision of the world (informed by recognition of Brahman).

> In Śaṅkara's view, the Vedic revelation negates the ultimate truth of plurality, the framework in which it appears and in which worldly ascertainment is possible. But this does not mean that it concerns only the ultimate metaphysical status of the world of plurality, without affecting its own internal conditions. Insofar as it speaks about transcendence, the Veda also speaks about what has to be transcended. There are no strict borderlines. The Veda 'reveals' reality as well as appearance in its soteriologically relevant details; and it precludes a systematic and unrestricted usage and development of the worldly means of knowledge even within this world.[13]

But how can the Veda touch a world that is only reached through reasoning and the senses? In my view, such a question expresses wonder and the power of doubt to generate metaphysical energy. Under the spell of strict content-coherence and a conflated author/*siddhāntin*'s certainty, Halbfass, the best of scholars, can hardly answer such a foundational question about Śaṅkara's Advaita. His cautious and eloquent rephrasing of Śaṅkara's Advaita is ultimately blurred, even self-contradictory. For in terms of contents, the Veda is not pure

---

[13] Halbfass 1991: 152.

metaphysics, nor does it change sense-perception (fire stays hot). It interferes with worldly plurality yet leaves it as it is. Our sense of wonder at Śaṅkara's wonder reenacts Śaṅkara's own.

As suggested above, consequent upon the distinction between Śaṅkara the *bhāṣya-kāra* and Śaṅkarācāya, the winning *siddhāntin*, is the renunciation of much scholarly work on the eight-century sage. For if Śaṅkara's and Śaṅkarācārya's theories of totality and the nature of its oneness, notions of the self (*ātman*) and its relationship to the individual soul, etc. are to be distinguished, then much that has been said about Śaṅkara's Advaita can be seen to reflect a vision that is blurred in significant ways. Therefore, though one must tread carefully here and distinguish between author and *siddhāntin* only when it is possible to reap substantial benefits, there are reasons to resist the current, paradigmatic conflation of author and *siddhāntin*.

We have a choice to make. The Advaita symphony consists of several discernible voices: the strains of the Advaita message (such as the oneness, omniscience, eternity of the self) echo differently if they emerge from the mouth of the loser than if voiced by the *siddhāntin* (this topic is further discussed in chapter 9). And a winner's victorious concluding statement has a different cadence if it is questionable or unconvincing (our argument in Chapter 2). The author is aware of the play of these voices in his text; through their juxtaposition he creates a space where his own doubts are articulated. The *siddhāntin* rejects plurality but the author does not know in what sense. Ultimately, what emerges is an author who becomes visible through his literary expression and expressiveness—a great scholar, energized by wonder and the yearning for truth, who recognizes the relevance of worldly phenomena and accepts the multiplicity of truth-values, while still recognizing Brahman's ultimate reality. But what makes Śaṅkara's suprising act of imagination possible? A *siddhānta*-Advaitin would never say *dṛṣṭāc câdṛṣṭa-siddhiḥ* (the unseen is known from what is seen). Neither would he imagine (as Śaṅkara does) the positions of his rivals as fully as he images those of his *siddhāntin*. Śaṅkara's Advaita metaphysics is that of wonder, not that of certainty.

Upon the collapse of conflation, the nature of the author comes to the fore along with the complex and intimate relationship between him and his *siddhāntin*. The sense of struggle is tangible, but the emphasis is on the organic, all-encompassing dimension of existence within which worldly phenomena and conventional multiplicity still leave their trace. *Pūrva-pakṣin*s, like snakes, do have a vital presence of their own. The author resists, as it were, immersion in the unchangeable self or Brahman. He is a philosopher asserting the difference of *viṣayin* and *viṣaya*, the two concomitant types of existence. It is impossible to identify the *siddhāntin*'s eternal Brahman as the sole reality with the author's imagination. The author's is one, and the exponent's is another. The forceful act of imagination is the clue to Śaṅkara's Advaita or Viveka-Vedānta; basing himself on a deep commitment to Upaniṣadic truth and the corresponding attraction of the one self (*ātman*), he still allows the play of wonder, curiosity and doubt to emerge and make their imprint.

The most important Advaita truth imaginable pertains to the relation of the individual soul (*jīva*) to the one omnipresent *ātman*. In my view, the source of the author's Advaita lies in the attempt to piece together the puzzle of the (impossible) connection of the individual soul with the one *ātman*. In other words, brooding over this connection generates the author's so called 'doubt' and engenders wonder, ultimately becoming a source of energy. In the process, Śaṅkara, the author of the BSBh, preserves his sense of an individual self, as do Uṣasta and Kahola. He fails, as it were, to lose that boundary between his dynamic, changing self and the eternal, unchanging *ātman*.

Śaṅkara the author of the BSBh lives an apparent impossibility; though the world of plurality cannot co-exist with the oneness of *ātman*-being, it is very much alive in the author's mind. Like a lamp, his vital imagination illuminates the world of plurality with a vividness and concreteness that is aware of itself, allowing us to witness the workings of a mind reaching toward wonder and truth.

EPILOGUE

THE USELESS KNOWLEDGE OF SELF AS THE HIGHEST GOOD: A NOTE ON ŚAṄKARA'S SECRET TEACHING OF VIVEKA-VEDĀNTA

If we heed the distinction between Śaṅkara and his multiple voices (in the shape of exponents and opponents), it is possible to assess the overall relationship between the author and the various creatures of his mind.[1]

As in the life of ordinary people, the real self of a pure *Vivekin* is often in need of concealment. Or perhaps there exists in men and women a measure of caution exercised from within, an expression of ambivalence regarding the truth of a real self that is extremely difficult to contain. The case of Śaṅkara is no different; a free thinker and great scholar, he seeks a truth that is very difficult (for others as well as, perhaps, for himself) to accept. The ultimate truth he speaks of is the *unbridgeable difference* between the oneness of the self and everything else (the objective world). It is an ice-cold negative proposition, as it were, and nearly impossible to maintain. Truth is incompatible with life as we know it. Like life itself, Śaṅkara's own speech-act in this assertion is self-contradictory. Only by means of an erroneous metaphysics can life go on and on. To assert that knowledge of the self (*ātman*) is, strictly speaking, true imagination made of a complex mode of consciousness (double attention) that has no use (*anupayoga*) in this world—this is Śaṅkara's "secret teaching."[2] The existential implication

[1] Since both exponents and opponents are Śaṅkara's "creatures of mind," we would expect that sometimes the opponent (*pūrva-pakṣin*) rather than the exponent would express his master's voice. Moreover, if this is indeed the case, the most secret or hidden part of the author's vision could be found in an opponent's view. I suggest that this is the case of Śaṅkara's view of the autonomy of reasoning (*tarka*). See BSBh 2.1.11.

[2] Śaṅkara's secret teaching and innermost voice consists of the following four propositions: 1) consciousness-made imaginations are the only reality; 2) true imagination is the one and only thing that may and should be known; 3) the distinction (*viveka*) of seer and seen underlies true "daylight consciousness," which is different from a blurred, "twilight state of mind" (see below); and 4) true imagination of oneself as Brahman ("knowledge") does not serve any other purpose.

is as obvious as it is tantalizing: either live in error or do not live at all. *Adhyāsa*, the superimposition of the self on the non-self and vice versa, is as wrong as it is life-giving. Even speech is self-defeating. Such a realization of truth generates the experience of an irreducible gap, an experience we label *viveka*. It is a subtle message, yet one of apparent, misleading simplicity, and trivially true, as it were.

One of the well-known propositions of the Upaniṣads is that knowledge of the real self is of paramount importance. One should listen to, think of, meditate on the self;[3] whoever knows the *ātman* satisfies every desire;[4] the self is the subtle, the real,[5] and so on. Obviously, Śaṅkara's conception of self (inherently dissociated from worldly apparition) is different from the Upaniṣadic notion of self as the primordial cause and origin of plurality. While the Upaniṣads state that knowledge of self is highly desirable, they also address numerous other topics. The connection of the seen with the primordial seer (*ātman*) provides an opening for much speculation and many observations. The majority of Śaṅkara's *siddhāntin*s express the Upaniṣadic vision of the self. Śaṅkara's innovation is the framing of his particular version of the Upaniṣadic self as the vantage point from which everything else is assessed, judged, and perceived.[6] Such framing implies a great deal. It means above all a dissociation of knowledge from any in-the-world goal (including the elimination of suffering and the achievement of immortality).[7] Knowledge of the self is not just very good and desirable, it is the only good. It is never a means to attain other goods in life but an end in itself.[8] True imagination of Brahman, significantly unspecified, is the highest good, independent of any purpose other than itself, as the *siddhāntin* asserts in BSBh 1.1.1: *niḥśreyasa-phalaṃ tu brahma-*

---

[3] BU 2.4.5.

[4] CU 8.7.1.

[5] CU 6.8.7.

[6] The cure of conventional, worldly existence (*saṃsāra*) is denied on this framing of true imagination as the exclusive perspective to assess the human condition.

[7] Although immortality is a characteristic feature of true imagination of self, the *siddhāntin* portrayed in BSBh 1.1.4 refuses to acknowledge instrumentality of true imagination in this respect. The Mīmāṃsaka opponent suggests that as the *agnihotra* ritual relates causally to gaining access to *svarga*, so the imagination of Brahman/*ātman* brings about immortality. The *siddhāntin* opposes this suggestion, insisting (in his master's voice) that knowledge of self is inherently non-instrumental.

[8] The universe created by true imagination is beyond the domain of means and ends (*sādhya-sādhana-bhāva*).

vijñānaṃ na cânuṣṭhānântarâpekṣam.[9] In this sense, Śaṅkara is a true philosopher and lover of wisdom.[10]

Rather than surrendering to innate drives for unity and integration, the philosopher exercises *viveka*, separation and distinction. Thus, in my view, Śaṅkara is a Viveka-Vedāntin (rather than an Advaitin). The argument, based on the introduction to the BSBh, is simple: If misperception or wrong knowledge (*avidyā*) consists of *adhyāsa*, then its opposite, *viveka*, or separation of the metaphysical subject (*viṣayin, sākṣin, ātman*) from objective reality (*viṣaya, dṛśya*), is true "knowledge" (*jñāna, vijñāna, vidyā, saṃyag-darśana*). The differentiating vision produces a quality of resistance that emerges from the empty field between the metaphysical subject (*ātman*) and everything else. It is perhaps the deepest and most disturbing challenge offered by philosophy to mankind.

The subtlest kind of separation is that which exists between the individual soul and the metaphysical subject. As *puruṣa* is infinitely different from the *sattva*-component of *prakṛti*, so the metaphysical subject is infinitely different from the *jīva*. *Viveka* means negation, resistance. Negation is not as satisfactory as integration. The philosophical mood wins over the innate drive for satisfaction. Śaṅkara inherits Yājñavalkya's *neti neti* rather than Uddālaka's *tat tvam asi* (*tat tvam asi* expresses the drive for unity rather than separation).

Given the exclusive nature of *viveka*, imagination of self and non-self, the author's state of mind is necessarily *gauṇa*, or "metaphorical," to be distinguished from a "merely erroneous" state of consciousness, which is characteristic of the rest of humanity. A new concept of truth and falsehood emerges; apparently erroneous (*adhyāsa*-inflicted) statements such as "I am sick," "I am going home," "I am thin," voiced by ordinary people are indeed "merely erroneous." Voiced by an Advaita-connoisseur, however, they are *gauṇa*-statements (true, although of

---

[9] Thibaut's translation at this point is somewhat misleading. Taking *niḥśreyasa-phalam* as a *bahu-vrīhi*, he translates: "The enquiry into Brahman, on the other hand, has for its fruit eternal bliss..." (Thibaut 1891: 11). Thus, according to this translation, knowledge of Brahman is instrumental in bringing about the condition of so-called "eternal bliss," a psychological condition of alleged happiness or joy. However, in my view, as suggested above, Śaṅkara's intention is to assert that knowledge of Brahman is the highest good (*niḥśreyasa*) (implied as a consequence of learning about Brahman).

[10] Knowledge of *dharma* (*bhavya*, action to be performed) is of excellent consequences (*abhyudaya-phalam*, BSBh 1.1.1), but knowledge of Brahman is not of this kind.

"secondary meaning," or figurative, as it were). Śaṅkara's simile of twilight as a moment of inadequate consciousness is telling; blurred and incapable of allowing one to make the distinction between the witness (*sākṣin*) and the witnessed, people live in confusion, mixing light and darkness, like one who gazes at a post (in twilight) thinking it is a man.[11] Even learned sages who allegedly distinguish between self and non-self "confound the words and ideas as common shepherds and goatherds do."[12] Keeping in mind the vast difference of *viṣayin* and *viṣaya* (see below), Śaṅkara is, in his own eyes, of a metaphorical, even poetic state of mind.

Separating consciousness from any trace or domain of an "in-the-world" dimension, the Advaita theory focuses on "true imagination" of the self; it is more coherent and forceful than illusory imaginations,[13] a mode of consciousness essentially "ineffective" (yet the highest good).[14] A reference to Śaṅkara's recurring association of magic and imagination[15] is in place here. A real magician (*paramârtha-rūpa*) standing on earth is different from a false one climbing on a string to the sky and holding a shield and knife (*yathā māyāvinaś carma-khaṅga-dharāt sūtreṇâkāśam adhirohitaḥ sa eva māyāvī paramârtha-rūpo bhūmiṣṭho 'nyaḥ*).[16] Keeping in mind the abysmal, irreducible difference between the witness (*sākṣin*) and every other phenomenon, the real magician is a poet who is aware of standing in the world. According to Śaṅkara's

---

[11] BSBh 1.1.4. *yathā mandāndhakāre sthāṇur ayam ity agṛhyamāṇa-viśeṣe puruṣa-śabda-pratyayau sthāṇu-viṣayau.*

[12] BSBh 1.1.4. Thibaut 1891: 43.

[13] Śaṅkara uses the term *apavāda* to denote replacement of a wrong conception (*mithyā-buddhi*) by another, correct one (*yathârtha*). Thus, in BSBh 3.3.9: "We, in the second place, have *apavāda* when an idea previously attached to some object is recognized as false and driven out by the true idea springing up after the false one. So, e.g., when the false idea of the body, the senses, and so on being the Self is driven out by the true idea springing up later—and expressed by judgments such as 'Thou art that'—that the idea of the Self is to be attached to the Self only." (Thibaut 1891, v. 2: 197).

[14] I think Śaṅkara is indebted in this respect to the Sāṅkhya conception of *puruṣa*, the inherently ineffective, unchanging subject.

[15] Scholars often do not distinguish between *māyā* as so-called "cosmic illusion," apparently unreal, and true imagination, which is reality. Thus, for example, A. Fort says: *māyā* both conceals and misrepresents Brahman, but is (inexplicably) derived from it, as unreal appearance requires a real basis" (Fort 1990: 5). Reflecting on true imagination, D. Shulman says: "It is the imagination that conjures up the real, penetrating past its outer guise, working on—actually half-dispelling—its surface manifestation with words" ("Rethinking the Imagination in Sixteenth-century South India: Notes on Ratnakheṭa Śrīnivāsa *Dīkṣita's Bhāvana-puruṣottama*," *Diacritics*, in press).

[16] BSBh 1.1.17.

own analysis, Advaita attention is of a double nature; a successful Advaitin maintains awareness of the real self and of worldly phenomena as two distinct entities. This is how speech and play are made possible.

Considering its meaning and implications, Śaṅkara's message of the highest good must have been kept secret, or at least somewhat concealed by the author's art of writing.[17] A so-called secret teaching is not so much secret as it is a mode of consciousness difficult to express (or contain) under certain circumstances. Lost among voluble scholars who speak of *ātman* and *anātman* and yet, living a twilight-consciousness, are incapable of truly making the distinction, Śaṅkara is a *vivekin* living in constant awareness of a world inherently unrelated to the "metaphysical" subject (*ātman*, Brahman). Devoid of the recognition of self and non-self, unable to recognize their true being in relation to these two poles, and immersed in confluent, false conditions, people are cut off from their realities. Indeed, the vast majority of Śaṅkara's exponents (*siddhāntins*) as well as opponents (*pūrva-pakṣins*) should be considered "functional false selves." Such selves reveal but also hide various aspects of the most precious and, in some respects, vulnerable real self.[18] In a sense, the false selves' propositions, though apparently mistaken, are metaphorical insofar as they preserve a measure of the real self's truth.[19] One recalls a statement of a leading psychologist of our time: "The False Self has one positive and very important function: to hide the True Self, which it does by compliance with environmental demands."[20]

We do not know much of Śaṅkara the man, yet if he had asserted that knowledge of self, in its absolute dissociation from the world, is the *only* worthwhile purpose in life[21] and is the ultimate good, he

---

[17] See L. Strauss, *Persecution and the Art of Writing*, 1969. I am indebted to Naphtali Meshel, who insisted that Strauss' conception is relevant in this respect of hiding an author's true intentions. Instead of speaking of persecution and, consequently, of contradiction and irreducible tension, I tend to speak of a positive relationship, a particular kind of protection, between false and true selves. See below.

[18] Secondary meaning (*gauṇa*, *lakṣaṇa*, *upacāra*) is one of Śaṅkara's primary methods of articulating his so-called secret teaching. Metaphor both hides and reveals ultimate truth. See below.

[19] The difference of error and *gauṇa* is of crucial importance for Śaṅkara. See below.

[20] Winnicott 1965: 146–7.

[21] Consciousness of Brahman, says the *siddhāntin* in BSBh 1.1.1, is the goal of man (*brahmâvagatir puruṣârthaḥ*), because of its power to destroy completely the useless

would have been in need of a measure of false appearance, a sort of concealment. A position such as Śaṅkara's pristine Viveka-Vedānta is hard to maintain openly while living in cultural environments that are inherently therapeutic (Bauddha, Sāṅkhya-Yoga)[22] or otherwise instrumental in their underlying presuppositions and promise (Pūrva-Mīmāṃsā). Indeed, such a teaching requires a very special audience, *mumukṣus* of proven despair (with respect of "life in the world"),[23] committed to the truth of imagination and freedom (*mokṣa*). A poetic audience such as this is rare indeed and mostly unavailable. In fact, the text we have tells us of this intellectual situation, sometimes by explicitly replacing the *siddhānta*-positions,[24] sometimes by pregnant silence,[25] and sometimes by the innermost voice when speaking of the principle of non-*adhyāsa*, or of attention concomitantly focused on the self and non-self in their difference.

A sense of freedom and choice informs Śaṅkara's exclusive selection of the Upaniṣadic message with respect to the imagination of self. Visualization of self is potent and free; its truth cannot be judged by correspondence to "external reality" or other types of imagination (or visualization). Freedom embedded in and implied by the nature of imagination constitutes the ground of Śaṅkara's creativity.[26] Consist-

---

illusory cognition which is the seed of *saṃsāra* (*niḥśeṣa-saṃsāra-bījâvidyādy-anartha-nibarhaṇāt*).

[22] The opening proposition of Īśvarakṛṣṇa's *Sāṅkhya-Kārikā* epitomizes the controversy between Śaṅkara and *Sāṅkhya-Yoga*: Opposing (counteracting) the suffering of three kinds, the quest for knowledge arises (*duḥkha-trayâbhighātāj jijñāsā*).

[23] See the opening section of the prose part of the Upad. "We are going to explain the method of liberation for the benefit of those spiritually fervant, desiring liberation (*atha mokṣa-sādhanopadeśa-vidhiṃ vyākhyāsyāmo mumukṣūṇāṃ śraddadhānānām arthinām arthāya*).

[24] According to BSBh 2.1.33, a *siddhāntin* in favor of creation (of plurality from the one Brahman) is replaced by another (higher voice, as it were) who judges Vedic theories of creation as untrue and made of illusory cognition (*avidyā-kalpita*). Such replacement of a *siddhānta*-position means, among other things, that the distinction of exponent and opponent is not clear-cut; a *siddhānta*-position becomes a *pūrvapakṣa*. The higher voice, the ultimate *siddhānta*, as it were, is the author's.

[25] There are different degrees of so-called pregnant silence. In some contexts, such as silence maintained over the potency of Advaita imagination in the removal of *duḥkha* (heard in the controversy with the Buddhists), silence is dense and strikingly tangible. In other contexts, pregnant silence is of a more subtle quality. The philosopher's (*tārkika*) assertion in BSBh 2.1.11 (see below) that groundlessness (*apratiṣṭhitatva*) of reasoning is a big advantage (*alaṃkāra*) generates a pregnant silence of the more subtle type.

[26] Imagination consists of two fundamental flavors: discovery and creativity. Śaṅkara's reflection on "knowledge of self" integrates these two dimensions of

ing of modes of attention and consciousness that are less complex than Viveka-Vedānta, other imaginations of self are more vulnerable and less viable than an *adhyāsa*-free state of mind. Imagining the imaginations of his opponents and exponents, Śaṅkara recommends choosing what he considers the true, essential Upaniṣadic imagination of the self concomitant with utter negation of any trace of objectivity. There is, however, a major difference between the Upaniṣadic conception of self and Śaṅkara's own. In a nutshell, the Upaniṣadic vision is creationist, based upon the transformation (*pariṇāma*) of the one primordial *ātman* into a this worldly condition of plurality. Śaṅkara focuses on the irreducible difference between *ātman* and worldly apparitions of plurality. In his view, I dare say, the Upaniṣadic theories of creation are of the twilight quality, *adhyāsa*-driven. His own state of mind is of the *vivarta* type of relationship between *ātman* and the world, a relationship in which freedom of imagination is palpably accessible. The freedom to imagine one's self is perhaps the hallmark of being truly human or conscious, in Śaṅkara's mind.[27] It is also, perhaps, the most difficult freedom to exercise.

In addition to the flavors of discovery and creativity that are manifest in imagining ("conjuring the real"), disembodiment (*aśarīratva*) is a third flavor of much importance in Śaṅkara's secret teaching of the self.[28] The association of disembodiment with true knowledge of self and freedom (*mokṣa*) is undeniably a feature of true imagination.[29] A primary exercise of *avidyā* is the superimposition of bodily attributes on the self.[30]

Choosing imagination is, in Śaṅkara's experience, the most important exercise of freedom in a man's or woman's life. Implied by his theory of *adhyāsa* (the core of his secret teaching), visualization of

imagination. On the one hand, a sense of discovery is implied (see, for example the *siddhāntin*'s insistence on knowledge of Brahman as *vastu-tantra*, dependent solely on the nature of the object to be known). On the other hand, absence of a corresponding, out-of-consciousness criterion of truth implies a measure of inherent freedom in creating one's self.

[27] See the discussion below on "beastly *adhyāsa*," according to the introduction to the BSBh. Beasts and human beings are the same in their exercise of superimposition.

[28] Śaṅkara's intention is that for embodied people (including scholars), an Advaitic imagination is of no use insofar as these people insist on "staying embodied."

[29] See BSBh 1.1.4; 1.3.19; 1.3.40; 4.2.14; 4.4.2; 4.4.12.

[30] See Śaṅkara's introduction to the BSBh: Attributes of the body are superimposed on the Self, if a man thinks of himself (his Self) as stout, lean, fair, or as standing, walking, or jumping" (Thibaut 1891: 8–9).

the true self is a matter of life and death, as it were. Such an association comes to mind in Śaṅkara's reflection on a passage from the Chāndogyopaniṣad 8.12.1, brought forth by a *siddhāntin* portrayed in BSBh 1.1.4. The Upaniṣadic passage refers to the disembodied condition of one who is free of both pleasure and displeasure: "Pleasure and displeasure do not touch one who is disembodied" (*aśarīraṃ vāva santaṃ na priyāpriye spṛśataḥ*). However, says an opponent (BSBh 1.1.4), only a dead person could be said to be disembodied (*śarīre patite 'śarīratvaṃ syāt, na jīvata iti*)! But no, says a *siddhāntin*. Only by virtue of wrong imagination does one identify oneself with a body (*saśarīratvasya mithyā-jñāna-nimittattvāt*). It is not possible to attribute embodiment to one who has renounced the wrong imagination of being a body (*na hy ātmanaḥ śarīrâtmâbhimāna-lakṣaṇaṃ mithyā-jñānaṃ muktvânyataḥ saśarīratvaṃ śakyaṃ kalpayitum*).[31]

The choice of imagination implies rejection of one possible world for the sake of another, more viable (and true) universe.[32] Renunciation of one type of imagination is necessary in order to conjure up another; the co-existence of Advaitic imagination and plurality is strictly impossible. This is the core of Advaita psychology. In this context, Śaṅkara's elaboration of the difference between the lower and higher imaginations is important. The highest (*niḥśreyasa*) truth is one; numerous are the lesser, environment-sensitive truths articulated by *siddhāntins* and *pūrva-pakṣins*.

Indeed, Śaṅkara's *siddhāntins* speak in many voices and are engaged in various environments that are different in tone and contents. Sometimes, for example, a *siddhāntin* speaks of the one strictly impersonal *ātman* or *nir-guṇa* Brahman, devoid of any characteristic sign (*liṅga*) as

---

[31] The dissociation of body and imagination (and dream) is closely related in the Upaniṣadic literature to self-understanding. See, for example, Indra's search for the self through the conditions of embodiment, disembodiment in dream-states (*svapna*), disembodiment in dreamless sleep (*susupti*), and disembodied, playful existence (ChU 8.7–12). The Chāndogya is explicit in its association of true imagination of self with freedom of embodiment. Prajāpati sums up the teaching of the self in the following passage (ChU 8.12): "This body, Maghavan, is mortal; it is in the grip of death. So, it is the abode of this immortal and nonbodily self. One who has a body is in the grip of joy and sorrow, and there is no freedom from joy and sorrow for one who has a body.....the wind is without a body, and so are the rain-cloud, lightning, and thunder....the life breath is yoked to this body, as a draft animal to a cart" (Olivelle 1998: 285).

[32] Conceptualization of true (Advaitic) imagination is free of contradictions; that of untrue imagination is self-contradictory. Under this presupposition, the exercise of reasoning by exponents and opponents continues unabated.

the origin and cause of the world.[33] Sometimes he speaks of *Īśvara*, an allegedly personal entity that is capable of delivering grace (*prasāda*)[34] as the creator and origin of the world.[35] Sometimes Brahman is the self, and sometimes it is *Īśvara*.[36] From one perspective, there is a difference between Brahman and the individual soul (*jīva*);[37] from another, there is no difference. Sometimes, the logical force of the Upaniṣadic quotations is compelling, bearing directly on the nature of the Absolute or the self; sometimes, such quotations seem to be merely associative or of an illustrative impact, a kind of textual exemplifcation. Sometimes, the *siddhāntin* asserts that *dharma* is of value, so that a *śūdra* may not approach the Veda; sometimes, *dharma* is of no significance (as a dimension of *saṃsāra*). Sometimes, an exponent speaks of the elimination of *duḥkha* due to the knowledge of self as being of primary significance,[38] and sometimes he sees such knowledge of self as the highest good in life, with merely cognitive parameters, of no other purpose (*prayojana*), and hence having no real impact on everyday life (*vyavahāra*).[39] Sometimes, the Veda is of absolute authority, and sometimes, it is made of *avidyā* (*avidyā-kalpita*), of mere instrumental significance. Sometimes, the world emerges from Brahman and hence is somewhat similar to it; sometimes, the absolute is totally unrelated to the world.

When we heed the numerous shades, hues, and philosophical positions voiced in the course of the BSBh, a question arises: Is the BSBh self-contradictory? Such a proposition is premature and obviously unwarranted. There seems to be a unified intention behind the composition of the BSBh; a certain sense of coherence does prevail in the text. But what is it? Strict, logical coherence is hard to find. Viewed according to their respective contents, different *siddhānta*-voices (engaged in various environments) would appear contradictory. In search of coherence among the multitude of Vedic expressions and positions, Śaṅkara himself addresses issues related to contradiction and coherence:

[33] BSBh 1.1.4.
[34] BSBh 1.1.5.
[35] BSBh 2.1.33.
[36] BSBh 2.1.1.
[37] BSBh 1.2.8.
[38] BSBh 2.3.45–47.
[39] BSBh 2.1.33. See below.

> ....Śaṅkara emphasizes repeatedly that the Veda itself adjusts its teachings to different levels of understanding and qualification, that it uses different methods of instruction, and that it addresses different interests and capabilities. The whole "work section" (*karma-kāṇḍa*) applies to those who are still in the network of "work orientation," that is, of reward-oriented nescience; but also within the "knowledge section" (*jñāna-kāṇḍa*), that is, the Upaniṣads, it speaks at different levels. It offers various meditational and devotional methods and "symbolic" devices (*pratīka*), such as the *oṃ*, to those who are of slow or mediocre understanding (*manda-madhya-pratipattiṃ prati*).[40]

Śaṅkara's vision of Vedic adjustment to different environments and needs could be applied to Śaṅkara's own literary expression. It is, as Halbfass suggests, a legitimate notion of coherence applicable to Śaṅkara's use of "examples" (*dṛṣṭāntas*) and other means of instruction and persuasion (such as metaphor).[41]

Suppose then that environments count and that a plurality of voices is assumed. Is there not an environment-free context in Śaṅkara's writing in which the author of the BSBh speaks self-consciously in his own voice? Indeed, Śaṅkara's introduction to the BSBh is an environment-free speech-act; no scholastic *pūrva-pakṣin* is in sight.[42] Even the Veda is not quoted. The introduction is devoted to one and only one topic: the difference between true and illusory knowledge (*avidyā*). The difference between true and distorted cognitions is the underlying and explicit theme, the subject of the entire introduction. The author discusses at length the nature of the major dynamics that are generative of illusory imagination (*adhyāsa*, "superimposition" of self on not-

[40] Halbfass 1991: 57.

[41] Halbfass' meticulous reading of Śaṅkara, although essentially conflating author and *siddhāntins*, recognizes the variations in these voices and creates a softer sense of coherence in the BSBh, a sense receptive to variations in environment and audience. See Halbfass 1991: 131–204.

[42] The only opponent present in the introduction raises a question that the *siddhāntin* is unable to answer in a satisfactory way: "But how is it possible that on the interior Self, which itself is not an object, there should be superimposed objects and their attributes? For everyone superimposes an object only on such other objects as are placed before him...and you have said before that the interior Self, which is entirely disconnected from the idea of the Thou (the Non-Ego), is never an object" (Thibaut 1891: 5). The *siddhāntin*'s response is somewhat ambiguous: "It is not, we reply, non-object in the absolute sense. For it is the object of the notion of the Ego, and the interior Self is well known to exist on account of its immediate (intuitive) presentation" (ibid.) (*na tāvad ayam ekāntenâviṣayaḥ, asmat-pratyaya-viṣayatvāt, aparokṣatvāc ca pratyag-ātma-prasiddheḥ*).

self and vice versa),[43] the beastly nature of ordinary men and women afflicted by *adhyāsa*, and the status of the Veda as a means of knowledge.[44] There is no mention of suffering to be avoided or eliminated. The cognitive, scholarly, philosophical bent and essence of Śaṅkara's teaching succinctly shows at the end of his introduction:

> Thus, there goes on this natural (*naisargika*) *adhyāsa* of no beginning and end. It shows in the form of wrong conception (*mithyā-pratyaya-rūpa*) and is the cause of individual souls appearing as agents and enjoyers (*kartṛtva-bhoktṛtva-pravartaka*). Such illusion of knowledge is seen to be the lot of everyone (*sarva-loka-pratyakṣa*). In order to have a release (*prahāṇāya*) consisting of true knowledge of the oneness of *ātman* (*ātmaikatva-vidyā-pratipattaye*), a release of the cause of nonsense (*anartha-hetu*), all the Vedānta-texts are introduced (*sarve vedāntā ārabhyante*). This is the purpose of all the Vedānta-texts, and we are going to show this with respect to this text called the *Śarīraka-Mīmāṃsā*.

Thus, free of the *sūtra-kāra*'s presence, the introduction expresses the author's true being as a philosopher who is intoxicated with the truth of the separation of seer (*viṣayin*) and seen (*viṣaya*),[45] maintaining a "pregnant" silence over other purposes in life. Knowledge of self is thus inherently useless by virtue of its being the exclusive and only good.[46] Such knowledge heals cognition, namely, the disease of fusion, *adhyāsa*, the dynamics of wrong imagination.

It is, I think, noteworthy that the author makes exhaustive use of the concept of *adhyāsa* only in the introduction to the BSBh; other

---

[43] The author provides four definitions of *adhyāsa* and discusses the meaning of his decisive intellectual move (to see in *adhyāsa* the only topic which matters).

[44] Scholarly fusion of author and exponents is another case of "wrong imagination," superimposition (*adhyāsa*).

[45] Wonder over the relationship of the seer and seen (and the irreducible difference of the "metaphysical subject" from the world) finds expression in some of L. Wittgenstein's notes on the subject. Thus, in the Tractatus:

> 5.632: The subject does not belong to the world: rather, it is a limit to the world.
> 5.633: Where *in* the world is a metaphysical subject to be found?

You will say that this is exactly like the case of the eye and the visual field. But really you do *not* see the eye. And *nothing in the visual field* allows you to infer that it is seen by an eye (Wittgenstein 1972: 117).

The philosophical self is not the human being, not the human body, or the human soul, with which psychology deals, but rather the metaphysical subject, the limit of the world—not a part of it (ibid.: 119).

[46] Prakśānanda, a follower of Śaṅkara, was of a similar view, according to S. Dasgupta: "Prakāśānanda holds, however, in his *Siddhānta-Muktāvalī*, that Brahman itself is pure and absolutely unaffected even as illusory appearance, and is not even the causal matter of the world-appearance" (Dasgupta 1997: 469).

references to this concept are few and casual.[47] In its style and straightforward assertion, the introduction stands apart as the most intimate testimony of "Śaṅkara's secret teaching."[48] Together with other segments of this teaching, such as the pregnant silence over *duḥkha* in the exchange with the Buddhists, the relegation of Vedic theories of creation to the domain of lesser truths of illusory imagination, and the resistance to the Mīmāṃsaka's wish to subordinate knowledge of self to the imperative mood or to gaining immortality, the introduction to the BSBh is definitive in its constitution of the author's innermost voice, or perfectly genuine, teaching.

Towards the end of the introduction, Śaṅkara compares people to animals in two regards: in favoring safety and pleasure to danger and pain, and in the exercise of *adhyāsa*. On the one hand, they are similar in their avoidance of danger and attraction to friendly offerings. Cows welcome a person with fresh grass in his hands and run away from one who is shouting and holding a knife. People behave likewise; they are attracted by pleasure and avoid risk and pain. This is sober, conventional wisdom. The secret teaching is different, strikingly unfamiliar, grotesque, almost bizarre: people and beasts are the same, since both kinds exercise *adhyāsa*, or the superimposition of self on not-self, and vice versa.

> Now it is well known that the procedure of animals bases on the non-distinction (of Self and non-Self); we therefore conclude that, as they present the same appearances, men also—although distinguished by superior intelligence—proceed with regard to perception and so on, in the same way as animals do.[49]

The apparent categorical mistake of "beastly *adhyāsa*" invites a pause for reflection. What seems to be the highest achievement of mankind (knowledge of self, free of *adhyāsa*) divides the creatures into those who do not exercise *adhyāsa* (a negligible minority of Advaitins like Śaṅkara) and those who are deluded, constantly superimposing subject on object and vice versa; the latter are no different from beasts. We see how deeply ingrained is the so-called secret, idiosyncratic conviction

[47] See BSBh 1.1.24; 3.3.9; 4.1.5.

[48] The space occupied by Śaṅkara's secret teaching in the BSBh is not great. Important concepts appearing in the introduction, such as *viṣayin* (seer) and *sākṣin* (direct visionary witness), are not present elsewhere in the BSBh.

[49] Thibaut 1891: 8. *ataḥ samānaḥ paśvâdibhiḥ puruṣāṇāṃ pramāṇa-prameya-vyavahāraḥ. paśvâdīnām ca prasiddho 'viveka-puraḥsaraḥ pratyakṣâdi-vyavahāraḥ.*

of Śaṅkara, in that he dares to make this categorical mistake of considering animals to be capable of superimposition. The secret teaching implied is the framing of true knowledge of the self as the highest and *only good.* Pending such knowledge, nothing really matters; all sorts of differences—so meaningful by conventional standards—are insignificant. Śaṅkara repeats that human beings are of superior intelligence (*vyutpatti-mata*), and yet, bereft of true imagination of self, they are like beasts. Such is Śaṅkara's harsh judgment of the human condition. It is concealed by a more conventional comparison with respect to similar patterns of the conditioning of human beings and beasts.

Of what character is an *adhyāsa*-free state of consciousness and verbal expression? How does Śaṅkara speak in his own voice? Secondary meaning, or "metaphor" (*gauṇa, lakṣana, upacāra*), is a concept central to Śaṅkara's self-understanding and a vehicle of the distinction between truth and falsehood. A metaphorical state of mind, says Śaṅkara in his real voice, is making an apparently false statement with true sounds. Combining *adhyāsa* theory with the notion of *gauṇa*, Śaṅkara provides a key to reading the entire BSBh. The presence of *gauṇa* in Śaṅkara's mind is made tangible throughout the BSBh. Indeed, almost every instance of Vedic speech is false if taken in its primary or literal meaning (*mukhya*) but true if meant metaphorically. As we have seen above, if the Upaniṣadic teaching of creation is taken literally, it is false (*avidyā-kalpita*); if it is taken as a secondary meaning (*gauṇa*) and a corresponding state of mind, it is correct, a worthy means of knowledge. Thus, the role of "secondary meaning" in Śaṅkara's mind is obvious;[50] it is a primary mode of access to Vedic speech as well as to an Advaitic consciousness of man and woman. Free of the primordial confusion of *viṣayin* and *viṣaya*, the successful Advaitin is either silent or speaks through secondary meaning, *as if* oblivious to the respective distinction. The Advaitic *jīvan-mukta* speaks and lives as an ordinary person, but awareness of the irreducible difference of subject and object makes his or her speech true rather than false. In my view, reflecting on the distinction between error (*mithya-jñāna*) and secondary meaning (*gauṇa*), Śaṅkara speaks in his innermost voice, expressive of his real self. In BSBh 1.1.4, he

[50] See BSBh 1.1.4; 1.1.5; 1.1.6; 1.1.7; 1.1.22; 1.1.2; 1.2.6; 1.4.15; 1.4.22; 2.1.17; 2.3.3; 2.3.5; 2.3.7; 2.3.8; 2.4.1; 2.4.2; 2.4.3; 3.1.4; 3.1.22; 3.1.25; 3.2.9; 3.2.3; 3.2.34; 3.3.8; 3.3.16; 3.3.34; 4.1.6; 4.1.3; 4.1.16; 4.4.4.

inserts the key to reading the entire gamut of voices by exponents and opponents voices in the BSBh:

> This objection we invalidate by the remark that the distinction of derived and primary senses of words is known to be applicable only where an actual difference of things is known to exist. We are, for instance, acquainted with a certain species of animals having a mane, and so on, which is the exclusive primary object of the idea and word 'lion,' and we are likewise acquainted with persons possessing in an eminent degree certain leonine qualities, such as fierceness, courage, etc.; here, a well settled difference of objects existing, the idea and name 'lion' are applied to those persons in a derived or figurative sense. In those cases, however, where the difference of the objects is not well established, the transfer of the conception and name of the one to the other is not figurative, but simply founded on error.[51]

The *as if* existential condition inherent in figurative speech and a figurative state of mind is protective of the real self and has tangible liberating effects. Thus, in the *adhyāsa*-free, *gauṇa* state of consciousness, we find the key to Advaita speech, spirituality, and theory of truth. Having cultivated an enhanced awareness of an existing, unchanging ground for the metaphysical subject (*ātman*)—absorbing the Upaniṣadic notion of *ātman*—an awareness concomitant with acute recognition of the complete, paradoxical dissociation of self and non-self (which is Śaṅkara's contribution to Advaita theory), Śaṅkara, the *viveka*-poet, comes to life. The author's voice is true either by virtue of primary meaning (*mukhya*) or by metaphor. The author, committed to his secret teaching, aware of the identity and oneness of Brahman/*ātman*—the author who distinguishes Brahman from anything else and remains firm in the conviction of the useless knowledge of self as the highest (and only) good—looks perhaps like everybody

[51] BSB 1.4.1; Thibaut 1891: 40–1 (*dehâdi-vyatiriktasyâtmana ātmīye dehādāv abhimāno gauṇo na mithyeti cen na, prasiddha-vastu-bhedasya gauṇatva-mukhyatva-prasiddheḥ. yasya hi prasiddho vastu-bhedaḥ, yathā kesarâdi-mānākṛti-viśeṣo 'nvaya-vyatirekâbhyāṃ siṃha-śabda-pratyaya-bhāṅ mukhyo 'nyaḥ prasiddhaḥ, tataś cânyaḥ puruṣaḥ prāyikaiḥ kraurya-śauryādibhiḥ siṃha-guṇaiḥ saṃpannaḥ siddhaḥ, tasya puruṣe siṃha-śabda-pratyayau gauṇau bhavato nâprasiddha-vastu-bhedasya. tasya tv anyatrânya-śabda-pratyayau bhrānti-nimittāv eva bhavato na gauṇau. yathā mandândhakāre sthāṇur ayam ity agṛhyamāṇa-viśeṣe puruṣa-śabda-pratyayau sthāṇu-viṣayau, yathā vā śuktikāyām akasmād rajatam iti niścitau śabda-pratyayau, tadvad dehâdi-saṃghāte 'ham iti nirupacāreṇa śabda-pratyayāv ātmânātmâviveke-notpadyamānau kathaṃ gauṇau śakyau vaditum. ātmânātma-vivekinām api paṇḍitānām ajāvi-pālānām ivâviviktau śabda-pratyayau bhavataḥ. tasmād dehâdi-vyatiriktâtmâstitva-vādināṃ dehādāv ahaṃ-pratyayo mithyaiva na gauṇaḥ*).

else. In this sense, his figurative speech protects his real self, veiling the difference between one who truly knows (imagining oneself) and others who do not. While speaking of wives and sons, pleasures and displeasures, jars and carpenters, servants and kings, spiders and cows, arrows and oil, he knows all this to be speech (and thought) other than those used by the rest of humanity. Given the fundamental distinction (*viveka*) of seer (*viṣayin*) and seen (*viṣaya*), every speech-act betokens *avidyā* (*adhyāsa*). Given the distinction between a real and a false self, and the corresponding difference between secret and overt teachings, *siddhānta* positions are often metaphorical, while *pūrva-pakṣa* positions are often "simply wrong." The author stands apart from both. In his self-understanding, he is the only ultimate *vivekin*, the free magician[52] standing on earth, silent amidst rather noisy *siddhāntins* and *pūrva-pakṣins*. "Deliciously free,"[53] playful, enjoying the protective as well as the liberating effects of *gauṇa* speech, he celebrates his separation from the rest of humanity, which is afflicted by *adhyāsa* (*avidyā*) and unaware of the falsehood of an ordinary, non-*gauṇa* state of mind.

[52] The relation between the Advaitic separation of *ātman* and the empirical ego and the notion of freedom and playfulness is beyond the scope of this essay.
[53] D. Shulman's expression.

BIBLIOGRAPHY

Primary Sources

Annamaya, *God on the Hill: Temple Poems from Tirūpati*, translated by Narayana Rao, V. and Shulman, D. New-York 2005.

Bhagavadgītā-bhāṣyam, 1955.

Brahma-sūtra-śāṅkara-bhāṣya. Delhi, edition 1987.

Brahma-sūtra-bhāṣyam. Bombay, 1948.

Brahma-sūtra-śāṅkara-bhāṣyam. Varanasi, rep. 1998.

Bṛrhadāraṇyakôpaniṣad-bhāṣya. 1983.

Kaṭhôpaniṣad-bhāṣya. 1983.

Complete Works of Śaṅkarācārya, in the Original Sanskrit. Madras, 1983.

Kauśītaki-Upaniṣad-bhāṣya. 1983.

Śaṅkara-dig-vijaya of Vidyāraṇya. Mylapore, 2000

Īśâdi-daśôpaniṣadaḥ, Ten Principal Upaniṣads with Śāṅkara-bhāṣya. Delhi, 1964.

The Early Upaniṣads, Annotated Texts and Translation by P. Olivelle. New-York, 1998.

Upadeśa-sāhasrī, A Thousand Teachings, Sanskrit and English, translated by Swami Jagadananda. Mylapure, 2003.

Secondary Sources

Bader, J. *Conquest of the Four Quarters; Traditional Accounts of the Life of Śaṅkara*. New-Delhi, 2000.

Bakhtin, M. *Problems of Dostoevsky's Poetics*. Chicago, 1993.

Booth, W. *The Rhetoric of Fiction*. Chicago, 1993.

Dasgupta, Surendranath. *A History of Indian Philosophy*. New-Delhi, Rep. 1997.

Frege, G. *Philosophical Writings*. Oxford, 1952.

Freud, S. *On Metapsychology: The Theory of Psychoanalysis*, in The Penguin Freud Library, v. 11, 1984.

Hacker, P. "Śaṅkara der Yogin und Śaṅkara der Advaitin, einige Beobachtungen," *Wiener Zeitschrift für die Kunde Süd- und Ostasiens* 12/13, 1968, 119–148.

Halbfass, W. *Tradition and Reflection; Explorations in Indian Thought*. New-York, 1991.

——. *Philology and Confrontation; Paul Hacker on Traditional and Modern Vedānta*. New-York, 1995.

Handelman, D. and Shulman, D. *God Inside Out: Śiva's Game of Dice*. New-York, 1997.

——. *Śiva in the Forest of Pines: an Essay on Sorcery and Self-Knowledge*. New-Delhi 2004.

Hopkins, Th.J. *The Hindu Religious Tradition*, 1971.

Ingalls, D.D.H. "Śaṅkara on the Question: Whose is Avidyā?" *Philosophy East and West*, v. 3, 1953, pp. 69–72.

——. "The Study of Śaṃkarācārya." *Annals of the Bhandarkar Research Institute*, 1952.

Iyer, M.K. *Advaita Vedānta according to Śaṅkara*. Madras, 1954.

Granoff, Ph. And Shinohara, K. *Monks and Magicians; Religious Biographies in Asia*. New-Delhi, 1994.

Granoff, Phyllis. "Scholars and Wonder-Makers: Some Remarks on the Role of the Supernatural in Philosophical Contests in Vedānta Hagiographies." *JAOS* v. 105, No. 3, 1985, pp. 459–467.
Grant, S. *Śaṅkarācārya's Concept of Relation*. Delhi, 1999.
Keith, A.B. *The Religion and Philosophy of the Veda and Upaniṣads*, 1925.
Kocmarek, I. *Language and Release: Sarvajñātman's Pañcaprakriyā*. Delhi, 1985.
Korner, S. *Kant*. Yale, 1982.
Krishna, D. (ed.) *Discussion and Debate in Indian Philosophy*. New-Delhi, 2004.
Larson, G.J. *Classical Sāṃkhya. An Interpretation of its History and Meaning*. Delhi, 1979.
Ludden, D. *India and South Asia: A Short History*, 2004.
Mayeda, S. *A Thousand Teachings; The Upadeśa-sāhasrī of Śaṅkara*. New-York, 1979.
Murty, K. *Revelation and Reason in Advaita Vedānta*, Waltair, 1959.
Olivelle, P. *Saṃnyāsa Upaniṣads: Hindu Scriptures on Asceticism and Renunciation*. New-York, 1992.
Ong, W.J. *Orality and Literacy: The Technologizing of the Word*. London, 1982.
Pande, G.Ch. *Life and Thought of Śaṅkarācārya*. Delhi, 1998.
Potter, K. *Śaṃkarācārya, the Myth and the Man*, in Williams, M.A., *Charisma and Sacred Biography*. Chicago, 1982.
Quine, W.V.O. *Word and Object*, 1973.
Radhakrishnan, S. *Indian Philosophy*. London, 1929.
Ricoeur, P. *The Conflict of Interpretations: Essays in Hermeneutics*. Evanstone, 1974.
Rukmani, T.S. *Śaṅkara, the Man and his Philosophy*. Simla, 1991.
——. "Śaṅkara the Author of the Brahmasūtrabhāṣya is not the Author of the Vivaraṇa". *Journal of Indian Philosophy*, 1998.
Schechet, N. *Narative Fissures: Reading and Rhetoric*, 2005.
Shulman, D. *The Hungry God: Hindu Tales of Filicide and Devotion*. Chicago, 1993.
Thibaut, G. *The Vedānta Sūtras of Bādarāyaṇa, with the Commentary by Śaṅkara*. New-York, rep. 1962.
Wittgenstein, L. *Philosophical Investigations*. London, 1974.

INDEX

adhyāsa vii–x, xiv, 12–13, 27, 36–37, 44, 86, 98, 102, 145, 158–159, 162–163, 166–171
avidyā ix–x, 6, 13, 15–16, 26, 33, 35, 37, 41, 46, 98, 102–103, 159, 162–163, 165–166, 169, 171

Bader, J. 74, 150, 152–153
Bakhtin, M. xii, 2, 15, 116, 140–141
Bhagavadgītā 116, 137
Bhagavadgītā-bhāṣya 16, 63, 91, 117
Booth, W. 3

Dasgupta, S. 12–14, 167

Frege, G. 124
Freud, S. 107–108, 113

gauṇa xiv, 35, 51, 159, 161, 169–171
Granoff, Ph. 16–17

Hacker, P. 27
Halbfass, W. x, xiv, 14–15, 27, 76, 96, 154, 166
Handelman, D. 102–103
Hopkins, Th.J. 13

Ingalls, D.D.H. 15–16, 87–88, 117

Jaimini 131–132

Kant, I. 123
Keith, A.B. 123–124
Kocmarek, I. 124

Ludden, D. 73

Mayeda, S. 25, 51, 72, 117
mokṣa viii, xiii–xiv, 1, 6, 16, 29, 33, 35–36, 38–40, 46–48, 56, 71, 91–98, 118, 126, 133, 135, 136, 162–163

Nakamura, H. 27, 117

Olivelle, P. 39, 164
Ong, W.J. 116

Pande, G.Ch. 27, 83
Potter, K. 36, 66, 74–76, 126–127
pramāṇa ix, 13, 20, 56, 60, 68, 109–110, 113, 135, 144, 168

Quine, W.V.O. 123

Radhakrishnan, S. 43–44, 85
Ricoeur, P. 124
Rukmani, T.S. 27–28, 84–85

saṃsāra 1, 6, 8, 33, 37, 40, 46–48, 61, 83, 89, 94, 108, 118, 125, 127, 134–135, 137, 148, 150, 158, 162, 165
Schechet, N. 80
Shulman, D.D. xiv, 38–39, 45, 102–103, 123, 160, 171

Thibaut, G. 37, 40–44, 53–54, 97, 108, 122, 128, 141, 151, 159–160, 163, 166, 168, 170

Upadeśa-sāhasrī vii, ix, xi, 8, 20, 23–32, 55, 58, 63, 74, 86, 89, 91, 113–114, 117–118, 140, 146, 148–150, 162

viṣaya vii–x, 8, 12, 24, 27, 35–36, 57, 86, 102, 156, 159–160, 166–167, 169–171
viṣayin vii–viii, x, 12, 27, 35–36, 86, 102, 156, 159–160, 167–169, 170
viveka viii, x, xiv, 6, 36, 139–140, 143, 145, 157–159, 170–171
Viveka-Vedānta viii, x–xii, 35–36, 139, 142, 153, 156, 157, 159, 162–163
Vyāsa 27–28, 38–39, 44–45

Wittgenstein, L. 123, 167

JERUSALEM STUDIES IN RELIGION AND CULTURE

The JSRC book series aims to publish the best of scholarship on religion, on the highest international level. Jerusalem is a major center for the study of monotheistic religions, or "religions of the book". The creation of a Center for the Study of Christianity has added a significant emphasis on Christianity. Other religions, like Zoroastria nism, Hinduism, Buddhism, and Chinese religion, are studied here, too, as well as anthropological studies of religious phenomena. This book series will publish dissertations, re-written and translated into English, various monographs and books emerging from conferences.

VOLUME 1 *The Nuṣayrī-ʿAlawī Religion*. An Enquiry into its Theology and Liturgy. Meir M. Bar-Asher & Aryeh Kofsky. 2002. ISBN 9004 12552 3

VOLUME 2 *Homer, the Bible, and Beyond*. Literary and Religious Canons in the Ancient World. Edited by Margalit Finkelberg & Guy G. Stroumsa. 2003. ISBN 9004 12665 1

VOLUME 3 *Christian Gaza in Late Antiquity*. Edited by Brouria Bitton-Ashkelony & Aryeh Kofsky. 2004. ISBN 9004 13868 4

VOLUME 4 *Axial Civilizations and World History*. Edited by Johann P. Arnason, S.N. Eisenstadt & Björn Wittrock. 2004. ISBN 9004 13955 9

VOLUME 5 *Rational Theology in Interfaith Communication*. Abu l-Ḥusayn al-Baṣrī's Muʿtazilī Theology among the Karaites in the Fāṭimid Age. Edited by Wilferd Madelung and Sabine Schmidtke. 2006. ISBN 978 90 04 15177 2

VOLUME 6 *The Poetics of Grammar and the Metaphysics of Sound and Sign*. Edited by S. La Porta and D. Shulman. 2007. ISBN 978 90 04 15810 8

VOLUME 7 *Islamic Piety in Medieval Syria*. Mosques, Cemeteries and Sermons under the Zangids and Ayyåbids (1146-1260). Daniella Talmon-Heller. 2007. ISBN 978 90 04 15809 2

VOLUME 8 *Greek Religion and Culture, the Bible and the Ancient Near East*. Jan N. Bremmer. 2008. ISBN 978 90 04 16473 4

VOLUME 9 *Morton Smith and Gershom Scholem, Correspondence 1945-1982.* Edited with an introduction by Guy Stroumsa. 2008.
ISBN 978 90 04 16839 8

VOLUME 10 *Interprétations de Moïse.* Égypte, Judée, Grèce et Rome. Edité par Philippe Borgeaud, Thomas Römer et Youri Volokhine. 2010.
ISBN 978 90 04 17953 0

VOLUME 11 *Syriac Idiosyncrasies.* Theology and Hermeneutics in Early Syriac Literature. Serge Ruzer and Aryeh Kofsky. 2010.
ISBN 978 90 04 18498 5

VOLUME 12 *The Secret Śaṅkara.* On Multivocality and Truth in Śaṅkara's Teaching. Yohanan Grinshpon. 2011. ISBN 978 90 04 18926 3